THE
INDEPENDENT
FILM &
VIDEOMAKERS
GUIDE

01

001

01

001

02

by Michael Wiese

1

Books by **MICHAEL WIESE**

Film & Video Marketing
The Independent Film & Videomakers Guide
Film & Video Budgets
Home Video: Producing for the Home Market

Books from **MICHAEL WIESE PRODUCTIONS**

Fade In: The Screenwriting Process by Robert A. Berman
Hollywood Gift Catalog by Ernie Fosselius

TO BUCKY

July 12, 1895 - July 1, 1983

Published by Michael Wiese Productions, 3960 Laurel Canyon Blvd., Suite #331, Studio City, CA 91614-3791,(818) 905-6367 in conjunction with Focal Press, a division of Butterworth Publishers, 80 Montvale Avenue, Stoneham, MA 01801, (617) 438-8464.

Cover and book design by Joe Feigenbaum
Back cover photograph by Geraldine Overton

Printed by Braun-Brumfield, Ann Arbor, Michigan
Manufactured in the United States of America

Library of Congress Cataloging in Publication Data

Wiese, Michael

THE INDEPENDENT FILM & VIDEOMAKERS GUIDE

Bibliography
A Michael Wiese Production Book

1. Motion Picture Financing. 2. Motion Picture Production. 3. Motion Picture Distribution. 4. Motion Picture Industry. 5. Pay Cable Television I. Title. 6

ISBN 0-941188-03-5

44461

791 . 4302

WIE

Acknowledgements

Filmmaking is a cooperative adventure. Of the many people who have collaborated with me over the past 18 years I would particularly like to thank filmmakers Stephen Arnold, Dorothy Fadiman, Ernie Fosselius, John Fante, Hardy Jones and John Knoop for their major contributions to the films mentioned in this book. I am also appreciative of David Sawyer (DHS Films), The American Film Institute, and The Movie Channel for the opportunity to work in New York.

I am especially grateful to Joe Feigenbaum, who brought the book cover to new heights by his type design and illustration.

My very special thanks goes to Morgan, my wife, for her support during the first writing of this book in 1981 (which she proofread and edited), and later, her remarkable patience during its three subsequent revisions, my four changes of employment and our move from California to Connecticut.

Reprinted by Permission

Hardware Wars Spoofs the Force by Ben Fong-Torres, from *Rolling Stone*, Issue No. 276, June 15, 1978. By Straight Arrow Publishers, Inc., Copyright 1978. All Rights Reserved.

Michael Wiese: Portrait of an Artist as a Young Filmmaker by Gayle Murphy, from *The Twin City Times*, March 26, 1981, Landmark Supplement.

Radiance: The Experience of Light by Bud Brainard, from *New Age*, Vol. 4, No. 5, October 1978.

New Film: Dolphin by Win Murphy, from *The Greenpeace Chronicles*, Issue No. 18, August 1979.

Dolphin, A Film of Intelligence, Love by Richard Simon, from *The Sacramento Union*, July 10, 1979.

Dolphin, A PBS-TV Special Probes Man's Best Underwater Friend, by Mara Purl, from *On Location, The Film and Videotape Production Magazine*, January 1981.

Hardware Wars Study Guide by Ernie Fosselius and Dorothy Fadiman, and *Radiance Study Guide* by Dorothy Fadiman, printed by Pyramid Films.

Hardware Wars Poster (Gay Barnes), *Postcard* (Ernie Fosselius), and *Catalog Copy*, printed by Pyramid Films.

The Wonder of the Dolphins Study Guide by Centron Films. *Dolphin Study Guide* by Michael Wiese and Hardy Jones, and *Dolphin Promo Flyers* by Michael Wiese, printed by Films Incorporated.

Dolphin Premiere Poster (Dustin Kahn), printed by Human/Dolphin Encounters, A Limited Partnership.

Printing

This book was written with an Apple II + Computer using Professional Easy Writer and Magic Wand word processing programs. The data on the disks was telecommunicated using a Hayes Smartmodem 1200 and ASCII Express Pro and Z-Term Pro programs to printer Braun-Brumfield Inc. in Ann Arbor, Michigan. The data was then phototypeset on the Mergenthaler Linotron 202. The text type is Times Roman. The headings are Helvetica. Special credit must be given to the perseverance of the Braun-Brumfield typesetting department during this my first experiment in telecommunication.

Introduction To The First Edition

I wrote this book because I want to see independent filmmaking survive.

To be an independent filmmaker you must be a jack (jill) of all trades. You need to be able to raise money, as well as understand the technical processes of filmmaking. And once you finish your film, there is the ordeal of finding a reputable distributor. It is truly a miracle that anyone does all of this.

For those just beginning, the 'how-to's' can be very difficult to learn. To assist in this process, I designed the *'No-Nonsense Film Seminars'* where I have had the opportunity to speak with hundreds of filmmakers. I discovered that, when it comes to making the kinds of films we believe in, we all have the same problems.

Fortunately, I have produced a number of short films and a television special that have been shown all over the world. They have received awards, garnered favorable reviews and some of them even made money. These films were not produced with grant money but were financed by people who believed in me and the films.

What I have done in this book is to outline the steps that I must go through every time I start a new film. It doesn't matter whether it is a short or long film, whether it has a low or high budget, the same principles still apply. I have tried to make the information very practical and useful. I am not interested in spinning yarns or discussing film theory. What I want is to see us all succeed in independently producing our films. Let me know if what follows helps you in accomplishing that goal.

Best wishes,

Michael Wiese

Sausalito, California
May 12, 1981

Introduction to the 1990 Edition

The purpose of the book hasn't changed. I still want to see independent film and videomaking survive.

The advances in the last few years in new production techniques and expanding (and contracting) markets have required that I revise this book. It is no longer possible to address just the *"videographers"* or just the *"filmmakers"*. What were once two very separate technologies have now merged to such an extent that it is necessary for *"communicators"* to understand and be willing to work in both mediums.

When I originally wrote this book I did so out of my experience as an independent filmmaker who had produced and distributed short and documentary films. I was primarily interested in PBS and the educational markets but I quickly realized that these would not support the scope of genres I had in mind. I had to gain a broader understanding of other markets, and other techniques. My first 16 years as a filmmaker resulted in 29 films totaling about 4 hours of screen time. In the next three years, my accumulated commercial and pay TV on-air work was 31 hours of screen time. Nearly 8 times more production! In the last 5 years I've been involved on the production or on the executive level with over 200 hours of programming. Something dramatic is happening. As a culture we are producing and absorbing more and more visual information. I've experienced this directly in my work. There are more outlets than ever before to deliver these film/video experiences.

This book is not totally revised because I didn't want to lose some of the feeling and insights of the original book which addressed the problems of first-time independent producers which I feel are still important. I have added new information (especially about cable buyers, television sellers and film/video distributors) that will empower both novice and experienced producers. My newer books, especially, FILM & VIDEO MARKETING (1989), brings even greater depth to the job of creating and marketing your work.

As a producer of various media (tv, film, video, books, games) I have a foot placed awkwardly in two different worlds. The first foot stands where I started in the "get-it-done-because-it's-important-to-me" world of no-budget, grass-roots production. My books are representative of an independently-produced and distributed work which do not require the "green light" of a major publisher. My second foot stands in the mass market where communication pieces reach mass audiences through world-wide video distribution. Both worlds are very satisfying. I continue to try to bring the two worlds together. The insights I've garnered through working for major pay broadcasters and home video companies I bring to the independent world. Simularily I try to instil the independent spirit and quest for values in the corporate worlds I enter. A friend recently said to me, *"your work is either very low-end or very high-end, but there's not much middle"*. Now I'm working on the middle.

It's time for independents to think bigger, to take more chances, to get out there and broaden their audiences, influence and income without giving up their values. I'd like to see this book give you practical solutions about how to finance, produce and distribute your work world-wide. In the accomplishment of your goals, I wish you every success.

Michael Wiese
Studio City, California
November 1, 1989

TABLE OF CONTENTS

TABLE OF CONTENTS

The Interview

Market Research

Producing

Budgets

Distribution

Markets

Promotion

Self-Distribution

Music Videos

Appendix

FINANCING

Independent Filmmaking

'The goal is to make films with integrity and then find outlets for them.'

Independent Filmmaking

What does it mean to be an independent filmmaker?

It means to be independent, free from the control of others and to rely on one's own abilities (for the most part) to produce one's own ideas on film.

Independent filmmakers have a 'concern' that needs to be expressed. They are self-motivated enough to turn their concerns into film and videotapes.

Hopefully, through these efforts, they will be rewarded with enough income from distribution to make more films. While this is not the reality for most independent filmmakers, it is certainly the ideal.

Many independents have chosen to work outside of the Hollywood or commercial film systems. Perhaps they want to make a different kind of film statement. Or perhaps they are unwilling to hassle with the politics, censorship and commercial pressures of the film industry. Maybe they like to be their own bosses. Or maybe they just haven't been invited to Hollywood yet.

Whatever the reason, independent filmmakers do want their work to be seen and earn some income. To this degree, independents must participate in the arena of the traditional film

3

world. They need to rent equipment to shoot their films, then the film must be processed and edited. Then, of course, there is the problem of distribution.

The goal then, is to strike a balance between the two worlds so that independents can make films with integrity and find sufficient outlets for this work.

This book makes the assumption that you are, or would like to be, an independent filmmaker and that you already have one or more ideas for a film project. And that these ideas are compelling enough to keep you going for the many months or years it may take to write a script, raise money, produce your film and then find a distributor who can begin making sales. It is a very long and tedious process. There are more separate steps involved in filmmaking than in just about any other business or art I can think of. To get through it, you have to develop a single, almost obsessive vision, of the completed work. Even after the film is finished you may be representing it, selling it, and expressing your enthusiasm in front of audiences who are just viewing it for the first time. This will take many years of your life, so choose your project carefully.

The next step is raising the money.

Sources Of Financing

'Things change when you use other people's money. You have to pay it back.'

Sources of Financing

Filmmaking is extremely expensive. Unlike the writer or painter whose material costs are minimal, the filmmaker quickly learns that fund-raising is one of the main ingredients for survival.

There are four basic sources of financing:

1. Your Own Money

2. Grants

3. Corporate Underwriting

4. Investors

Your Own Money

That's how I started. But it didn't last long. After working at numerous part-time jobs, I simply couldn't earn enough for the equipment rental, film and processing, mixes and answer prints. It took many months to make the films and because of financial limitations they were technically very ragged. However, I was able to make the many mistakes necessary to learn the craft of filmmaking. They were expensive mistakes. Fortunately, I was not spending someone else's money. Some

5

of these films never went into distribution. If you have your own money, you may want to spend it learning to make a film before risking an investor's money.

Grants

Ahhh, grants. They are wonderful when you get them. Awful when you don't. After 9 years of writing proposals to the AFI (American Film Institute), I finally received a grant. I was absolutely thrilled. Someone else finally believed in me enough to send money. It gave me a new confidence in my own abilities.

More recently, I have been a finalist in WNET's Documentary Fund and CPB's (Corporation for Public Broadcasting) grant cycles. Being a finalist gets you very excited. I could almost spend the money. In my imagination, I began scheduling the production. Then the grants didn't come through. Six months later and I was back to 'square one'. While it was an acknowledgement that I was a finalist, it isn't enough to order film from Kodak. I would rather get an instant 'no', than a lingering 'maybe', but that's the nature of the grant game.

Some of these organizations receive 1000 or more applications for each grant. There may be 90 finalists and 12-25 winners. Not very good odds. But then, it is money that you don't have to pay back.

Grants are the way to go if your film is non-commercial and has no hopes of ever earning back its cost. But expect to spend a lot of energy and many months waiting for an answer. It certainly doesn't hurt to apply for every grant you can, because you have to write budgets and proposals anyway, but you should be well aware of the odds. (Reagan's budget cuts to NEH, public schools and PBS will make grants even more difficult to obtain.)

6

(*Get The Money and Shoot* (1981), by Bruce Jackson, $15, from Documentary Research, Inc, 96 Rumsey Road, Buffalo, New York, 14209, is an excellent guide to the film grantsmanship game.)

Corporate Underwriting

Many large corporations, like Mobil, McDonald's, or Xerox, have foundations which give grants. Of the thousands of corporations (listed in the books in the Bibliography), only a handful regularly give money to Public Broadcasting. One of the best ways to discover who is giving money is to watch your local PBS station for a week and write down the credits. You will have a list of about 15 major funding sources.

Corporations give money away to enhance their own image. To receive underwriting your program will need to satisfy this objective.

Secondly, your project will need to be presented in conjunction with a PBS '*station of entry*' which has agreed to broadcast and distribute your program to PBS. Most of these 'stations of entry' have their own projects that they are trying to get underwritten. If they take on your project they may be competing with themselves for the same scarce corporate dollar.

This process can take many months or years. Our 'station of entry', KQED-San Francisco, and I sent proposals to over 70 corporate foundations for *DOLPHIN*, which was a finished show. It had already received high ratings and excellent reviews in a San Francisco test broadcast and been purchased by Japanese TV and the BBC. It took nearly 6 months to find underwriting. A more recent film proposal on emerging styles of '*fathering*' which I was producing with Bill Jersey (a director with Academy and Emmy Award nominations) was sent to 50 corporations. About 45 responded saying that they thought it was a *'wonderful treatment of a timely and important issue'* but the bottom line was that not one provided the funding. After nearly a year we had no choice but to scrap the project.

Investors

As a filmmaker, your idea or concern is quite immediate. You feel something very strongly. You want to make a film. You want to begin right away.

If a project is commercially viable, and you think it can make back its production expense (and then some), raise the money from private investors.

Things change when you use other people's money. You have to pay it back. Not legally, but morally. If you don't, it will be much more difficult to raise money again.

After all, the investors who help you launch your film will be known entities to you, not anonymous people who send you checks and expect nothing in return. Some you may never see again, others may become friends and telephone or write you when they expect a return on their investment. Hopefully your answer will be, *'it's on its way'*.

This book is designed to help you raise private monies and do so in a way that is honest and keeps the investors' needs in mind.

'Will you be able to complete the film? How can you let them know that?'

Financial

1. Will it return my investment? By when?
2. Will it make money? How do you know that?
3. How much of a tax loss can I claim?
4. What are the markets for the film?

Intrinsic

5. What are the social, emotional or spiritual values of the film? Who is the audience?
6. Do you (the filmmaker) have integrity? Will you do what you say you will? Will you be able to complete the film? How do I know that?

Participatory

7. How can I (the investor) participate in the project?

These are the basic questions that will need to be answered whenever you meet a potential investor. Some of these questions will be asked. Others will be thought. The filmmaker's job is to answer these questions completely.

People invest in movies for all kinds of reasons. At present there are about 70 people who have invested in one or more of my films. Once I thought that if I could come up with a *'personality profile'* of my investors, then it would be easier to find

9

the 'investor type' for future projects. It didn't take long to discover that there is no one type of investor.

People invest because they want to make money, or they believe in what the film is trying to say, or because they know and respect the filmmaker's previous work. Or it is for a combination of all these things.

However, most will want their questions answered.

Answering the Questions

'Will it return my investment? Will it make money? How do you know that?' This book is designed to help you thoroughly research these and other financial questions.

'What are the social and spiritual values of the film?' Since the film is your concern and close to your heart you will need to provide this answer yourself.

'Are you a filmmaker with integrity?' Your actions and the quality of your presentation will answer this often-thought but rarely-asked question. One of the best ways to answer it is to design your project so you can finish it on time and within the budget and have it be a financial and artistic success. If your past films have demonstrated that you can do this, then you have a *'track record'* and that will help immensely. If not, then simply be forthright and honest about your abilities. Most of all, be prepared before going out to find investors so that you can answer all their questions.

'How can I (or my daughter who wants to act) participate in your film?' Make it very clear from the start. They can't participate. At least not in the way they may secretly desire. They are participating by investing. That is really all you want from them. Do not hint that they are entitled to more than that. They are not. They are the investors. You are the filmmaker.

Your legal contract with your investors, called a *'Limited Partnership Agreement'*, not only limits their financial liability (they can't lose more than they invest), but it specifically excludes them from participating in the business management of the production. That is your domain.

Too Much Participation

Once I was invited to Las Vegas to meet an accomplished musician who (along with his friends) said he'd be willing to put $500,000 into producing a sailing film. Sound good? It did to me too. After sitting around his pool, dining in a nightclub (accompanied by a harpist) and touring the casinos, a hidden agenda became clear. I gradually learned what he *really* wanted. It was, a) to sail his new boat on film (which he had not yet learned to dock), b) to bring his wife and daughter along and, c) to compose the music score (his first).

Now if he wants to take a vacation on his new boat with his family, okay, fine. But I'm not willing to endanger a film expedition by bringing along extra bodies who are not working on the film.

As much as I wanted to make a sailing movie I knew that if I agreed to anything more than bringing him along (without the boat and family) I was inviting doom as, 1) it would be downright dangerous to use his boat with him at the helm and 2) although he was an fine musician he'd never composed music for a film and I had no indication his music would be right for the film.

When I told him my needs and those of the production, his enthusiasm faded and I was on the next flight home. I felt relieved. I had a close call with a potential investor who wanted to do more than make a movie.

There may, from time to time, be a situation where a camera-man or actor or writer wishes to invest in the film. Then, by all means, accept that person as a 'limited partner'. But because there is useful talent for the film, not because someone has 'bought' their way in.

You can very easily create a sense of participation for your investors. Simply stay in communication with them. Every few months send out a newsletter about the progress that is being made on their film. When you hire that special actor, or composer, or finish your music, or when you have made your first distribution deal. You can invite them to the premiere (reserving the best front row center seats) and the party afterwards. If the film will be on television, let them know so they can tell their friends. When the film wins awards or favorable reviews, send them xeroxed clippings for their scrapbooks.

By sharing with them your sense of excitement as the film progresses you can give them a sense of participation that they will truly appreciate.

PRESENTATIONS

How To Give A Successful Presentation

'The goal of the presentation is to have people invest.'

Purpose

Before you can make a successful presentation you must know what you want. You must have a result you want to produce. Without actually setting a goal for yourself you will have no way to measure your own effectiveness.

The main purpose of a presentation is to raise money for your film or video project. Once you tell yourself and the prospective investors the truth about what you want, you stand a much better chance of getting it. The goal of the presentation, therefore, is to have people invest. If someone invests, you have a measurable result.

The purpose of the presentation is not to screen your films, have a party or socialize. If this happens you may not produce the investment you are looking for. You need to be very focused in your approach. Write a script for the presentation with a good beginning, middle and end.

Visual Impact

Human beings are primarily visual creatures and receive most of their information through sight. This is important to remember because it will most likely be the visual aspect of your presentation that will make the greatest impact.

15

Studies have shown that people are influenced in varying degrees by the following:

55%	Visual	(What is seen.)
38%	Vocal	(What you say; the content.)
7%	Verbal	(How you say it.)

(If the presentation is made on the phone, then it is 85% vocal and 15% content.)

Another way to understand this is that the impact of a presentation comes through *'style'* and not *'content'*. Sad, but true. It is *'personality'* that sells a project.

Your presentation needs to be very visual and have a style that expresses your project. Naturally, there needs to be substance to your project as well.

Personal Appearance

The audience of investors, whether it be 50 people in a room or two people over dinner, will only get what you give them. So you need to be aware of everything that enters their conscious and unconscious minds.

Their eyes will fall on you first. Within seconds, you will be judged and evaluated, solely on your appearance, before you utter a single word! Therefore, you must be dressed and groomed in a manner appropriate to the tastes of the people you will meet.

A Personal Story

During the late sixties and early seventies, I made films that were as *'far out'* as possible. I wanted people to know how *'far out'* I was. These films were seen in museums around the country by hundreds, maybe thousands of people. A small audience.

When people asked me what these far-out films meant, I said, *'They mean different things to different people. Everyone has his own experience. My opinion is only one interpretation. I don't want to influence you with it. You'll have to figure the film out for yourself.'* (I think I had heard Fellini say that and figured it was a pretty good answer.)

Finally it hit me. What did I really want? Did I want to be 'far out' and misunderstood? Or did I want to make films that communicated something? The latter seemed more important. I saw that the strange, mysterious and far-out image I spent so long in cultivating, both in my films and appearance, got in the way of what I really wanted. To communicate. Some artists don't like to hear me say this. They think that being understood and looking relatively normal somehow means selling out. Fine. But I don't see it that way. I see it as putting your ego far enough in the background to produce a film that is clear in its intent. Today, if someone doesn't understand something in one of my films, I figure that it's my job to make it clearer and I take another look at why it might not be working. As for my personal appearance, I do not want it to interfere with what I need to do to produce a film, which is work with all kinds of people.

Unfortunately, many filmmakers with wonderful projects never get funded because they are more concerned with making a statement with their appearance.

The question is one of purpose: do you want to 'be you' or do you want to get the job done and raise money for your film or video project? If you fail at raising money because of an inappropriate appearance, you can go back to your *'starving artist'* friends, pat one another on the back and complain how genius is misunderstood.

17

The point is to be understood. Position your project and yourself in its most favorable light so that it has every conceivable chance of being understood. An inappropriate appearance may disqualify you in the first few seconds.

This may be common sense, but it is one of the most frequent barriers to fund-raising that I've seen among filmmakers who have come to me for consultation. They will go to endless lengths to make their films look great and then neglect their own appearance, thinking that somehow it is not that important.

Mock-Up Presentations

To find investors, cast actors and crew, do publicity and the many other duties associated with filmmaking, you are going to have to do a lot of talking. And, you're going to be giving presentations of all shapes and sizes. If you are uncomfortable speaking in front of groups, the best way to overcome this is to mock-up or rehearse your presentation for friends that will critique you on the following:

1. **Being there.** You need to really *'be there'*. Be present, right here, in present time, not off in your head thinking about anything else than what you are doing right now. It may be uncomfortable and you (your mind) would rather scurry to safer places, but that won't allow you to make an effective presentation. (How could it, if your mind is millions of miles away and your investors are left with your empty body?) Be well grounded in what you are saying. Your eyes should not dart nervously side to side.

2. **Eye contact.** Eye contact gets the attention of your listener. Your eyes reveal everything about you. If you are sure of your project, eye contact will convey that confidence better than any flip chart of profit projections. If you are not prepared, your eyes will communicate that.

Make eye contact, first with one person (for about 5 seconds), then move on to another. By meeting as many eyes as you can, you will keep the people interested and receptive. Each person will feel you are speaking directly to him.

3. **Awkward movements.** Your friends will notice if you clench your hands in a nervous manner. Your hands can be expressive and complement what you want to say with graceful, expansive gestures appropriate to your own style. They should not be distracting.

4. **Voice.** Record your voice. Many people are pleasantly surprised when they hear what they sound like. Any 'ummms' or 'ands' can be deleted from your presentation. Learn to generate enough energy to project your voice out into a large room.

5. **Smile.** Your smile is very important. It expresses goodwill. If your presentation is lively and naturally humorous (without being a comedy routine) it will relax your audience.

Your dress, your posture, voice, hand gestures, movements and particularily your eyes, communicate a lot about you to your potential investors. There are many ways you can use these things to help rather than hinder you.

The Setting

---

*'Take full control of the room.
Remove anything that does not
support your purpose.'*

Room Ambience

Select a room that is clean, well-lighted and has comfortable
(but not too comfortable) seating. It should be in a part of town
that is safe and easily located. Include a map along with your
invitation.

Screening Rooms

Screening rooms are good for presentations because you may
show film clips. Investors can see the screening room's sound
recording equipment, dubbers, and mixing console. Since
most people have never been in a professional screening room,
it is very exciting for them to see where movies are made. It
gives them a sense of being part of the movie-making world
and establishes credibility. Screening rooms can be found in
most major cities and booked for $25-50 per hour.

If the screening room is located in an unfamiliar part of town,
station someone outside to let people know they are in the right
place.

Make people's total experience as pleasurable as you can. You
don't want them to have trouble parking because they will
bring that negative experience in the door with them and it will
influence their response to your presentation. You want them
to feel that you will take as good care of their money as you

21

have of them, so be conscious of these small details. It is one of the easiest ways to let people feel your sense of style and grace. All of this happens before you've said a word about the project you want to do.

Private Homes

If you use private homes for presentations, you can prepare (in advance) your sample film clips and transfer them on videotape. Rent a videotape player, plug it into a television set, and the private home can serve the same function as a screening room.

Take full control of the room. Remove anything that is distracting and does not support your purpose. The worst thing you can do is have a clock on the wall behind you.

Go as far with this idea as you can. If possible, even light the room, by moving lamps or ceiling lights around, so that there are no dark spots where investors may sit and become drowsy. Arrange flowers, lay out a wine and cheese table, open a portfolio or a prospectus on the coffee table. You may want to have your friends (assistants) greet people. Make people feel as comfortable as possible.

Restaurants

When you do presentations in restaurants make sure you will have minimal distractions. It should be quiet so that you can be heard and leisurely enough so that you can sit and talk after eating. Survey the restaurant before meeting there. Since you cannot control the environment, you must be very careful in your selection. You may only get one chance.

Attitude

'You must exude confidence and place no responsibility on the potential investor.'

'Inner' Environment

Once you have created a pleasant and supportive 'outer' environment, you can do the same thing on your 'inner' environment.

What is your overall attitude? How are you expressing yourself psychologically? Or simply, where are you coming from? Try to find out your own point of view because it will subtly influence your communication to your investors.

Many filmmakers come from *'survival'*. The tone of their presentation says to the investor, *'Please help me. Without your money, I can't do my film.'* (Or, *'I need you to survive.'*)

This attitude puts all the responsibility on the investor and may easily frighten him. If you were an investor would this kind of attitude give you a feeling of confidence in the filmmaker?

Investors want to know that, with or without their backing, you are going to make your movie. You must exude confidence and place no responsibility on the potential investor. You simply want to know if they'd like to invest.

Although you may never use these words, the tone of your first telephone call to a potential investor may sound like this:

'We are making this film. (Present tense, not we 'will' make this film, we 'are' already making it.) *We've been working on*

23

it for x months. What we have accomplished so far is . . . The film will be finished in . . . .months and distributed like this. . . . We have sold x shares and raised $ x. We need to raise $ x more. Does this sound like something you'd like to invest in?'

The style is very straightforward. It shows the potential investors that you are moving forward, that you have already accomplished something and you know where you are going. It provides all the information necessary to decide whether or not to invest. The information takes less than 3 minutes to deliver, during which, the potential investor can decide to attend a one-hour group presentation or to meet with you to gather more detailed information.

Questions and Answers

After you do your formal presentation, with a group or a single person, allow some time (keep it brief) for questions. Be so well prepared that you can answer anything they might ask. (When you do your mock-up presentation for your friends, have them ask difficult questions.) Do not give a presentation until you are prepared and have a prospectus with budgets, market research and income projections prepared. You will also want to have a first draft of your script completed. Nothing speaks more of your professionalism than being prepared.

If you don't know an answer to a question, for heaven's sake, don't lie or make something up. Write it down and tell them that you will get the answer. Then do so and call them back. If it is a financial or legal question, ask the person if he/she would like your lawyer or accountant to call. (Be sure your accountant and lawyer are willing first!)

Minimum Effort

Make it as easy as possible for someone to invest. The legal documents should already be prepared by your lawyer so that all that is required of an investor is a signature and a check.

Groups

Groups of people create a synergetic effect. If you do a very successful presentation it will be even more so. People who were on the fence about investing will be swayed because of the enthusiasm in the room. They will sense it is a good investment and want to join in. If, on the other hand, the presentation is awkward and goes poorly, then the audience as a whole may decide not to invest. Stack the odds in your favor by being conscious about your purpose, projecting a personal style and grace and creating a supportive environment in which to do your presentation.

Groups communicate something else. If you can put together an investors' meeting of 20, 30 or 40 people, you can certainly handle a crew, a press conference and the other group tasks associated with filmmaking. If you are not good at presentations then team up with someone who is. Not everyone's personality is suited to public speaking. If the thought of getting up in front of a group terrifies you, practice until you can do it easily. If it still terrifies you, then get someone else to do it.

The Wise Guy

I don't know where they come from but there always seems to be one at every presentation. They show off by challenging you with questions. They want you and everyone else present to know that they are smarter than you. I suppose they would rather be the one making the film. But they aren't. Whatever their motivation, they can be a real bother. Worse yet, if you aren't prepared for them they can throw you off. Which you certainly don't need. You want to look your best. (For mock-ups your friends can portray the *'wise guy'*. It will help you to be firm and keep the presentation on track.)

If these wise guys ask questions that you don't know the answer to, simply say you don't know and go on. Don't totally ignore the wise guy. Give a courteous answer and then move on. Do not let them dominate the situation. It's your presentation.

Saying 'No'

Sometimes these wise guys will actually want to invest. I recommend against it. You can sense when someone will be nothing but trouble. You've got a movie to make. You don't need more problems than you've already got. Say 'no'.

I know that (after spending the last dozen pages on how to raise money) it sounds absolutely mad to tell you to say *'no'* to some investors. But this is a very important point. You are about to enter a relationship with another person. If, at the outset, it looks like it will be trouble, be assured that this person will later wreak havoc by wanting to read the script, inspect the books, or whatever. Don't let this happen. Not because you've got anything to hide, but because you simply don't need the hassle.

I've had experiences with these wise-guy types that have brought me nothing but trouble and wasted my time. Don't get me wrong. I am not talking about investors that are accomplished in business and can contribute their expertise. I welcome investors like that. I am talking about these yo-yo's who think because they've invested a few thousand in your film that they have the right to mess around with it. They don't.

I remember a time when I had a large stack of unpaid lab bills and a staff to pay. There was $20 in the checking account and not a prospect in sight. Except for a 'wise guy' like I just described. It was tough. I had to tell him *'no, you can't invest in the film'*. An inner voice was screaming, *'Wiese! You fool! You're broke. Take the money!'* But another part of me knew I made the right decision. A few days later, the needed money came from someone else.

Not only is it a great boost to your ego to say *'no'* but it helps you prove to yourself that money isn't scarce. You don't have to take it just because it's there.

Support

Investors are support. They are supporting you with money (physically) and emotionally. Each investment carries with it an *'intention'* that goes into film as well. I don't know how to describe this without sounding mystical because, to me, it is mystical.

DOLPHIN was financed by a large group of investors. I have met almost every single person. I can feel their support, as a group and as individuals. Some have sent me clippings about dolphins, or written suggestions for titles. Others shared their knowledge of business, or have shown the film in their communities. All of them have supported the film and made it what it is in the world.

The Money for DOLPHIN

Before beginning *DOLPHIN* I never thought I was very good at raising money. Not big money. So, I asked a friend (who had raised millions in real estate) if he could raise the money for *DOLPHIN*. He felt absolutely confident that he could, and encouraged me to get on with the business of making the film.

27

For a reasonable commission (5%), he would raise the money. (You can already guess the punchline.)

We took a full crew to locations in Hawaii; topside and underwater cameramen, recording equipment, diving gear, an underwater piano, etc. We stayed in hotels for about 10 days. We rented boats and helicopters. When we had shot all our film supply and filled up my credit cards, we returned to the mainland and sent the film to the lab.

I called my friend. I was sure by now that he had raised the money. I told him about the film, the lab bills, the deferred crew payments and the credit cards. Expectant of good news, I asked him how much he had raised. He told me, *'not a cent'*. He said that while raising money for real estate ventures was a *'snap'*, he simply didn't know how to raise money for a film.

I was flabbergasted. That's when I went out looking for money. It was one of the worst/best things that ever happened to me. I was thrown back on my own abilities. Raising money was something that I had avoided and now it was imperative that I learn.

I found that I had to clearly communicate what the film was about, who would see it, and where it would be sold. I had to seriously evaluate the project in terms of what it could earn back. I had to tell people what I wanted: money. It surprised me when it came. One in every five people I called on invested.

Where to Find Investors

'They are not the rich, fat-cats of your imagination.'

Where To Find Investors

Investors are where you least expect them, all around you. They are not the rich, fat-cats of your imagination. They are real, accessible, friendly people. They are more likely your friends, and your friends' friends.

People say to me, *'Well, I don't have rich friends.'* So? Neither did I. That shouldn't keep you from finding backing for your film or videotape.

Think for a minute. Who do you know that knows about money? Who has a small or large business? Who owns a house or works for a large corporation? Do you know a doctor, a dentist, a lawyer, a retired businessman, a young entrepeneur? All you need is one, and you're on your way.

Go to him or her with your idea (prospectus). Or invite several people to a presentation. Enlist their help. Although they may not invest, perhaps they'll give you a name or two of their friends who will. Ask if you may use their name when you call their friends. They will probably say 'yes', but ask their permission anyway.

Get at least two referrals from everyone you talk to. If they like you and your idea this will not be difficult. (If they don't invest they still may be willing to help you find other people who will.) If they do invest, then they will want to help you (and protect their investment by seeing that the project is fully funded.) Before you know it, you will have a long list of people to call.

29

You will be very surprised when you find investors. They will not be who you expect. Many people may have some savings or resources you never knew about until you asked them to invest. Not only that, they may be pleased that you included them!

About 'No'

You will get many *'no's'* when you ask for money. That's okay. It is nothing personal. And it's going to happen. No big deal. They simply do not want to invest. You must go on to the next person, and the next until you get a 'yes'. *'No's'* can make you feel bad. You'll think no one cares. *'Yes's'* will make you feel great. It's much easier to make the next call if you just received a 'yes'. You will have to go on after the 'no's' as well. It is the 'no's' that cause most people to give up.

I like to tell myself *every 'no' brings me one step closer to a 'yes'.* That seems to help.

When you get a 'yes' it strengthens your position. Then you can say, *'We've raised 'x' dollars and we only need another 'y' dollars.'* When you have sold most of the shares in the film you'll be more confident and the last shares will be easier. When a number of people have already invested, new investors feel safer, and rightfully so. People begin to feel that they have made the right choice.

'Maybe's'

You don't want them. A 'maybe' will drive you crazy. At least with a 'no' you know where you stand. With a 'maybe' it is unresolved, incomplete and psychologically draining. You want to find out if someone is going to invest. If they don't want to, go on. *'Life is too short.'*

30

Some people like to hang out with filmmakers. It makes them feel creative, important. Lunch after lunch goes by. But enough is enough. You are not there to socialize but to raise money. Make that clear.

If you haven't provided enough information for them to make a decision, do so. If you have, then it's time to get an answer. Get yourself off the hook and onto new prospects.

You've Got to Ask

If you want someone to invest in your project, you've got to ask. Chances are, they are not mind readers.

Many filmmakers are afraid to ask for what they want. You may be having a great time with someone over lunch and feel you don't want to spoil it by asking for money. What's the point then? You are really wasting your time and energy. You need to make it clear in the beginning why you are meeting.

The same thing is true at a large investors' presentation. You have not asked them to a nice film show and a wine tasting ceremony. (Although this may happen.) You have invited them to a meeting of prospective backers. The purpose is to have them learn about your project and find out if they'd like to invest. If you don't make this clear at the outset and then spring the big question ('Do you want to invest?') on them at the presentation they will feel tricked. And you won't get the investment you need.

Presentation Budget

Have money to live on while you are fund-raising. Give the appearance of being successful. If you are to attract money you have to look like you don't need it. Playing the 'starving artist' (even if you are one) usually doesn't work. Your potential investor will figure that even with the money your project will not succeed. You must already look like a *'success'* on your way to another success.

It will cost money to create a presentation. Perhaps a few hundred dollars. Maybe more. You need to be aware that you will have these costs and include them in your budget under *'pre-production'* or *'presentations'*. It costs money to raise money. It is a legitimate business expense. You will also incur similar expenses when your film is finished and you are meeting with distributors and the press.

Among these expenses are screening room rental, slide shows, equipment rental (slide projectors, videotape players, projectors), printed invitations, color xeroxes, typesetting, legal fees, xeroxing and binding proposals, flowers, wine, cheese, and travel.

Presentation Structure

> *'Your talk is a relaxed and fun sharing of information. Its purpose is to sell yourself and your project.'*

Invitations

As you call friends, friends of friends, and make 'cold calls' you can list all those people that you have invited to the group presentation. Some will be invited to lunch. It is up to you to be selective. Some people you will only invite to a group presentation.

Remember you are setting the tone for what is to follow. In calling your prospective investors make it absolutely clear that the presentation is for people who may be interested in investing. Let them know that you will be discussing the film, its marketing and why you think it will be successful. Let them know if you will show clips from your work-in-progress and how long the presentation will last. (I suggest 1 to 1-1/2 hours or less. Then stick to your time limit!) Tell them that refreshments will be served.

You can also send invitations. I usually have an artist prepare calligraphy on good paper. I also include a detailed map of the location. I ask that they RSVP (or I confirm their attendance with them a day in advance). This way a guest list can be made up and you will know when everyone has arrived.

33

Advance Preparations

First and foremost is the presentation itself. Every moment is planned in advance. All the equipment is tested. All visuals such as slides, film clips, flip charts, and graphs are readied. Prospectus' are xeroxed and bound. Be sure you have enough for everyone. The room is booked and 'dressed' as necessary. Friends and associates are asked to assist. Their responsibilities are carefully defined. (Help with parking, greet people, take people's coats, hand out prospectus', serve wine, collect enclosures, etc.)

Rehearsals

The most important aspect of the presentation is the talk itself which you should rehearse at least 4-6 times from start to finish. (If you will give the talk with another person, then rehearse it together. Know who will cover what.) Have your friends time the presentation and critique it. Rewrite it and rehearse it until it works! It's important to rehearse the whole thing without stopping. Then have your critique and make your changes. Then rehearse it again.

The Presentation

The presentation starts when the guests enter the room. (Actually it starts when you meet them or speak to them on the phone.) You might invite them to the wine and cheese table first. You may hand out prospectus' or you may wait. Whatever you do, start the presentation on time.

Keep in mind that your talk is a *'conversation'* with the group. Do not read it. Speak it. It is not a lecture. Use note cards if you like, but do not depend on them. Memorize your presentation so the cards are just a reminder. Your talk is a relaxed and fun sharing of information. Its purpose is to sell yourself and your project.

The Beginning

Like any good book or film your presentation (and prospectus) will have a beginning, middle and end.

After saying *'hello'* and making some brief, informal remarks begin with something bold. A thought-provoking statement or a startling fact. Something that gets their undivided attention. You might flash a strong image on the screen and leave it there for the first few minutes.

Preview your point of view and intention. But keep it short and get to the heart of your talk. (Let people know they may ask questions at the end of the talk. If you don't do this they may interrupt you and break your concentration.)

The Middle

The middle of your talk should expand the group's understanding of your project.

Sometimes it's possible to follow the same order as the information in your prospectus. If you make it clear to your audience that this is what you are doing then they may feel that everything is being covered and they won't have to read every word of the prospectus when they get home. This may help to speed up their decision-making process. The danger with handing anything out during your talk is that you invite people to read it rather than have their full attention on you. This demonstrates again that you need to use everything you can to captivate your audience.

Develop your points in a clear order with one thought leading to the next. Don't jump around. Be sure all your points support your purpose. (Motivate people so that they will want to invest.) But don't be too serious about it. Keep it light. Don't be afraid to make a joke or have fun (when appropriate). You may weave in personal stories, analogies, experts' opinions, and fascinating details to emphasize your main points. Feel free to use colorful graphics and flip-charts to illustrate your points. This can be anything from cartoons to graphs as long as it is appropriate. When you rehearse your presentation, ask your friends to tell you what was boring and what was fascinating. Discard what didn't work. Finds ways to make your talk forward-moving and fresh. Your enthusiasm and energy are selling points.

The Ending

The ending should be crisp, clear and, most of all, memorable. End with a bang! Review your main points, which support why people should take action (that is, invest). Again, don't get serious, keep it consistent with the rest of your talk. Finish with confidence.

Questions and Answers

At this point you may or may not wish to answer questions. It may diffuse the momentum you've built. On the other hand, some important questions may need to be answered to further sell your project. Answer your questions in a way that expands and supports your own point of view and involves your entire audience, not just the person asking the question. Address your answer to everyone so you don't lose the whole group's attention. If questions are slow in getting started then ask a question yourself. *'People often ask me . . . . . . '* When the questions do begin, keep an *'open'* body posture, arms at your side. Do not cross them in front of you or put them in your pockets because (in body language) this is a defensive and guarded position. It will communicate that you are trying to hide something. If you don't know the answer to a question, say so, don't fake it. Offer to get back to the person who asked the question. Most of all, keep the answers short and concise. Keep the same confident and personal tone as in your original talk. At the end of the questions, bring everything together in a concise closing statement.

You may wish to hand out the prospectus during your talk. If you do, be sure to tell people that you will cover everything in the prospectus. Tell people they may take the prospectus home with them. This will allow them to relax and not feel they have to read it during your talk.

If film and videomakers put as much creative thought into the process of giving talks and presentations as they do into the design and execution of their works they would find they have much more success at raising money for their projects.

Film Clips

If your project has already begun you may want to show film clips or videotape to interest people in the project.

In some cases, it is not a good idea to preview this work-in-progress. Investors are not filmmakers and they may be disturbed by a scratchy workprint or spotty unmixed sound track or videotape with rough-cut *'glitches'* (flashes at the cuts between scenes). Because an unfinished work can look so bad, people may assume you are not a very good filmmaker. I've heard people ask if the lines (drawn on workprint to indicate dissolves and fades) would be on the final version! Unless you plan to do a lot of explaining, which makes you look like you are apologizing and puts you in a bad light, you may wish to hold back on showing rough-cut clips.

37

With *DOLPHIN*, we had already shot some exquisite underwater scenes of wild dolphins and decided to chance a showing. My creative partner, Hardy Jones (a former newscaster with an excellent voice), recorded a narration. We added music (from records) and performed a *'live mix'* of the three sound tracks (sync, music and narration) while the potential investors watched! Fortunately, editor John Fante, who knew where all the sound was placed, hit all the cues and none of the splices broke. It looked pretty good. (We wiped off the grease-pencil dissolve marks.) The *'film'* had a beginning, a middle and an end. It gave a memorable experience of the film we were making. At this point we had spent about $13,000 photographing, recording and editing the *'pilot'* cut.

Later we transferred this *'pilot'* to videocassette using a Rank Cintel flying spot scanner and color-corrected each scene. We added video-generated titles and previewed the resultant cassette in additional investor presentations, saving screening room expenses.

If you do use a film clip, it should not be too long. It should be like a *'coming attraction'* and make the audience want to see (and invest in) the film to come.

If you do not have footage to show you may wish to screen other films you or your partners have made. Keep them consistent in style or subject matter with your current project so that they do not detract from the mood of the presentation.

Show the film or videotape early in your presentation because it will act as a *'grabber'* and set a tone that the evening is about filmmaking.

Enclosures

Once the presentation is over you will want to find out how

you did. That is, have you found anyone who will invest. Since people tend to be uncomfortable talking about their financial intentions in front of others I provide an *'enclosure'* that can either be slipped in the back of the prospectus or handed out separately. This is a more private method for people to let you know if they will invest.

The enclosure will be filled out by everyone and returned at the end of the presentation. It also allows investors to communicate to you about investing or needing more information. This way, those who say *'no'* need no follow-up and those who say *'yes'* can be clearly identified. The forms can be gathered and then people may be invited to partake of the refreshments.

Enclosure Sample

Your project's title

—— *I wish to invest in 'title'. Amount: $___.*

—— *I do not wish to invest at this time.*

—— *I would like some more information about the project.* *Please call me.*

Name:_____ Phone:_____

Thank you.

At this point the presentation is over. People can stay and socialize if they like. You can answer questions privately but be aware that this can create a feeling of exclusion for others. So I say that I would like to chat with everyone afterwards but that I don't want to answer any more questions about the project.

Conclusion

If you have made it to this point in the long and arduous process of being an independent film or videomaker you have a lot to be proud of. You have overcome the fear of public speaking and introduced yourself and your project to discriminating investors. You have clearly outlined your film's purpose, your distribution plans, and projected the project's future earnings based on your market research. (Consult the chapters that follow). You have taken a major step towards realizing your goal.

When you look at the returned 'enclosures' you'll have a pretty good idea of exactly how much you can expect from the investors. Hopefully in the days that follow you will be depositing checks in your limited partnership's bank account. (I was surprised when we collected over $50,000 from investors at our first *DOLPHIN* presentation. It paid all those outstanding lab bills and crew debts and allowed us to begin the next major phase of our project.) If you are clear, confident, enthusiastic and you have a project that merits being made (either commercially, emotionally, politically, or spiritually) you will find people who will invest. If you receive any money at all after giving your presentations you are well on your way in establishing your own independence as a film or videomaker and transforming your ideas into reality.

THE PROSPECTUS

The Prospectus

'It is everything anyone needs to know about your project.'

The Prospectus

The prospectus is a bound booklet of all pertinent information about your film or video project. It is everything anyone needs to know about you, your project and its profit potential.

It is written in simple, easy-to-understand language. The prospectus for Broadway plays and Hollywood movies are legal documents. What I am calling a prospectus has financial information in it, but it is a non-legal document. The Limited Partnership Agreement is a separate legal document which accompanies the prospectus. (More on that later.)

What follows is a page-by-page description of the prospectus. It may be used for any size film or video project, be it a documentary feature, a series, or a short. You may modify this format for grant applications as it will contain all the necessary information most foundations require. This is also necessary for live presentations, so if you have not assembled this information before your presentation you are not ready to give one.

Cover

Right off, most prospectus' I've seen miss the boat on the cover. Of course, it has a title (and your name) but it should also have a picture. Many don't. Perhaps it's because many filmmakers read those script format books that say only put the title and your name on the cover. That's well and good for

43

scripts but the prospectus is a selling tool. And since we are visual artists, a strong picture that expresses the mood, tone or content of your film can be very useful. The *DOLPHIN* prospectus had a full-page, color-xerox of dolphins on it. Right away, an investor knew what to expect. Furthermore, every time a prospective investor looked down at the prospectus on his coffee table, there were those smiling dolphins, reminding him (selling him) on the film.

Why not insert pictures of your subject throughout the prospectus? The effect could be quite powerful. This will give your project the feeling of being something quite special and it is!

When you give someone the prospectus, pay close attention to how they use it. Most people will read the page headings and look at the pictures, and once they satisfy themselves that the information is there, they turn to the next page.

Then there are the *'literary'* types. They read every word and don't pay much attention to the pictures. By studying how prospective investors look at the prospectus, (and assuming they are right-handed) you can tell what kind of *'mode'* they operate in, how they process information and how they perceive the world. If they concentrate on pictures (right-brain) then they are probably more responsive to feelings, music, imagery. You can then discuss the project from that point of view. They will respond more favorably because they understand things in terms of emotion, music and imagery. If you notice that some people *read* the prospectus very carefully, word by word (left-brain), then you can focus on cerebral ideas, numbers and budgets, schedules, language and marketing plans. Obviously the world isn't so easily divided into right- and left-brained people. Most will respond to both dimensions of the prospectus so it needs to be well-balanced.

Title

The title works better if it is short. A recent study of books found that the average best-selling title is 1.8 words. (So how do I explain the title of this book? It's not a best-seller!) The title should engage the reader's mind and conjure up an image or idea that is consistent with the film you are selling. I suggest an 'active title' rather than a 'passive' one. It is all right to use a *'working title'* until you find exactly the right one. Type the title in capital letters throughout the prospectus for reinforcement.

Statement of Purpose

The very first sentence is a statement of the film's purpose. It is an expression of your intention in making the film.

The first paragraph of the proposal on *OUR FATHERS* written with Bill Jersey was:

'OUR FATHERS is about men discovering how to be fathers. It is about their growth as individuals, and the growth of their children.'

For *DOLPHIN* we wrote:

'To create an informative, entertaining, and inspiring motion picture which effectively communicates existing relationships between humans and dolphins.'

'To transform public awareness about these intelligent creatures and to bring about an end to the senseless killing of dolphins and whales.'

A clear and simple purpose will keep you on track. You can always refer back to it with any new idea and see if you are being consistent. If you change your purpose mid-stream, your film will reflect this in a negative way.

Spend plenty of time with your partners in defining and writing down your purpose. When you agree on it, you will have a much better chance of making a concise film and communicating clearly. If your purpose is pages long then you don't have it yet. Keep working on it until you get it down to a sentence or two. You'll never regret the time this takes and your film will be better for it. Your purpose will motivate everything: the way your film is written, how it is shot, what you include and what you don't include, what motivation the actors are given and so on. Everything will come out of your purposes. We have all seen a great many films where there was no purpose.

Project Summary

You can use a few paragraphs or as much as several pages to summarize your film or video project. You can also present an outline or finished script along with your prospectus. If that is the case in your situation then keep the summary short.

Treatment

How will you treat your subject? What style will you use? What format? Is it a one-hour film? A 15-minute video? Drama? Docu-drama? Animation? Music Video? What is unusual or unique about your project? Does it present a balanced or biased point of view? (Both are valid.)

Research

This is an optional section. It contains facts and statistics about your subject. It may be a summary of your own research or the research of others. It may be a letter written by an expert or consultant about your project.

Project Background/Progress To Date

This page (which can be rewritten and replaced as things progress) describes the work you have already accomplished. Has a treatment been written? A script? Have actors, crew or experts already agreed to participate? How much of your budget have you raised? (With *DOLPHIN*, we had already shot about 20% of the film before we gave presentations. We included this information in the prospectus.) Whatever you have already achieved should be mentioned. This will show that you are already well on your way to completing your film. Your prospectus is not a fantasy. It is not an idle promise. You are already getting something done.

Have actors, crew or experts already agreed to participate? How much of your budget have you raised? (With *DOLPHIN*, we had already shot about 20% of the film before we gave presentations.) Whatever you have achieved can be included. This will demonstrate the project is already happening.

Production Schedule

The production schedule is a month-by-month chart of production activities. Before you write a production schedule you must know how long it will take for research and writing, booking crews and actors, finding locations, shooting, editing, recording music, processing and so forth. It will probably take you 50% longer than you plan. Since a longer schedule will reflect a higher budget, it is better to raise the amount that you will actually need to make the film.

Most projects go over budget because they take longer to make than expected. If you are making a dramatic film, you calculate your schedule on a finished script, and compute how many total days or weeks it will take to shoot.

47

My production schedule (for the prospectus) is very simple. It lists the months in the left-hand column and the work to be accomplished in the right-hand column. I avoid technical terms like *'A & B rolling'* because the prospectus is read by non-film people.

It might look something like this:

JANUARY	Interviewing
FEBRUARY	Script Writing
MARCH	Pre-Production Scheduling
APRIL	Principal Photography
MAY	Principal Photography
JUNE	Editing-Assembly
JULY	Editing-Rough Cut, Record Narration
AUGUST	Editing-Fine Cut, Record Music
SEPTEMBER	Mixing Sound Track, Titles
OCTOBER	Cut Original, Lab, Test Prints
NOVEMBER	Screenings for Distributors
DECEMBER	Negotiations for Distribution
JANUARY	Negotiations for Distribution
FEBRUARY	Distribution-Promotion, Printing
MARCH	Distribution-Promotion, Mailing

The production schedule ends when the film goes into general distribution. Include the time it will take to find a good distributor. This will show your investors that you know what the job requires and that you are not just going to shoot some film and move onto something else.

Budget

The budget is a very clear statement of what it will cost to make the film. It is based on the production schedule and includes every detail and cost of the entire process. Remember to include monies for pre-production, presentations, and the costs incurred when you are looking for distributors (shipping, travel, phone, prints, etc). Be sure to include something for your own time or you will find that when you reach the last stages you are suddenly cash poor with work still remaining on this project. If you are not paid, you may quickly come to resent your situation and make the wrong decisions. (If I were an investor I would want know that my producer's personal finances were in order when he or she signed that irrevocable distribution contract; that he or she were making the best deal possible. I want to be sure that the producer was paid for a long enough period of time.)

Write two budgets. (No, you're not keeping two sets of books.) Both will have the same total. One is a *'detailed budget'* which generates the second, a *'summary budget'*, for the prospectus. You include the summary and not the detailed budget not because you are hiding anything but because a summary budget gives all the necessary information. It will avoid opening a can of worms. (How you wish to allocate the production funds is your business. It is also your investors' business. You can always show the detailed budget to the investor upon request.) What you want to avoid are a whole set of questions that raise more questions and inadvertently put you on the defensive when you have to explain yourself. An investor may ask *'how come you are renting a van for 6 days when the shoot is only 4 days long?'* and so forth. (Answer: *'to pick up and return equipment before and after the shoot.'*) Basically, I do not wish to encourage discussions with investors about the inner financial workings of the production.

Note: To fully discuss budgets would require a whole book in itself. (So I'm writing one!) I expect to publish *FILM & VIDEO BUDGETS* in early 1984. Budgets are so important I encourage you to read the book, which covers a wide variety of different kinds of production budgets from student films to music videos, film and videotape documentaries, low budget features, commercials and industrials—something I am regrettably unable to do within the context of this book.

Summary Film Budget

A 24-Minute Film

A. TALENT	5,382
B. PRODUCTION PERSONNEL	5,366
C. FILM STOCK AND LABS	3,161
D. PRODUCTION EQUIPMENT	1,900
E. EDITING AND FINISHING	9,496
F. NARRATION AND MUSIC	1,215
G. OFFICE	3,480
TOTAL	30,000

Financial Overview

This page covers the basics of what is contained in the Limited Partnership Agreement. It is only meant to give a very general overview of the financial structure of the partnership. It could be as simple as this:

'FIRST FAMILIES', An Hour Television Special on America's First Families, by 'FIRST FAMILIES PRODUCTIONS', a Limited Partnership. General Partners: John Doe & Jane Doe and 10 Limited Partners.

50

Minimum Investment: $10,000. Total Budget: $100,000. Each $10,000 investment equals 5% of the net profits of the film.

The total capital contribution of $100,000 shall be repaid in full from all income received through the sale and distribution of the film. Once repaid, the General Partners and Limited Partners shall share in the profits 50/50.

To date, $30,000 has been raised. An additional $70,000 is required.

This non-legal page simply represents what is found in greater detail in the legal document. The example given is purely hypothetical, as limited partnerships may be used to raise more or less money, and profit sharing may vary.

Its purpose is to give an investor a quick overview of the financial aspects of the project. (Consult your lawyer about the inclusion of this page in your prospectus.)

Market Research/Trend Indicators

This section shows that you have done your homework and studied the markets for the finished film. If you find similar films with strong gross incomes you can use those as examples in your prospectus.

The more detailed this page can be, the better, because it will show the real chance for success for your proposed film.

In the *DOLPHIN* prospectus, we mentioned that the *National Geographic Whale Special* had the second highest audience ratings in PBS history and that this demonstrated the public interest in dolphins. (That turned out to be true, *DOLPHIN* also received very high ratings.) We indicated that since this

51

program had a budget of $250,000, we expected to sell our show to PBS for a similar amount. (This, unfortunately, did not turn out to be true. Had we fully studied the realities of our situation, and not what we hoped would be true, we would have found that there is a great difference between what PBS will pay for an *'acquisition'* and a show which they themselves produce. The $250,000 budget was the total underwriting budget which included station overhead, promotion and production costs. It was not the amount paid to the producers for the 'acquisition' of their show. This was a major oversight and a great shock to everyone when we found that we would not receive anything close to that amount for *DOLPHIN*. Everyone's expectations had been raised in the prospectus and presentation and it was months later before the awful truth became known.)

Here is another example of *'trend indicators'* research. Once I wanted to produce a health-related film on the handicapped. Four films had already been made on similar subjects and were distributed by four different distributors. Some films have been out for 10 years, others for 3 years. They have all grossed between $175,000 and $750,000. Given those strong past performances on my relatively low budget, I sensed that it would be profitable to do this film. Although the subject itself was worthy of production, I also knew that in order to survive as a filmmaker I had to find markets for my proposed film.

I called all four distributors because I was afraid that, with four other films already out, the market might already be saturated. They all told me they thought there would be an even greater market in the future and expressed interest in distributing my film should I produce it.

I also researched television distribution for my idea, both in this country and abroad. While it took several days and a small fortune in phone calls, I gathered enough information to make a fairly sound financial assessment of the profit potential of my proposed film. Since a profit is possible, it was feasible to present this film to potential backers. If I learned it was not a profitable venture, my option would have been to search for grants.

Do a thorough job in your market research. Be careful that your desire to make your film does not influence the *'supportive'* evidence you present. It's hard to believe that your film will not be profitable. Maybe it will. Find out. The truth is, very few independently produced shorts and documentaries ever make their money back.

Distribution Markets

This section in the prospectus gives a basic description of some of the markets where the film or videotape or television program may be licensed and distributed. Your film or videotape may be released in several different markets and formats thereby increasing your income. Since most investors are not familiar with these markets they need to be described in the prospectus. My descriptions are rather simple but may serve as foundation paragraphs for your own prospectus. The markets that you plan to distribute should be backed up with actual figures in the income projection tables. Consequently your investor will want to know about these markets in some detail. The various markets that specific distributors service are:

Theatrical Markets. This refers to income from theatrical motion pictures that play in commercial movie theaters. Films can play for a day in a single repertory theater or as long as several months in a hundred theaters depending on its popularity. The box office revenues are shared with a theatrical distributor once 35mm print costs and advertising are deducted. Only a few dozen low-budget, genre pictures (horror, exploitation) reach the market each year.

Non-Theatrical. This traditionally means the educational market and includes schools, libraries, health, business and industry. Income is derived from the sale of 16mm film prints and video cassettes. Unfortunately for producers this market has diminished significantly in the last decade. Seven companies now account for 80% of all business and industry sales. Media buyers are converting to video because the cost of programming is considerably cheaper to purchase.

Videotape. This is the fastest growing sector in the entertainment industry. VCRs are in 30% of all American TV households. Programming includes Hollywood feature films, childrens, music video, instructional, documentary, x-rated and a wide variety of original programs made-for-home video. England, Australia and Japan are the largest of the international markets. By the end of 1985 there will be 100 million VCR players worldwide. This market offers the most opportunity for independent product in a variety of genres.

Videodisk. The CED videodisk player has been discontinued. A few program duplicators still manufacture disks for the dwindling universe of 700,000 disk players. Laser disks and hardware are still being manufactured and offer superior sound and picture quality. The interactive ability that a new generation of hardware offers mades this an exciting format to watch. This market, however, is part of the video market because video distributors usually handle all video formats of product (Beta, VHS, Laser and the upstart, 8mm). Other than features, and some industrial training programs, few programs find their way to disk today.

Network Television. Outside of sitcoms, game shows and specials network television is closed to independent film and videomakers. With few exceptions, the three television networks, (ABC, CBS, NBC) use their own news' departments to produce documentaries.

Syndicated Television. Syndication is a fancy word for 'distribution'. Syndicators (distributors) license programs to stations on a station-by-station basis. These stations may or may not be affiliated with the networks. The prices that the syndicators receive are based on the time of broadcast, the show's demographics, and the size of the potential viewing audience in the broadcast area. Often, in lieu of payment for programs, syndicators will offer the programs to the stations free in exchange for some of the advertising time, which they will then sell themselves. This is called *'bartering'*.

PBS. PBS (Public Television System) is an association of 281 stations that buy programs in several different ways. This is described in more detail in a later section. PBS has a significantly smaller audience than commercial or network television and shows high-quality, specialized programs. rarely is a program shown on both PBS and a commercial network.

Foreign Television. Foreign countries with television systems, state or commercially owned, may also license your program. A specially prepared *'M & E'* (music and effects) sound track and English language script must accompany a new 16mm film print. The foreign broadcaster re-narrates the film and dubs in the voices of the actors in the native language.

Pay-TV. At present there are 90 million US homes with television. About 76 million of these homes are *'passed'* by cable. Some 34.2 million homes receive *'basic cable'* which improves the reception of network tv and carries 'basic' cable networks (such as *MTV, ESPN, CNN, Nickelodeon*, and local cable stations). There are a total of 30 million homes that receive *'pay'* cable. These homes pay approximately $15 per month for each premium service (such as *THE MOVIE CHANNEL, SHOWTIME*, or *HBO*). A producer may license material to Pay-TV, on an exclusive or non-exclusive basis, for so many *'plays'* or showings in a limited period of time. Programs are sold to pay-TV before any other television market. The subscriber base has actually diminished among pay-tv networks. Licensing fees have fallen. Nevertheless cable provides some ancillary market for independent productions. Query the potential buyer before producing your program or you may end up with a show that's difficult to sell.

Stock Footage. This is an *'auxillary'* market. Stock footage from your production may be licensed to other producers for use in their programs. If your material is unique or unusual, then this may be another source of income for you. Stock footage is sometimes acquired by already existing shows, such as *SATURDAY NIGHT LIVE, BLOOPS AND BLUNDERS, IN SEARCH OF, PM MAGAZINE*, and *20/20*.

Release Schedule

Since there are a number of different markets that your tape or film could sell to you need to include in your prospectus a release schedule—in essence a marketing plan that shows how you will release the program in each market. The order is very important as a poorly designed release could result in a loss in potential earnings. Basic rule of thumb: first sell to the highest paying buyer and work your way down.

A release schedule for a theatrical film might look like this;

Market	Release Date
US THEATRICAL	January 1986
FOREIGN THEATRICAL	July 1986
HOME VIDEO (US)	June 1986
FOREIGN HOME VIDEO	January 1987
PAY-TELEVISION (US)	June 1987
NON-THEATRICAL	October 1987
NETWORK TELEVISION	June 1988
FOREIGN TELEVISION	January 1989
STOCK FOOTAGE SALES	After June 1988

The logic of this pattern or schedule is that it starts with the higher paying and more specialized markets first and then expands into wider distribution.

The theaters show the film first where people pay as much as $5 per ticket to see it. A film that performs well can receive a higher home video and pay TV price.

If a film does poorly it moves into home video quickly to maximize on what little publicity it has had. A film that does well theatrically at the box office usually isn't released in home video for 4-6 months.

The foreign theatrical release can come 3-9 months later and, in English-speaking countries will utilize the same film prints.

Foreign television rights may be sold soon after the US television rights. If a show is popular here and has good ratings it may help foreign sales, but not always. (*DOLPHIN* was sold to several foreign networks because the PBS broadcast was successful.)

The pay television release occurs about 9 months to a year after the theatrical release. The *'pay per view'* potential of cable may squeeze in before the home video release. Most pay per view systems are trying to convince the studios to release before home video. The success of this strategy has not yet been tested.

Since, in the case of popular films, there may be re-releases of some titles, the network broadcast may not occur for 3 years or more. Obviously any tv sale will hurt pay broadcasts and home video sales so domestic television holds the last window before television syndication. Recently, networks are producing their own movies.

The non-theatrical release of features, (to college campuses, etc.) yields little money and can occur anytime after the theatrical release. Sometimes the non-theatrical release can be coordinated with a networks or PBS broadcast. A mailing can be made to schools and libraries letting them know a certain film can be seen on television. The broadcast is like a *'free preview'* and the distributor does not have to go to the expense of sending out preview prints since the potential buyers can see it on television.

On the other hand, potential buyers may videotape the program and sales can be lost. (When we license *HARDWARE WARS* to pay-TV we make it contractual that they cannot publish the exact broadcast time in their program guides. We do this because we want people to rent the videotape and not tape it off the air. It's hard to tell how much this helps.

Lastly, there is the sale of stock footage. This is a market for unusual documentary footage and does not apply to most films. You obviously want to take full advantage of the material first. If you sell your program's stock footage prior to your television it may devalue your own show and its use. (On the other hand, showing selected clips on tv talk shows will increase public interest in going to the theatrical showings of your film. In this case clips are shown for free.) Not every sale will be in your film's best interests so you need to be careful what you sell. (We sold dolphin footage to *THOSE AMAZING ANIMALS* only after *DOLPHIN* had been shown on PBS).

Once you determine your release pattern you will have a better sense of your expected income. If you are licensing your program to pay TV you will not be able to sell the rights to commercial television until the pay-TV license expires. Your income projections will reflect your release schedule so be sure this information is consistent in the prospectus.

The market for documentaries and shorts are considerably more limited than features.

Income Projections

The income projections are a market-by-market breakdown of anticipated profits over a specified time period. This is the one page most popular with investors and hence it should be well supported by research so that it is not *'pie in the sky'*. You may wish to footnote this page, stating the assumptions you have made, based on your market research and how you obtained these figures.

Resumes

Resumes are important to include in your prospectus because they give your investor the confidence and assurance that you have assembled a competent and experienced team to make the film. If you are including the resumes of many people then it is best to condense them to the essentials rather than have 5 different resumes with varying formats. Be sure to include the top credits and awards of your associates. You may also include *'letters of participation'* from scholars, resource people, consultants, hosts and actors. This demonstrates that top people are willing to participate in the film.

MICHAEL WIESE

3960 Laurel Canyon Blvd., Suite #331
Studio City, CA 91614-3791

Summary Background: *Entertainment executive with twenty-two years experience as producer/director of films, television, pay TV and home video. Author/publisher of film/video books.*

RECENTLY RELEASED

Producer/Director, **SHIRLEY MACLAINE'S INNER WORKOUT** for Vestron Video. On Billboard's best selling video charts: 150,000 units sold.

Author, **FILM & VIDEO MARKETING**, a comprehensive guide (512 pages) to film and video marketing and distribution techniques for low-budget features and home video programs.

Co-Inventor, **GOIN' HOLLYWOOD: THE MOVIE-MAKING GAME**, an irreverent comedic board game as seen on Entertainment Tonight, MTV, USA Today, LA TIMES.

NEW PROJECTS IN DEVELOPMENT

SHIRLEY MACLAINE'S "GOING WITHIN" (Two hour meditation audio tape for Bantam Audio.)

Executive Producer, **HOME VIDEO SPORTS SERIES** (Vestron).

Producer/Director, **PEAK IMMUNITY**, one hour video based on revolutionary new therapies by Dr. Luc De Sheppard which cleanse and strengthen the immune system.

Writer, Producer. **SURVING THE DREAM** (A Video Novel) *"Mysticism, magic and madness"*—an adventure travel memoir of life in a Balinese village in 1970.

1988-89

NATIONAL GEOGRAPHIC TELEVISION
THE SMITHSONIAN INSTITUTION
BUCKMINSTER FULLER INSTITUTE
THE AMERICAN FILM INSTITUTE]
MYSTIC FIRE VIDEO (Joseph Campbell, "The Power of Myth")
NAUTILUS JAPAN
PBS-WNET

PAST EXPERIENCE:

Executive-In-Charge of Production for Vestron on **STRAWBERRY FIELDS,** an animated feature film ala "Yellow Submarine" with Beatles' songs performed by Michael Jackson, Cyndi Lauper, Robert Palmer, Stevie Ray Vaughn and Crosby-Stills-Nash. Voices of Debra Winger and Steve Guttenberg. (An ITC, Vestron and CGL co-production.) (3/85-8/88)

VESTRON VIDEO
3/84 to 8/87
Vice President of Non-Theatrical Programming. Founded the original program division and developed, acquired and/or produced over 200 original programs in comedy, sports, childrens, music video, how-to, and specialty genres. Gross whole-sale receipts from original programs acquired and produced have exceeded $60,000,000.

Negotiated the **NATIONAL GEOGRAPHIC VIDEO** deal which brought Vestron the forefront of "quality programming". The series has sold 2 million units. Followed with the acquisitions: **NOVA VIDEO, RAND MCNALLY VIDEOTRIPS, SMITH-SONIAN WORLD** and **AUDUBON VIDEO.** Released the first "instant publishing event" best-sellers such as **"LET'S GO METS", "SECRETS OF THE TITANIC"** and others. Executive producer on **ARNOLD PALMER: PLAY GREAT GOLF, NEW WAVE COMEDY, NON-IMPACT AEROBICS,** etc.

Negotiated and acquired home video comedy programs from **ROBIN WILLIAMS, WHOOPI GOLDBERG, BILLY CRYSTAL, BETTE MIDLER, JOE PISCOPO, STEPHEN WRIGHT, ROBERT KLEIN, FATHER GUIDO SARDUCCI, BOB GOLDTHWAIT, STEVE MARTIN** and many others.

Executive Producer, **THE BEACH BOYS: AN AMERICAN BAND,** Vestron feature.

SHOWTIME/THE MOVIE CHANNEL
10/82-11/83
As <u>Director of On-Air Promotion and Production</u> oversaw the creation and production of over 1200 on-air segments. Yearly production budget of $3,000,000.

DHS FILMS
2/82-10/82
As <u>Head of Production</u> oversaw all television production for 17 senatorial and gubernatorial campaigns including those of Senator Moynihan, Governor Babbitt, and Senator Lautenberg. Produced 175 tv spots, 60 radio spots and 2 documentaries in 9 months. Budgets totaled over $3,000,000.

THE AMERICAN FILM INSTITUTE
1982 - 1989
As <u>seminar leader</u> conducts *"Independent Film and Video: Financing and Marketing Techniques"* for producers throughout the U.S, England, Australia and New Zealand.

FOCAL/BUTTERWORTH PUBLISHERS
As <u>author and publisher</u> wrote four and published six best-selling film and video books used by professionals and in college film courses throughout the U. S.

- o <u>FILM & VIDEO MARKETING (1989)</u>
- o <u>HOME VIDEO: Producing for the Home Market (1986)</u>
- o <u>FILM & VIDEO BUDGETS (1984)</u>
- o <u>THE INDEPENDENT FILM & VIDEOMAKERS GUIDE (1981)</u>
- o <u>FADE IN: The Screenwriting Process</u> (Berman)
- o <u>THE HOLLYWOOD GIFT CATALOG</u> (Fosselius)

- o Publishing, SHOT BY SHOT: VISUALIZING FROM CONCEPT TO SCREEN (Katz)
- o Writing, RAISING MONEY FOR FILM & VIDEO

MICHAEL WIESE FILM PRODUCTIONS , 1972-1988
<u>Producer and/or director</u> of 27 shorts and documentaries including **"HARDWARE WARS"** (Warner Home Video, HBO, Pyramid) and **"DOLPHIN ADVENTURES"** (Vestron Video, PBS, BBC, Disney Channel, Discovery Channel, and 30 foreign television networks.)

Press Clippings

Newspaper articles that discuss the project you are currently working on lend a sense of reality to the project that goes beyond your written presentation. Something about the printed page—somebody else's printed page. If no article have been written you might solicit one or two that will support what you are doing. The following article was written when I was working on a film about "Divorced Dads". Lots of dads called in so the article—besides getting attention for the project— was a subtle casting call and lent credibility to the project.

Publicity when it appears in magazines and newspapers help generate new publicity. After a while it begins to feed on itself. Articles will appear on their own without having to be solicited by your publicist. A few months back an article appeared in the LA Times about one of my projects. Two weeks later the entire piece was picked up by PEOPLE Magazine. The magazine press create a lot of their stories from regional newspaper pieces.

DIRTY DANCING, for example, got to the point where the press was feeding on the press. It was a publicist's dream. (There is a case study of DIRTY DANCING that goes into the marketing of the successful independent film in FILM & VIDEO MARKETING.)

Note:

In creating your prospectus remember that it is <u>your</u> prospectus. These are only ideas about what kind of information you may want to include. You can structure it to best represent your project and help you raise money, get distribution or publicity.

When I was an executive at Vestron in charge of buying programs for home video distribution I received numerous proposals that were formatted exactly like what I've suggested in this book. Now, some of those submitting probably didn't know I wrote the book and some probably did. I found myself with one producer who was flabbergasted when I rejected his program. He said, "*But Mr. Wiese, I did exactly what you said in the book.*" I had to tell him that writing a prospectus doesn't guarantee acceptance by a buyer. Plus his program idea was dreadful.

The presentation is vitally important. The contact of the program is important. But the real "yes" will come from a buyer <u>if it meets with the needs he or she is trying to fill</u>. The prospectus is only a presentation format where you put down all the vital statistics of a program. I've bought programs or co-produced program ideas that were one-page letters. But that's also because it was clear upon meeting the producer that he or she could deliver the goods.

Michael Wiese /Sausalito filmmaker looking for divorced fathers by Karen King

Divorce is on a constant rise all across the nation. We've seen the statistics and heard the many reasons why. But what is seldom dealt with is how divorce is affecting men and their relationships with their children.

Sausalito filmmaker Michael Wiese — producer/director/writer — has decided to take up this issue in "Divorced Fathers" — the pilot for a proposed television series on fathering in America.

Still in the research stage, Michael is looking for divorced fathers who are willing to talk about their experiences. So far he's had over thirty men come to him — all with very different stories to tell.

"The one thing that's really surprised me about these guys," says Michael, "is

Michael
Wiese.
photo by
Tina
Gallison

that they all have such moving stories . I thought only women's stories could bring me to tears, but some of these guys' experiences are intense."

It also surprised him that men are willing to open up to other men; something that isn't ordinarily encouraged in our society. "The men all have an experience they want to share, but sometimes they just aren't ready to talk. That's why I have them come to me. After I spoke with one guy he suggested I call a friend of his who's just been through a divorce. I said no, you tell your friend about me."

The idea for this series on fathering, to be aired on Public Broadcasting, came from Bay Area filmmaker Bill Jersey. A divorced father himself, Bill began working on this project about 5 years ago. When Michael heard about Bill's proposed television series, he was intrigued and for the past six months, they've been researching together.

"The question I want to raise," says Michael, "is what does it mean to be a father. I don't have any children myself, but I think I could make a better mother than father because we all know what makes a good mother and what makes a bad one. But what makes a good father besides being around?

"In fact, the whole question of masculinity needs to be addressed. We've got to find out what being a man really means, and I think divorce often leads to a re-evaluation of that. During the years of the Women's Movement, there's also been a Men's Movement, but where women came to the foreground, men, who have always been in the foreground, withdrew. Women started turning to other women and men turned inward which can cause a terrible resentment or hatred for women and relationships."

Michael has been making films for the past 15 years and has formed his own production company in Sausalito. He recently produced the television documentary special "Dolphin" for PBS. About this current project, he speaks with warmth and sincerity. When I asked him how long the pilot would take to complete, he said "Maybe a year or so, but I'd really like to study the men over a period of 15 years to *really* get to know them and see what eventually happens between them and their children."

Michael and Bill want to speak to fathers who are going through divorce, as well as those who've been divorced for many years and now have a stable relationship with their children. They're interested in the changes men have to go through because of a separation, maybe doing things for the first time, and coming to a new understanding of the significance of being a father.

Divorced fathers who would like to share their experiences with the filmmakers may write FATHERS, Box 245, Sausalito 94965 or call Michale Wiese at 332-3829.

SAUSALITO FILMMAKER Michael Wiese was a drummer in a band when he was, first, a prize-winning photographer for his high school newspaper and then, later, a cub news photographer for his home-town daily. But the beat that pulsed through his being as a musician finally rebelled at the static constraints of still photography. "I got tired of pictures not moving," Wiese says simply, explaining his switch from single frames to rolling footage.

Although movement is what a motion picture is all about, it doesn't necessarily mean that the subjects being photographed have to move, Wiese notes. One of Wiese's latest films, Radiance: The Experience of Light (1979), winner of five film festival awards, evolved from a multiple-slide show, Do Saints Really Glow? It was inspired by an aura-like phenomenon that co-producer Dorothy Fadiman had experienced 12 years before she met Wiese. It is a motion picture made from still subjects. The movement of the film is gently tracked with music and a poetic narrative, all sensitively put together by Wiese, to produce what a critic called "an aesthetic high if there ever was one."

"Editing comes very easy to me because I was a musician. The whole process is really creating a rhythm for still photos. There's a beat I'm working for. A visual beat," Wiese explains.

If the music in his soul accounts for Wiese's effective editing abilities, his early familiarity with a camera (starting at the age of 11) and a good, substantial education in film science and filmmaking at the Rochester Institute of Technology (Kodak country) and the film school at the San Francisco Art Institute (where he graduated with honors at age 19), respectively, have led to his emergence as an extremely capable cinematographer.

As a matter of fact, Salvador Dali thought enough of Wiese's work to present his first film, Messages, Messages, at its premiere in the ballroom of the posh St. Regis Hotel in New York. The 25-minute "surrealistic art film," as Wiese describes it, was a critical success, garnering four awards at four different film festivals in this country, Canada and France. The film was also selected for showing in "The Director's Fortnight" at the Cannes International Film Festival.

However, Wiese and co-producer Steven Arnold faced the age-old problem of independent filmmakers — distribution of their film and money. The two decided to show their own films. They rented the old Palace Theater in San Francisco, held a press screening of the film and then, after the journalists had done their job, opened the doors to the public who, gratifyingly, filled the 2,000-seat house.

The owners of the theater were so impressed by the turn-out that they convinced Wiese and Arnold to produce a series of late-night film offerings. The two obliged and their "Nocturnal Dream Shows" offered camp, foreign, and their own experimental films to after-hours cinema seekers.

To Wiese's dismay, "old Betty Boop movies pulled better than the more serious films" and, after two years of promoting and programming, Wiese gave in to the enchanting influence of Japanese cinema that had been beckoning him for several years, packed his bag and headed for Kyoto where, for four months, he "took quiet strolls."

When his money ran out, Wiese set up "Global Dream Shows," a Far East version of his far-out venture in the Palace Theater. The Japanese appeared delighted with his multi-media presentations and had no problem understanding Wiese's presentations which were essentially silent films with a sound track.

From Japan, Wiese headed for Singapore, Java and the idyllic island of Bali where he spent half a year as the adopted son of a friendly village whose residents helped him build a thatched house where he painted, tried his hand at shadow puppetry and learned to play the gamelan, a Balinese xylophone. He ate eels with his new-found friends, but drew the line at "pigs that were served with their fur on."

"Here I was, an ordinary Illinois boy surrounded by extraordinary people," he says with a gentle smile. His affection for the Balinese was enduring and when he returned to the United States, he was able to sell some of the islanders' paintings he had taken with him. He sent the money back to the Balinese for a school house and additional rice fields.

From Bali, Wiese returned to Japan briefly, then continued on to India, East Africa and Greece in his quest "to experience the world and find out who I was" before returning home to make Silver Box, a cinematic photo album of "precious memories" that had, over the years, contributed to the growth and development of the young filmmaker. Perhaps because it was so personally introspective, Wiese stopped showing the film: "I got embarrassed."

Work as a part-time typist in a San Francisco law office kept body and soul together in the mid-70's until runner Mike Murphy backed Wiese in Extraordinary Powers, a 13-minute, synchronized sound film that "explores mind-body connections with some of the fastest men and women runners in the world."

Extraordinary Powers marked a very important turning point in the filmmaker's career. "I had always had to pay for my own films before by working at part-time jobs. This was the first time someone else believed in me enough to put up some money as well as kind wishes."

Another "believer" came forth almost immediately in the form of the American Film Institute which awarded Wiese a $10,000 grant to make I Move, an ode to motion, both freely spontaneous and consciously disciplined, a reflection of Americans' growing awareness of both mental and physical well-being.

It was quite a switch in style and subject matter for Wiese to join forces with Ernie Fosselius for the production of Hardware Wars, which Examiner critic Stanley Eichelbaum described as "a delightfully batty, 13-minute parody [of Star Wars] which is expected to be the biggest short film of the year [1978]." Eichelbaum was right on both counts. The little gem (that cost $8,000 to make) is batty as all get out and, three years after it was released, is still going strong as a feature in its own right.

The idea was hatched by Fosselius and revealed to Wiese during a hilarious lunch in a Chinese restaurant. To illustrate his concept of using household appliances as galactic weaponry in a spoof of George Lucas' cosmic classic, Fosselius snatched the silverware off the table and whirred it above Wiese's head as he described the adventures that would involve a cast of zany characters including Darph Nader, Augie "Ben" Doggie (last of the Red Eye Knights) and the heroine, Princess Anne-Droid. "He had me on the floor for half an hour," Wiese recalls with delight.

Hardware Wars boasts 11 topnotch film festival awards and was among ten short films considered for an Academy Award two years ago.

Moving along from the ridiculous to the sublime, Wiese next met up with Hardy Jones, a former writer/producer for CBS News. The two met at a Buckminster Fuller seminar that Jones was producing at Pajaro Dunes. He and Wiese shared a common fascination with dolphins and the notion that "man and dolphin could be friends." They both agreed with Fuller that "Nature wouldn't have given the dolphin its large brain unless she were doing something very important with it." Wiese had also "met a dolphin on a San Francisco beach in 1967 and I thought it communicated with me."

Hence, Dolphin was conceived and plans were laid to journey to the mammal's home waters and make a film not just about them, but with them.

When the crew of Dolphin arrived at its destination just off the Bahamas, they were welcomed by a school of dolphins who accepted them as unthreatening, new playmates. As a matter of fact, the friendly dolphins appeared to enjoy the music played for them by sound man Steve Gagne on a special, submersible keyboard he designed specifically for the film. As he played, the stars of the show cavorted gracefully with the divers and were filmed in sequences that appeared as a beautiful underwater ballet to critics who have been enthusiastic with their praise for the unusual film that is being shown on television throughout the world.

His plans for the future include a full length feature "about an ordinary young man who travels to the South Seas and to whom extraordinary things happen." Wiese says with a look of mystical merriment on his face.

How is it that he can manage to live in Marin and still be a successful filmmaker?

"It is very, very hard. The good news is that people here are quite helpful and supportive. The bad news is that the resources are very limited. My professional life is moving slower being here than if I worked in Los Angeles, but I am totally satisfied in my personal life living in the Bay Area. That's the trade-off."

Michael Wiese:

portrait of an artist as a young filmmaker

story by gayle murphy

67

Contact Address

It is amazing how many prospectus' neglect to list the address and phone number of the person to contact for further information. Both should appear on the front or inside cover of the prospectus.

Enclosure

The last page in the prospectus is the enclosure, which is a questionnaire that lets you know whether someone wishes to invest or not. This is not bound or stapled to the prospectus because it will be returned to you after the presentation or by mail. (A sample is included in the section on presentations.)

Binding

Do not bind the prospectus in such a way that you can't take it apart to insert updates. As the project progresses you will want to update many of the pages.

I've seen proposals bound in leather, wood, plastic, metal, cloth, and even mylar. Forget it. It's a waste of time. If your idea won't hold up on its own, no amount of fancy binding is going to sell it. In fact, spending money on binding is a poor choice of priorities when these precious funds could be used elsewhere, like on the screen. Either use a simple cover stock or a clear plastic report binder with three hole punch binding which costs about 59 cents. The great thing about binders is that you can take them apart to update your prospectus with new information. Let the title and the art work on your cover, be it a xerox, photograph, or drawing, do the selling, not the binding.

THE INTERVIEW

'You may wish to venture from the independent path at some time in your career.'

From Independent to Employed

Not only is it valuable to know how to present your project in its best light but it is also to your advantage to present yourself favorably through your resume. Your resume will be valuable, not only for inclusion in your prospectus but, heaven forbid, also should you look for employment in the future. You may wish to venture from the independent path at some time in your career. That's what happened to me.

For 16 years I was an independent film and video producer. In 1981, after a long stretch of not being able to raise money for a variety of projects, I took my first staff job as a segment producer for a *'live'* television show in San Francisco. My next job was as Head of Production with an agency in New York that specialized in producing media for political campaigns. And then I joined *THE MOVIE CHANNEL*, a Pay TV service, where I supervised the production of *'interstitial'* or break programming.

In my last two positions, I was responsible for hiring writers, field producers, directors, artists, editors, and crews. I sat on the other side of the interview table and had to evaluate the person seated directly across from me. Here are some observations that will assist you not only in giving presentations, addressing groups and holding press conferences, but also interviewing for work.

69

Know The Job

Research the job before interviewing. Too many people apply for jobs without knowing anything about the company or corporation, or the work that will be required of them. It wastes everybody's time and rarely do they succeed in getting the job. This research should be thorough enough for you to determine if you want to work for your potential boss or corporation. Learn all you can about what will be expected of you, who had the job before you, what happened to them, etc. Often, your interviewer won't have the time to describe the job in detail. You'll have to find out in advance. You can do this by talking to current and past employees. The more you can learn, the more you'll have to talk about. This will give you a leading edge. The more *'interested'* you are, the more *'interesting'* you'll be to them.

Go well in advance to the building, floor or even room where the interview will take place. Get the *'feel'* of the place. You can learn a lot about a company just by sitting in their reception area for half an hour. You can do this without an appointment. What you'll observe will give you a very good idea of what the people and company are like. In this way, at least the environment will be familiar to you when the interview begins. This isn't always possible but the more relaxed you are the more you can be yourself and the better chance you have.

Job: Landing The First One

When I applied for my job as a television segment producer I'd already learned (from the secretary on the phone) that many people had already applied. They were about to make up their mind and hire someone. It sounded like they had plenty of people although they said, *'yes, go ahead and mail your resume and then we'll see'*. I knew then and there that it was a long shot. My chances were slim and I didn't have much time.

I had to do something outrageous. I had to stand out. What did I have to lose?

Before I hung up I said that I'd hand-deliver my resume (to speed up the process). I also learned that the senior producer, who was doing the interviews, was in the studio. I figured if I hurried I might get a chance to see him. Even though I didn't know how.

Twenty minutes later I arrived at the studio armed with a brief letter. It said I was waiting in the lobby and would be there for an hour and asked if the senior producer would be willing to come out to meet me.

Unfortunately, I hadn't anticipated the studio security guard. With dramatic flourish I handed him the letter and said that it was urgent. I said the senior producer was expecting it. (Well, he was! Sort of.)

It worked. A few minutes later his secretary came down to pick up the letter. I did everything possible to get her on my side. I told her that I really wanted to interview for the job and could she ask the producer to meet with me right now. About 15 minutes passed. Just as I thought it was hopeless, she came back down and took me to meet the producer.

We talked for a few minutes. I quickly understood the job. I told him about those parts of my background that applied. (Everything else is irrelevant in an interview.) He asked if I'd seen the show. (I hadn't.) ***Rule Number One: Know The Job.*** Unfortunately I didn't. In fact, I'd only heard about the opening less than an hour earlier and had *never* seen the show.)

I said I had. (I was getting in deeper and deeper.) He asked if I had any ideas for it. I told him that I had quite a few. (I really did, whether they had anything to do with his show I couldn't say.) When he asked me what they were I told him that I didn't want to just bounce them off the wall but what I would do is write them down and present them to him in a more organized fashion. He agreed and asked me to submit them two days later.

I hurried home. Watched the show. Then prepared some 50 ideas for possible segments. (I also took the time to call people who'd worked for this producer before who could fill me in on his tastes, the inner workings of the show, and so on.) A day after he read my ideas, he hired me.

Now I don't suggest this approach to everyone. I felt I had to take the chances I did to get the job. Time was running out. Rarely will I go to an interview that unprepared. None of what I did was pre-meditated. It was totally spontaneous. It came out of my sheer desire to *'go for it'*. If I were on the receiving end I'm not sure how I would have responded. Perhaps this kind of persistence, aggressive humor, and *'chutzpah'* were qualities I'd look for in a producer. Maybe I'd figure if they can get in my door they can certainly get in other doors to do their job.

Job: Head Of Production

In New York (when I was on the hiring side of the interview desk) I met an uninvited production assistant (dressed in jeans and a t-shirt) that slipped past a very formal reception area, traversed two long hallways, ducked past my secretary and bolted into my office before anyone could say *'boo'*. I felt like my office had been invaded. I never did hire him but even today I think about this guy. He certainly made an impression.

On another occasion, a young producer who had interviewed with me said he'd bring in his videotape later. I clearly told him that I couldn't screen it when he brought it in but to drop it off with the receptionist and I'd watch it as soon as I could.

72

Instead, when he returned he convinced the receptionist it was urgent (sound familiar?). The receptionist's call interrupted a meeting I was having. I passed on the word that I'd be glad to view the tape but that he should leave it at the front desk. Instead, the producer found his way to my office and came right in. (So much for my open door policy.) I was not a very happy guy. He obviously didn't want to do what I had *clearly* asked. I wouldn't hire a guy who couldn't follow simple instructions. Now, on the outside what he did was not too terribly different from what I did a few years earlier. But there is a difference. It's a matter of appropriateness. I listened. I assessed the situation. He overlooked some very direct cues.

You've got to be aware of the signals the potential employer puts out. Sometimes the cues are loud and clear, other times subtle. What I did to get a job and what these other two guys did are not very different in form. I played it close to the line, but didn't go over it. I respected the people I met. I listened and watched and decided how far to go. Perhaps I was lucky. But I think not. It was a matter of being appropriate and sensitive to the situation.

More Tips

Other things to remember when going for an interview. Dress appropriately. Maybe that means shirt, jacket and tie. Maybe that means going casual. I'd suggest playing it safe. Dress up a tad more than you think necessary. It shows respect. If you play it on the conservative side your chances of going wrong are reduced.

Do yourself a favor. Go to your interview fresh. Get a good night's sleep. Give yourself plenty of time to get to the interview (be a few minutes early, never late). Don't rush to get there, not only will you be hot and sweaty, but you'll be off balance. Be sure to eat. Not so much that you're sleepy, but enough so that your stomach doesn't growl. You should feel confident, awake, relaxed, and be in good humor. (It's okay to smile in an interview. Don't let it get too serious. Most people like to have a little fun at work.)

Closing The Deal

Once I understand the job (and, if I really want it), I look the interviewer in the eye and come right out and say it. *'I want this job. What do I need to do to get it?'* Now you have to be truthful about this or it won't work. You have to really want the job. (Not *'need'* the job, that's very different, but *'want'* it.) This is usually so disarming to the person you say it to, it will have an effect. Hopefully a positive one. Most people pussy-foot around and never come right out and say what they want. I prefer the direct method, if it's truthful. You let people know where you stand.

It's also always better to apply for a job when you already have one. It increases your value in the employer's eyes. It may also increase your salary 25-50% over what you're currently making. If you come off the street then you'll be lucky to make what you did at your last job.

Don't 'Need' The Job

Like anything else, it's better not to come from a position of *'need'* when applying for a job. It's like taking out a loan at the bank; if you don't need the money, they'll loan it to you. So, you ask, *'how do you show you don't need a job when you really do?'* You have to create a feeling of abundance for yourself, that you have plenty of choices, that this job sitting right in front of you is only one option available to you. You have to have a lot of self-worth and really feel it, so that the interviewer will too. Not a cockiness or arrogance but good

74

feeling about yourself. It's entirely up to you to generate this feeling within. And it's very important the feeling is real for you. I generally reflect on my own abilities, or all the good work I've done, or remember a time when I was productive and happy about a job I had. It will help. If your interview has the tone about it that you 'need' a job you probably won't get it. People don't give jobs to people who 'need' them. They give jobs to people that will do a good job for them, that will be fun or interesting to work with, that they can be proud of, or will make them look good. People want to hire winners.

The 'Attitude' Going In

As an employer I can tell a lot about someone from how they describe their previous jobs. One fellow came to me and told me how he'd been burned by his bosses. *'They didn't understand. They weren't fair. They didn't know what they were doing.'* I began to wonder, if he ever worked for me, what would he be saying down the line? Would I be another in a long string of insensitive, unfair tyrants? Probably. He was all set for that to be so. Did he have a problem with authority? In taking direction? I didn't know and I didn't want to be the one to find out.

To Show Or Not To Show

Another guy came in to interview for a job as an assistant editor. Nice, young, friendly guy. Well-dressed. Intelligent. Looked good. He told me that the only editing job he had was cutting coming attractions (trailers) for a Pay TV service. I said that was okay. (The job he was interviewing for really didn't require much experience. At this point I was pretty certain I would hire him.) He asked if I wanted to see a cassette of his work. I said, *'it really isn't necessary, but if you like, why not?'*

75

When the cassette arrived it was all X-rated trailers. We're talking trash. We're talking smut. It was so raunchy that I couldn't tell whether he could edit or not. I was so surprised by the *'content'* that I paid no attention to the editing job.

I couldn't believe that he'd show me this. What in the world was he thinking of? It was totally inappropriate to show the tape for the job he was applying for. Was it a joke? Did he think I would like it? What was going through his head? I was all set to give him the job but he blew it. He really misjudged the situation. Could I trust him to represent the company should he have to deal with outside suppliers or other employees? I didn't know. I passed on him.

The Moral: Only show work that is appropriate to the job.
The potential employer doesn't need to know (and probably isn't interested in) anything else. Additional information may muddle and confuse the situation. You have to be selective in what you show and tell. If you don't have the right reel to show, show nothing at all.

(The funny thing is, that for years and years I worked very hard to build up my *'reel'*. I had always thought that I'd needed it to get a job. But in landing my last three jobs I sold myself on me alone.)

Just Browsing

Another attitude you might want to explore when interviewing for work is one of *'just browsing'*. I figure that if I am going to take a job it had better be one I really like, with people I like and with opportunities. With only one or two meetings this may be difficult to ascertain. Like a romance, each person will project *'images'* about the other. Now of course these images will not be true. Each person is really someone else. After a while the images will wear off and the people will quit project-

76

ing onto the other person. This also goes on during interviews. Somehow you have to get through this veil of expectations to see who and what is really there. Who is this person who'll be your boss, or your partner? What is the job? Not the job description or what they think it might be. What is it really? This may take several interviews or more to get to the point of whether you want the job or not (if it's offered to you). Explain your desire to learn about the person, the company, etc. Don't feel you have to rush into anything. Don't put yourself under so much pressure to 'get a job' that you'll take something you wish you hadn't later on. Remember that you are interviewing them as much as they are interviewing you. Take your time to pick a job that you can really feel good about. Everyone will be better off in the long run.

MARKET RESEARCH

Market Research

> *'It is critical to find out whether
> your ideas, once made into films,
> will have a market.'*

Market Research

This is probably the most important but neglected aspect of the whole filmmaking process. For years I avoided studying marketing. I felt that by dealing with such commercial concerns I would somehow compromise my creative and artistic efforts. This was simply not the case. It is critical to find out whether your ideas, once made into films, will have a market. It is a matter of survival.

I guess what I was afraid I might find out (and later did) was that many of my ideas were not in fact marketable. They were good ideas but too limited to have much of an audience. That's fine, but if you want to make those kinds of films it's best to raise the money through grants, contributions and not through investors who will expect to be paid back.

Once you get an idea for a film, research how the film will be used. What will be the most successful markets for your film or videotape idea?

Try to answer these basic questions in depth. Then present your findings in the prospectus under *'market research'*, *'trend indicators'* or *'income projections'*. Without knowing answers to these questions, you are not only fooling yourself about your film or videotape's potential but you may be misleading others as well.

81

1. *What, specifically, is the subject of the film?*

Once you have determined the purpose of your film, this question will be easily answered. While you are at it, you might brainstorm on other related ideas around your main subject area. You may be surprised to find a wealth of other ideas, spinoffs or other media that you could produce at the same time, thus economizing and creating additional income through other sources. Perhaps your one idea will lead you to a series. In the end, you will need to clearly identify the primary subject of your film.

2. *What is the length of the film?*

The answer is not *'as long as it wants to be'*. That is a fine way to make personal and artistic films and tapes but not media that someday will be bought and sold in commercial marketplaces. If, for example, you are making a television program, then you must stick to the standard times. If you don't, you'll surely come up with a *'white elephant'*. Commercial prime time is different from non-prime time. A *'television half-hour'* could vary between 22 and 26 minutes. A *'PBS half-hour'* could be 26 to 29 minutes long. If you make a film with an unusual length you'll have great difficulty in selling it. You must adhere to the standards for a particular market. It's best to know your exact running time before even scripting your project.

3. *In what formats (16mm, 3/4" video, 1/2" video, broadcast, videodisk, etc.) can your film or tape project be marketed?*

Don't automatically assume that your project will be distributable in all formats. You've got to do research to find out. Different markets use different formats. The business and health markets are using 3/4" videotape more and more. However, public libraries and schools still rely on 16mm films because they've already invested in projectors. Home consumers use videotape players and prefer VHS to Betamax by about

82

70% but this could change. Perhaps videodisk will become more popular in the next decade.

Don't think that if you shoot and edit in videotape you can make a tape-to-film transfer and have a high-quality product to distribute to the 16mm educational market. Perhaps someday, but right now the quality is usually not high enough to make sales. Film buyers are accustomed to looking at 'real film' and prefer it. This could change as technology improves. All the more reason to know what format the market requires.

Foreign television requires a 16mm film print (and not a video master!). There are so many different tape standards, the foreign networks prefer to make a 16mm film-to-tape transfer themselves. They'll also require a separate *music and effects track* ('*M and E*' track). US television requires a high-quality 1″ or 2″ master. Be absolutely sure you know what formats your product will best be distributed in and budget accordingly.

4. *Who are the distributors that may potentially distribute your film?*

I've listed many non-theatrical distributors, home video distributors and Pay TV program buyers in the appendix in the back of the book. This list will give you a healthy start in exploring possibilities for your films and tapes, even if they are only in the idea stage.

You may find similar films already in distribution on the same subject as yours. Don't let that discourage you before looking into the matter deeper. The film could be very different, or old and in need of revision.

I once wanted to do a film on the *'future uses of the human brain'*. I thought this would be an exciting subject, one that fascinated me anyhow. In searching through distributors' catalogs I found no films on the brain. Then, in Encyclopedia

Brittanica's collection (I think it was theirs), I found a film on the brain. I was greatly disappointed but I figured at least I'd rent the film and see what it looked like. To my amazement I found that the film was made in 1955, was in black and white, and compared the functions of the brain to driving a car! So despite my initial disappointment, the market was begging for a new film on the human brain. (As it turned out I didn't make that film for other reasons.) But it goes to show that it's a good idea to research any similarities in depth.

5. *What are the influences on the buyer?*

By that I mean, what will make them want to buy, or not buy, your film or tape? Price is certainly a factor. If it is an educational film and public monies have been cut in media centers' budgets then that is an influence. Perhaps it is a videotape for home consumer use but if we are in a recession, then that's a factor. Or perhaps the potential buyer of your film perceives its value lower than the price you've given it. How can you increase the consumer's perception of the value of your film or tape? (Recognizable names is one way.) It's wise to look into the markets you are interested in before leaping. Many small educational distributors are going out of business. The school and library market has dwindled in the last five years and can no longer support many distributors. Others are expanding into videotape and cable television markets.

The consumer videotape business is booming. Both rentals are growing and the 'sell-thru' market is finally taking hold. Feature films are the most popular genre. Children's programming may soon be 15% of the market. X-rated product still sells. Only a few 'how-to' tapes (Jane Fonda) have been best-sellers.

Another influence on buyers is advertising and promotion. The more ways they come into contact with your program, the more likely they will buy (or rent) it, particularly if they derive some benefit or value (information, entertainment, etc.)

84

6. Do you have any competitors? Who are they?

By going through film and video distributor's catalogs. You will quickly find programs similar to yours. Don't despair. View these films, they could be very different from yours. When you find a distributor that you think could market your program, call them up. Learn everything you can about their business. Gather valuable information. Act as if you are already producing your program. This way you won't have to worry about the idea being stolen. Most distributors aren't producers and will be glad to help you design your program. Don't work in a vacuum. A distributor is closer to the market than you are. He can suggest ways to make your program more marketable before you spend money. Speak with foreign television distributors who can give you insight into the international market.

Listen closely to what the distributor says. That doesn't mean you necessarily have to '*go commercial*' or compromise the film you want to make. The distributors know their markets. They know what sells and what doesn't. And since they may someday handle your film, they will usually be very willing to discuss your project with you. This free information can help you immeasurably in the planning stages. If you are afraid to explore these areas, you may limit your chances for success. This does not mean that you should go and tell everyone about your idea. Just the contrary. Keep your ideas and thoughts to yourself; don't dissipate your energy and focus. But what you can do is draw information from distributors who can help you. You'll learn about marketing and establish value contacts for distribution later.

7. What share of the market do you expect to reach? Of this market, how many do you expect to sell to? How will you reach them? Why will they buy?

This question can only be answered once you determine how

large the market is for your product and how many others you'll be competing with. Try to assess how many 16mm prints or video cassettes you can sell.

Study lists of mailing lists. This may give you an idea of how many users, renters and buyers you can reach through direct mail. Marketing studies have shown that if you use a good, well-focused list, 2-3% may respond to the first mailing and possibly another 1% or more with a repeat mailing to the same list. If you have a high sale to preview ratio (like 1:4), then you can begin to calculate how many sales are possible. You also can check similar films in the same subject area to see how many films were sold (and in what period of time).

It's easy to fool yourself. Just because there are 30 million homes with videotape players in the US that doesn't give you any indication of how many you will sell. Some producers think that if they only sell 1% of those VCR owners a tape they will be millionaires. Wrong! What they fail to realize is that, at present, most sales are to the 20,000 mom-and-pop video specialty stores and not the consumer. (At least not yet.) Most people do not buy tapes. They rent them from the video store. So the real customer is the video store—a universe of 20,000, not 30 million! A big difference. Inaccurate assumptions about the marketplace and how it operates could spell disaster for your income projections and the outcome of your endeavor. Learn enough about the market so that you can make reasonable assumptions.

8. What is the retail price to the consumer? Is the program competitively priced?

Distribution catalogs list film and videotape prices by length. The pricing standards in the educational and consumer markets are easily determined. 16mm film prints sell for $15-20 per minute. 3/4' videocassettes for the medical, industrial or educational market sell for about 70% of the 16mm film price. (Obviously the distributor does not want to compete with himself by selling tapes at greatly reduced prices even though their unit cost in tape is significantly less.) Business training tapes can sell for as high as $1500 per hour. The non-theatrical rental grosses diminish yearly. A five minute short film, for example, might rent for $20 ($4 per minute), while an hour film would rent for $45 (less than $1 per minute). That's quite expensive when you can rent a feature length movie on video for $3 per night! Be careful. New media, like video, can wipe out markets. Gather current information.

The retail cost of video tapes are $9-89. Prices are falling each year. The average cost in 1985 was $43. Some sell for as little as $9.99. Only with economy of scale can a distributor afford to sell tapes at a low price. He is hoping that by selling in volume he will make a profit. Producers that self-distribute have trouble getting their duplication cost down to $10 per tape. (And that doesn't include the cost of production.) It's difficult to complete with the major manufacturers when consumers can buy feature films at low prices. Why would they pay more for your tape? These and other factors must be carefully considered when you price your product. Study what already exists.

Market Research Among Distributors

Some distributors *pre-test* an idea before shooting a foot of film. They write a script with accompanying graphics or storyboards. They make a presentation of this film mockup to educators and media buyers. With the subsequent feedback from their potential buyers they rewrite the script and prepare for production. This way they know exactly how to design a film that will have a market. The buyers have told them their exact needs. This approach delivers a very high sales ratio. Exten-

87

sive pre-production research generates maximum return on investment. Independent filmmakers would benefit by using similar techniques and by studying their potential markets in advance of production. Again, you must separate *'what you would like'* from the market realities or you (and your investors) will be greatly disappointed.

Thinking Big

Some independent film and videomakers may have a mental block that keeps them from earning more income with their films. Instead of setting out to make a 20-minute film or videotape of your *'concern'* you may be better off to think of other formats for your ideas. Consider yourself not as a *'filmmaker'* or *'videomaker'* (which is too limiting), but as someone who has an idea they wish to communicate. Think of yourself as a *'communicator'*. You are a 'spokesperson' and can communicate your concerns in a much larger arena. Having freed yourself from the impulse to make your idea manifest in only one form (a 20-minute film) you will discover you suddenly have a much broader audience, more power, and much more influence. Not only will you increase your audience but your will expand your idea's earning potential.

That is not to say the original format (a 20-minute film) might not be the *'primary'* product, but there are also many other forms for you to use. Why limit your possibilities?

For example, distributing your idea via broadcast television, foreign television, on 16mm film, on videotape and videodisk are all possible formats. Everytime you give a tv or radio interview you communicate your 'concern'. Press releases, posters, newspaper ads and commercials are all ways you can communicate. As George Lucas has shown us with his *Star War's* mechandizing, even lunchpails, calendars, pencils and dolls are a forms of communication (and great income).

88

Besides, it will probably take the income from several markets to pay back your production cost. So why not plan your marketing strategy early in the game?

Thinking big will greatly increase your impact and your income.

PRODUCING

Producing

'Many filmmakers find they are much happier doing other jobs.'

The Producer

A producer is involved in a film or tape from the conceptual stages of the project, beginning with the pre-production, research, and writing, through the casting, shooting, editing, and post-production. But that's not all. The job continues with negotiating the distribution contracts and arranging for the promotion and exhibition of the piece.

The producer is the first one on a project and the last one off. I am still responsible for managing the on-going business of films that have been in distribution for many years. It is my job to collect the royalties from the distributors and disburse them to the investors and my creative partners. Some films will require attention as long as they are earning income, which could be 10 years or more.

When a project is just getting off the ground the producer represents the film to potential investors during the fund-raising. When the film is in production, the producer keeps the ideas alive with his/her co-workers. The conceptual idea for the film may have been created by someone else (like a writer or director) but it is the producer that stays with the job the longest.

The public thinks of a producer as the one with the big cigar and a roll of money. That's not so, at least among independents. He/she is the one responsible for raising money and paying the crew. The producer keeps the production on schedule. Much of the job is an administrative one.

93

It is not a job for everyone because it requires a certain stick-to-it-ness. Many filmmakers find they are much happier doing other jobs like writing, camerawork or editing. A producer's job has a lot to do with the business of filmmaking. If you do not have the personality to handle the business (financing, promotion, publicity and advertising) involved with producing films, then find someone who does. These aspects are crucial to the success of any film.

Relationships

Good working relationships with people are more important than any idea. This may sound a bit extreme but it's true. In filmmaking, it is people cooperating with each other that make ideas real.

Many people have wonderful ideas for films but can't work with others. Their ideas will probably not be realized in a film, which is very much a cooperative effort.

Many of the people you meet will continue throughout the years to make films. Their skills, talents and contacts will grow as will yours. Once you have built working relationships with these people you will want to continue to work together. The best way to begin is with agreements.

Agreements

An *agreement* is a tool for establishing and maintaining good communication—a clear understanding of what one's responsibilities are and what the exchange is. Agreements (or contracts) are the place where this is acknowledged and written down.

Very often two or more people will begin a film or tape project with very different ideas of who will do what and who will get

94

what. They'll work for many months, having very different expectations about responsibilities, about money, screen credits, and profit sharing. These aspects of the working relationship need to be clearly and firmly established from the outset.

For one thing, it clears the minds of everyone involved. You no longer have to struggle to get what you want because you have all already agreed on salaries, credits, profit sharing and responsibilities. Your energy can go towards working as a team and not manipulating or fighting with one another over who gets what.

Do not be afraid to put your cards on the table and say what you want. Encourage your partners to do the same. Out of these discussions you can determine what is the most workable agreement for everyone.

An agreement is something you all create and agree to. It is not something that is created by someone and forced upon someone else. Everyone may not get what they want. Compromises may need to be made, but at least everyone will have created the agreement and will support it. There is nothing worse than someone sabotaging the film because they aren't getting what they want. Written agreements align everyone and allow the film to get made.

Create agreements very early on. If it turns out that someone does more work than someone else, then revise your agreements. Have a basis on which to build. An agreement is something you can refer back to 12 months later when you all have forgotten what you agreed to.

Similar agreements can be created for the crew and other participants in the film. They can state what their responsibilities are and what the exchange is (money, percentages and credits).

The period of employment is established. Travel and other reimbursements can be clearly defined.

Many people in film and video projects have fights because there wasn't a clear understanding in the beginning. Everyone had a different idea about who would get what. It is extremely destructive to the morale of the cast and crew and the film-making community as a whole. Written agreements can alleviate much of the misunderstandings and subsequent bad feelings that arise when artistic people join in creative and business ventures.

Most important: write agreements with your best friends, your wives and husbands now. You'll avoid the worst of situations later.

Rights

Written agreements (which are legal contracts) extend into the area of 'rights'. You will have agreements with your creative partners (writers, directors, associate producers) and with anyone who contributes anything to your film.

(Note: Have your lawyer write your agreements, contracts or release forms. Rights need to be secured for everything that is used in your film.)

This is true for photographs, slides, art work, paintings, graphics, music, lyrics, poems and in some cases, props and locations.When it comes to licensing your film to television or signing distribution contracts, you will need to confirm that you own the 'rights' to everything in the film. Therefore, you will need to secure these various rights along the way.

96

Sample Release Form

This is a sample release form. It covers the appearance of everyone in the film and material that individuals and companies furnish, such as stock footage, photos, sound effects, art work, etc. Additional lines or notes may be written at the bottom of the form to clarify credits or payment. (Major participants in the film project should have their own agreements.) This form is for incidental participation and was adapted from a public television station release and is consistent with their legal requirements. The language is simplified wherever possible. *Note: Do not use this release form without consulting your lawyer in regard to your specific needs.*

'DOLPHIN' Release Form
(Your film's working title)

Michael Wiese Film Productions
(Your name & address)
Box 406
Westport, CT, 06881

Dear Michael (your name),

I am willingly participating in your film production, 'DOLPHIN' (film title) about human/dolphin interaction. (Film's subject.)

I grant you permission to film me and use my voice and physical likeness in your film without restriction in any form you wish, be it film, video or print media, or any future media market such as videodisk, etc.

I expressly release you and your agents or representatives or any institution transmitting or exhibiting the program from any claims arising from such use or distribution.

97

I confirm to you that any material furnished by me for the program (for example: music, writing, creative services, film footage) is either my own, or its use for the film has been authorized to me without any restrictions from any third party. Consideration, if any, for such material has been separately stated in a written instrument or added below.

I agree to be fully responsible for my own participation in the production, and hold you harmless from any liability, loss or expense arising from the use of my voice or likeness in the production. I also consent to the use of my name, likeness and voice, and any material about me, for promotional, publicity, or organizational purposes.

BY:
   (Signed)

Print Name:
Address:
Telephone:
Date:

Example of additions. *'I understand that I will receive end title credit in the film as follows: "_____."*

Or, *'I understand that I will receive $____ as full payment for the one time use of my _____ (specify what) in the above mentioned film.'*

Music Rights

Music rights can be difficult and troublesome to secure. Music that has already been recorded on records involves getting signed releases not only from the recording artist, but from the composer, record company, and publishing company. Furthermore, the musicians' union requires that you pay *'re-usary fees'*. (In the case of an orchestral piece, those fees alone could amount to $3000.)

Do not, as so many have, take music from a *Beatles* album, edit your film to it and expect to get the rights later. Even if it's *'okay with Paul'* and it's a non-profit project, you probably won't. The larger record companies simply won't bother with you.

You may also wish to deal directly with small, independent record companies that are owned by the recording artists themselves. You can make an arrangement for the rights with one person and be done with it. Good classical music may also be found by contacting small European record companies. If you try negotiating with the larger companies (EMI, Deutch Grammophone, Polydor) you will encounter the same difficulties as with a large US record company.

A very simple and effective way to handle music rights is to hire a composing student from the music department of a local university to do the score. Not only will he/she be delighted to get the experience and a modest fee, but he/she will probably do a very conscientious job. You can then either record union or non-union musicians. If your budget can afford it, you can hire a professional composer. You can find their listings in local production directories.

You can also go to a music library and pay *'needle-down'* license fees for music. The rates vary depending on how many selections you choose, the total length of your film and the market (educational, television, theatrical). The fees are called 'needle-down' because you are charged every time the needle is put down on the record and you use that music. These fees are very reasonable ($50-200) and while, in my opinion, much of the music is absolutely awful, if you listen to enough of it, you will find some good selections. Music libraries also have sound effects you can license.

You can find these music libraries advertised in trade papers such as *Variety* or in your local yellow pages. The sound department of your local film laboratory or recording studio may also have music libraries, although the largest are in Los Angeles and New York.

Other Rights

The rights to use art work, paintings, still photographs or other copyrighted material may be obtained by paying a flat fee ($15-150) to the owner of the material. The same is true with stock footage which is purchased on a per foot basis. ($15-25 per foot is an average figure to use when preparing budgets.) US National Archive film material, such as NASA footage, may be obtained for free since it is publicly owned. You will, however, pay the laboratory duping costs and shipping.

Copyrights

Copyrighting your film is not as mysterious or difficult as you may be led to believe. The steps are relatively simple:

1. Be sure to have a title on the head or end credits of your film that reads, '© *1984, Your Name*' or '*Copyright 1984 by Your Name. All Rights Reserved.*' The ©, within the circle, protects you internationally. The copyright '*bug*' will protect your material even before you actually receive your copyright registration number. By putting this on your film, people will automatically assume that it is copyrighted and that is a perfectly legitimate practice.

2. Write or call The United States Copyright Office, Performing Arts Section, Examining Division, Library of Congress, Washington, DC, 20559 and request *form 'PA'*. This is the form that you will need to copyright your film or videotape.

3. When you receive the form, fill it out. Even if your film is financed by a partnership, you can copyright it in your own name (or jointly with your creative partner). Copyrights are a

statement of ownership and so you are therefore claiming ownership in behalf of the partnership.

4. Return the form, along with a $10 check made out to 'Register of Copyrights'.

5. Send one copy of your film or videotape to the Copyright Office. The print should be a *'final'* copy in good condition. You may also request and fill out the *'Motion Picture Agreement'*. By doing this, they will return your film print or videotape, with the agreement that you will return it to them within 30 days, (if and) when they request it. (They probably won't.) In the past, the Copyright Office required two film prints which they would keep. If you had a long film to copyright, it could easily cost $1000 for their prints alone.

And that's all there is to it. You will receive a copyright registration number and form in a month or two which you may put in your file or safety deposit box. A few months later, you will receive a stack of complimentary library cards that have your film title, producer's name and brief description of your film along with a Library of Congress identification number. That's kinda fun. You will no doubt begin to feel pangs of immortality!

If you have any questions call the Copyright Office. The people are very friendly and quite willing to help you. They are sticklers, however, when it comes to filling out the forms exactly right. If you don't, the forms will be returned to you.

One part of the form that can cause some confusion is No. 6, *'Compilation or Derivative Work'*. In this section you list any material that is owned by someone else that you got permission to use in your film or tape. This includes stock film footage, paintings, sound effects, music, and so forth. For example, on the *DOLPHIN* copyright form, one line reads, *'Coin/*

101

Sculpture/Painting Pictures used by permission Bettman Archives, NY.'

In the second section of this form you are to *'give a brief, general statement of the material that has been added to this work and in which copyright is claimed'*.

This is very confusing. What they want you to do is list all the *'elements'* in the film that you wish to copyright. You can write; *'photography, editing, continuity, script, new music, sound effects and all other cinematographic materials excluding pre-existing material listed above.'* That means that you have copyrighted every element in the film, as well as the film as a whole.

The Limited Partnership Agreement

This is one legal form that is used to finance business ventures of all kinds. The purpose of this section is to describe the basic aspects of a Limited Partnership structure and not, in any way, to provide legal counsel. Please consult your lawyer to determine whether this business form is appropriate for you.

The Limited Partnership Agreement is a common business form and most lawyers are familiar with it. They may already have their own forms (*'boilerplate'*) which will be adapted to your specific project so the expense ($500 to $1000) should not be too great.

The Limited Partnership Agreement is so named because the partners are *'limited'* in terms of their liability. If the film goes over budget they have no legal obligation to contribute more money. Limited partners are also 'limited' in creative power. They may not make artistic decisions or manage the business.

The General Partners (you and possibly another) are responsible for managing the business, producing the film or

102

videotape, and getting it distributed. The General Partner is personally responsible for loaning or securing more money should the film go over budget.

The limited partners invest monies which are spent in production. In exchange for this investment they receive a percentage of profits (and losses), usually in proportion to their capital contribution. That is, the greater their investment the greater their percentage of profits.

Once the film is in distribution and begins earning income, the investors start recouping their original investment. Once the original investment is repaid in full then profits, if any, are shared between the investors (the limited partners) and the producer and the creative partners (the general partners).

In many limited partnerships the share of profits is divided 50/50. In more recent years, probably because of the depressed economy, producers have tried to make their packages more attractive by offering investors a 130% return on their investment *before* profits are shared. That means, if someone invests $10,000, they will receive $13,000 before the general partners (producers) share in profits. Since it can take several years for repayment to occur, even when a film is successful, this additional 30% is an enticement to the investor to invest in a film and not the money market. Of course, this is only an incentive and doesn't mean anything unless the film actually earns money.

If the film is not completed or is unsuccessful in distribution, then the partners can claim 100% of the losses. (The general partners do not share in losses since they have not put up any money.) It is a further enticement if the investors receive a greater share of profits (say 60%) than the producers after the original investment is returned.

A producer (general partner) can also be a limited partner. Say,

103

for example, that you've invested $10,000 actual cash in developing your project. Instead of paying yourself back from the budget you decide that you will become a limited partner and receive a proportionate share of profits like any other limited partner. Often investors will ask, *'how much of your own money is invested in the film?'* The idea being that if you really believe in the film you'll put your money where your mouth is. I don't necessarily agree with this reasoning but I understand it from an investor's point of view.

Your lawyer will register the limited partnership in your county and state. It is your responsibility (as a general partner) to provide income statements to the limited partners each year. (Your accountant will help.) Tax returns show each partner's capital account and profit (or loss) for the year and are sent to the limited partners. To keep on your investors' good side, send their tax statements to them as soon as possible after the close of each year as they must include this information in their own tax reports.

The Limited Partnership Agreement describes how the business will be conducted. It describes your responsibilities and what will happen if you die, neglect your responsibilities, encounter a limited partner who wants out and other sobering thoughts. It states what method will be used to return the initial investment to the investors. It is a good idea to have your accountant and lawyer consult with one another when writing up the Limited Partnership Agreement so that the best legal and accounting practices can be integrated. Since the agreement states how business will be conducted, you may refer back to it from time to time for procedural matters.

This document should be prepared *before* you begin raising money. You will give the Limited Partnership Agreement only to those who are seriously interested in investing in your project. They will probably have their own lawyer and accountant read it before they will invest.

104

Your lawyer will probably advise you to number each copy of the agreement and to record who you give it to and what the relationship is between you and the recipient (friend, acquaintance, relative, etc.) By law, there are restrictions on how many limited partners you may actually have as well as how many people you can approach for investment. You should ask your lawyer how to proceed. A limited partnership is not a *'public offering'* and cannot be advertised, nor can you mail out Limited Partnership Agreements to just anyone.

Make it clear to potential investors that films are a tremendously risky investment and that *there is a great likelihood that they could lose all their money*. While it is very exciting to think your project may be the next *Raiders* the real possibilities are 1) the film will never be finished, 2) it won't find a distributor, 3) it won't have wide distribution, 4) the public won't like it, 5) the theater will cheat the distributor and not report all ticket sales, 6) the distributor will cheat you, 7) the check will get lost in the mail on its way to you, or 8) all or none of the above.

'Investors who cannot afford to lose all their money in a film venture should not invest.'

It is better to be very conservative in your estimates of profits than raise everyone's expectations. You can print the horrible truth about movie investing in bold type in your prospectus and Limited Partnership Agreement so no one can say you didn't warn them of the risks.

If the project fails, your investors will lose everything and you will not be indebted to them. I've made films that have not fully repaid their investors and even though I legally do not owe them any money I still feel a sense of responsibility toward them. They believed in me, in the film, and it failed to make money. This has made me even more sensitive when preparing new projects for investment and has dampened my

105

boundless enthusiasm when it comes to painting bright vistas for would-be investors. Unlike some producers, I just can't (as they said in *Shogun* after someone died a violent death) *'karma, neh?'*, turn and walk away. So, if you're like me, be forewarned.

You want to do everything to see that your investors do not lose their money. That means choosing the right projects, conducting market research, preplanning and careful budgeting, striking good distribution deals, and continuing to promote the film well into your old age. If the film is successful (which could be defined as simply returning the original investment), your investors may be willing to reinvest in your other projects.

Producing As You Go

Some filmmakers raise the first $50,000 of a $100,000 project. That's just enough money to get into serious trouble. What can happen is that the money is spent and they are unable to raise more. I've met many filmmakers who have been in this predicament for years! Something they once loved and thought would be so enjoyable to produce is something they now resent. It is a considerable risk for your investors if you start before all the money is raised.

How you proceed should be clearly stated in your Limited Partnership Agreement. Some agreements require the money be deposited in an escrow account (and collect interest) until the full budget is raised. If the budget is not raised before a specified date then all the monies, including interest, are returned. Other partnerships allow some or all of the collected money to be spent before all the money is raised.

The advantage to beginning before you have all the money is that you will have something to show to potential investors and you will continue to move toward your goal. With *DOLPHIN*, we spent $13,000 before we had raised any money! (We had 30 days to pay our bills.) As it turned out the 'pilot' film we made helped us raised the rest. But our first shoots could have been a disaster.

The disadvantage of raising only a part of the total budget money is the pressure you will feel holding two jobs—one as a producer, the other as a fund-raiser. If, as you are proceeding, the film looks good, then money will be easier to raise. If it looks bad, then money will be difficult to find. Unfortunately even the best films look awful in the early stages. I hate to screen my works-in-progress for anyone, especially investors. Without color correction, dissolves, titles and a sound mix it's hard for anyone to 'imagine' what's not there. Besides, a minute after you've made your disclaimer about what is not there and the lights go out everyone will believe they are watching a real film. People are conditioned like that. After all, who but filmmakers sit around and watch unfinished films? Even though you tell them, psychologically most people will think they are watching your finished film. The result will be that the investors will think you don't make very good films!

BUDGETS

Budgets

'You can make movies on a small budget. It all depends on the skill of the producer.'

Budgets

The budget is one of the most important pages in your presentation. It must realistically anticipate every cost in your production. An error can cause severe repercussions. Writing a budget means researching costs and becoming creative when you breakdown your shooting script. You must find the most economical ways of doing things. If you are honest and very conscientious about preparing your budget your certainty will be reflected in both your written and live presentations. If you have fudged here and there, underestimated, padded or are in the dark about costs, you may run into trouble. If not now, then later. Some of the most difficult questions you will receive in your presentations will be about the budget. These questions will come from investors who have little or no experience with how films are made.

Do not write the budget until you know your film inside and out. Once you have a shooting script (hopefully a final draft) you can realistically determine how many days it will take to shoot, what kind of shooting ratio will be required, and so forth. Without a tight script you are just pulling figures out of the air.

For very rough purposes, 16mm documentaries cost $1500-2500 per minute. *But do not use these figures to estimate your budget.* Instead, do a very detailed budget based on your actual expectations. Your own films and videotapes could cost much more or much less. There are so many variables that using a rule-of-thumb only invites trouble.

While it is not within the scope of this book to cover budgets in great detail I did want to provide some thoughts that may prove useful to those of you who are embarking on first-time projects. (For a more detailed examination of all kinds of budgets, please see my book, *Film & Video Budgets*).

Negotiations

'It's all negotiable'. Remembering that will make a great difference on your bottom line. An exciting thing about movie-making is that there are few rules. It is an entrepreneur's business. You can make movies with a small budget. Or with a big budget. It all depends on the skill of the entrepreneur (producer).

Approach negotiation with an attitude that *'people already want to work with you'*. The people you want to borrow or rent equipment from already want to loan or rent it to you. The owner of the restaurant you want to use for a location would like nothing more than to have her restaurant in a movie. This will put you in the right frame of mind when approaching people. In reality, they may not want to have anything to do with you. It doesn't matter. You'll find people who will. It's a game. It's a treasure hunt. Have fun with it. Maybe you have $10,000 to rent a location for one day. But, you probably don't. Sharpen and develop your skills as a negotiator. You know how much you have to spend. But that doesn't mean you have to spend it all right here, right now. The more you can save in each area the more you have to spend elsewhere . And believe me, that *'elsewhere'* is just around the corner.

Some people will want to work for what you can afford. Others won't. Don't let that stop you. Go on to the next name on your list. If you represent your film as *'no one is getting paid'*, make sure that's true. Don't pay one person and not the others. The news will travel faster than you can say *'action'*. It'll create bad feelings all around. Even though it's your business, a crew will question how you can pay one person and not others. Be consistent. Either pay no one or pay everyone something, even if it's very little. If the cast and crew perceive inequities you'll pay dearly (in screwups and on-set delays). Tell the truth. If you can't pay people, tell them that. Don't lead people on. In our business, honesty is greatly appreciated.

For talent, services, materials offer *less* than what you are willing to pay. You may be surprised when people accept your first offer. Some won't and you'll be forced to pay *more* than you planned.

The Four Rules

There are four basic rules to keep costs down.

1. ***Question every price.*** I don't care what the price tag says. There's always room for reductions. Always ask if the price could be lower. What if you rented it for more days? Over a weekend? What if you video edited at night? On weekends? Be creative. Offer the supplier money or other values that they may not ordinarily receive. Is there any promotional value in what you are doing that they could share? Don't accept the first quote. Somewhere, someone will do it cheaper and perhaps better.

I once needed a special effect for a commercial. The first quote was $4,500. The fellow said, *'Bub, there's only one way to do this effect.'* I wasn't convinced. My second quote was $2,000. My third quote was $600. As I went from quote to quote, I learned problem-solving techniques. I figured out how to do the effect for $300. That's 6% of the original estimate!

Remember, every price is flexible. It's not unusual to receive anywhere from 5% to 50% off. But you have to have the courage to ask.

2. *Shop around.* Take the time to ask lots of questions, make phone calls, interview technicians, visit studios. Get out your production directories. Explore. Ask people for recommendations. Make lists of contacts. Check out every lead until you're an expert on people, places and prices. Then spend your money.

3. *Collect information.* If you question every price and shop around, then automatically you are collecting information. Often it's the information about a technical process or approach that you are paying for. Most information is free. But you have to be inclined to do some research. The more you learn, the more options you'll have. Filmmaking is problem solving. Lots of problem solving. The more time you spend in preproduction collecting information, the more you'll save (and the more you'll be worth as a producer, director or production manager).

4. *Give yourself time.* Too often producers and production managers don't have (or take) the necessary time to research every aspect of their production. They get forced into corners. They end up paying high prices to get the job done. This happens again and again in commercials. The client needs it done right away. It's rush, rush, rush. Rush charges double or triple costs. The suppliers love it. It's the same amount of work for them. They just may have to work at night or on weekends. They know that when clients are in a hurry they'll spend more money. Don't let this to happen to you. If you're a production manager you know that it's cheaper to hire a unit manager,

114

production assistants, location scouts, or field producers for a few extra days (or weeks) of preproduction.

Careful planning will make for a smoother, more cost efficient production. Some production companies operate with a *'crisis mentality'*. They rush around unnecessarily. Decisions wait until the last minute. There's no time for prep. Everyone works late, works weekends, skips meals. I guess emergencies make people feel like they are doing something important. Makes them feel like martyrs. (The job isn't any better because they stayed up all night to do it. It says to me they didn't plan their time well.) I don't think they're heroes. I think they're stupid. They've misused time and energy. Furthermore, the cast and crew quickly perceive this lack of professionalism. It damages morale.

Money-Saving Tips

Every single decision you make on a film costs money. Therefore, if you examine every step, you'll eliminate waste and create savings. These are a few thoughts on how to keep expenses down.

1. ***Prepare a detailed script.*** The cost of writing a detailed script is minimal compared to what it costs *'being creative'* on a set with a dozen people standing around. Storyboard every nuance in advance. The action, dialogue, technical requirements, camera angles, color schemes, costuming, blocking, lighting, sound, etc. The more planning before the cameras roll, the more you'll save. Most productions could use more planning.

2. ***Communicate with your department heads*** (director of photography, production manager, lighting director, costume designer, set designer, soundman, etc.) There should be many

115

preproduction meetings where every script detail is discussed. The department heads can take notes, do their own research, come up with questions for future meetings. Once you are in production there should be daily meetings to prep the next day's shoot. When people know what is expected of them they perform their best. If they sense (or see) that the director doesn't know what he or she is doing then they lose respect and enthusiasm for the project. Eveyone wants to work on a first-class film. You can make it first-class by planning and holding meetings with your staff.

3. **Don't spend money on unnecessary things.** This may seem obvious but many first time filmmakers with little or no money spend it on the wrong things. Maybe you can't afford to pay a cameraman. Maybe you need the money for film and processing. Then you must get a cameraman for free. Be smart. Your money is well spent if it appears on the screen.

Perhaps you receive a grant from *The American Film Institute*. While $20,000 is not much, there are ways to stretch those dollars. The AFI name, for example, has prestige. People will work for free, or donate locations and equipment because it is *'an AFI film'*. This holds true for any grant you may receive. People understand that it is not a commercial project. They will be much more willing to participate for little or no money. Don't spend what you don't have.

4. **Buyouts.** When you hire cast and crew, do so on a *'buyout'* basis. In simple terms, this means that you pay a flat daily rate regardless of how many hours are worked. Or, you pay a flat weekly rate. Then you know exactly how much the cast and crew will cost at the project's outset, and you will avoid over-time charges.

You can also negotiate lower rates for cast and crew if you are able to offer long term employment. For example, if a cameraman's rate is $500 per day and you need a cameraman for a

116

week, an offer of $2,000 may be acceptable. You've saved $1,500 right there. And, rather than rent the camera equipment from a rental house, hire your cameraman's gear for less than what you'd normally pay.

5. *Options.* The normal practice is to *'option'*, rather than *'buy'*, literary properties. If you can't get the project off the ground then losses are minimized. Perhaps your option was even free.

Put a crew *'on hold'*. Only *'confirm'* when you are absolutely certain the shoot will take place. If you don't put them *'on hold'*, you could be liable for full salaries if the shoot doesn't take place for whatever reason.

When you are selecting stock music for your film or tape, only pay the *'search'* and transfer fees. Never pay the license fees until you have a fine cut of your film or until you are absolutely certain that you will use the music.

6. *Consultants.* Consultants can save you tremendous amounts of money. You can hire as a consultant a production manager or assistant director to break down your script and prepare a budget. Their ideas alone may save you thousands. Or hire a script consultant to review your script for possible problems. A dialogue or comedy writer may improve certain scenes. A consultant can help with distribution, marketing or publicity. There are consultants for everything. You pay for their knowledge. A consultant can guide you away from costly mistakes.

7. *Narrators and actors.* When you hire a narrator or actors try to negotiate a flat fee that includes *'pickups'*. You will probably have lines you'll want to redo. This won't become apparent until you start editing. A line may be too long or too short. Maybe it doesn't sound right. You'll want to go back in

117

the studio and rerecord certain sections. This can be costly unless you negotiate for these pickups in advance.

8. *Equipment*. Rent equipment over the weekend. A weekend rate is the same as a one-day rate. You get two days of shooting for the price of one. (Be careful, however, if you have to pay crew overtime for the weekend.) You can also strike deals with video editing houses to edit at night or on weekends. Use equipment during off-hours and you can receive price breaks.

9. *Props and Costumes*. Can you get props or costumes in exchange for an on-screen promotional credit? Maybe? Try it. Also, you don't always need full costumes. I've filmed costumes which didn't have backs or bottoms. Silver paint turns cardboard into metal. Cheap costume jewelry can photograph better than the real McCoy. Try local thrift shops for period costumes and props. On *MESSAGES, MESSAGES* we used a $20 roll of white butcher paper for seven sets! We changed the look merely by relighting it. A little movie magic goes a long way.

10. *Editing*. Will transferring your film to videotape for editing provide any savings? Perhaps.

11. *Film*. In my student filmmaking days, we couldn't afford film. We'd get '*short ends*' from the local TV station. Today most TV stations shoot videotape so you may ask for old videocassettes. For short-ends, try commercial production houses.

12. *Editing Table Mixes*. With an editing table and tape recorder you can do a rough sound mix. You can listen to a simulation of your sound mix and hear '*holes*' that need to be filled. You can make creative decisions and not have to feel that you're playing '*Beat The Clock*' against expensive studio rates. This allows you to fine-tune your cue sheets before the real mix.

118

13. *Opticals and Titles.* If you shot on film but plan to show your program on television, you might want to do all your opticals (effects, dissolves) and titles on videotape. This will reduce your post-production time, give you a greater variety of opticals and speed up the titling process.

14. *Video Edit Sessions.* Work out an equipment schedule before you go 'on-line' so that you are paying for equipment only when you are using it. On-line editing rates can be $450 per hour or more depending on the equipment you schedule. Do not bring a Chyron (title generator) in until the end of your session for titling. Only book a Quantel or an ADO (optical effects) for the actual time you will need it. Don't have any equipment sitting around unused. You'll just have to pay for it.

If you are using many tape rolls and constantly changing reels, it might be cost effective to rent another playback machine at $75 per hour rather than spending $450 per hour changing reels and slowing down the session. An assistant can stay ahead of the script and keep the machines loaded with the appropriate rolls. Always come prepared with editing cue sheets with all your time code 'in's and out's'. Make a copy for your editor.

15. *Health.* Pushing your crew, cast and editors to their physical limits may save time but you run the risk of burning them out. Nothing is more destructive to your crew's motivation than being exploited at every turn. Skipping meals and sleep is damaging to their health and reflects poor planning. When a principal cast or crew member is sick you're out of business. Keep your staff in good health; it will pay off.

These are just a handful of suggestions for keeping expenses down. As you develop your script and budget you will discover many more on your own.

16MM FILM BUDGET

24-Minute Film

1.6 Ratio

A. TALENT

Producer	3	MONTHS	800	2400
Director	2	WEEKS	500	1000
Writer	1	FLAT FEE	500	500
Lead Actor	4	DAYS	158	632
Support Actors (3)	2	DAYS	125	750
Extras (5)	1	DAYS	20	100
				5382

B. PRODUCTION PERSONNEL

Camerman	6	DAYS	350	2100
Assist Cameraman	5	DAYS	100	500
Soundman	3	DAYS	200	600
Gaffer	3	DAYS	150	450
Production Assistant	6	DAYS	90	540
Still Photographer	1	DAYS	150	150
Stylist/Makeup	2	DAYS	150	300
Per Diem	33	TTL DAYS	22	726
				5366

C. FILM STOCK & LABS

Raw Stock	13	ROLLS	65	845
Developing	5184	FEET	.11	570
Workprint	5184	FEET	.152	788
Coding	10368	FEET	.015	156
¼″ Tape	7	ROLLS	8	56
Mag Stock	15552	FEET	.03	467
Transfers	3	HOURS	40	120
Still Film	10	ROLLS	7	70
Process Stills	10	CONTACTS	9	90
				3161

D. PRODUCTION EQUIPMENT

Camera Rental	1	WEEK	500	500
Lens Kit	1	WEEK	100	100
Magazines, Etc.	1	WEEK	50	50
Lighting	1	WEEK	100	100
Recorder, Mikes	1	WEEK	150	150
Camera Supplies	1	WEEK	100	100
Props	1	FLAT	500	500
Location Expenses	2	FEES	200	400
				1900

120

E. EDITING & FINISHING

Editor	6	WEEKS	450	2700
Assistant Editor	4	WEEKS	300	1200
Editing Table	6	WEEKS	250	1500
Editing Equipment	6	WEEKS	75	450
Edit Supplies	1	WEEK	150	150
Sound Mix	4	HOURS	150	600
Art Work	1	FEE	132	132
Titles	6	TITLES	50	300
Negative Matching	1	FEE	500	500
Answer Prints (2)	900	FEET	.33	594
Internegatives	900	FEET	.65	585
Release Prints (5)	900	FEET	.1	450
Cases	5	CASES	7	35
Video Transfer	.5	HOURS	240	120
Video Dubs	4	KC'S	45	180
				9496

F. NARRATION & MUSIC

Narrator	1	FLAT FEE	400	400
Recording Studio	1	HOURS	100	100
Tape Stock	.5	ROLL	30	15
Music Rights	10	MINUTES	50	500
Sound EFX	20	EFFECTS	10	200
				1215

G. OFFICE

Office Rent	3	MONTHS	80	240
Supplies	2	MONTHS	40	80
Equipment	3	MONTHS	65	195
Telephone	3	MONTHS	75	225
Shipping	3	MONTHS	50	150
Xeroxes	3	MONTHS	30	90
Bookkeeping	1	FEE	500	500
Accounting	1	FEE	1000	1000
Legal	1	FEE	1000	1000
				3480

Sub total	$30000	30000
Contingency 10%	3000	3000
TOTAL	$33,000	33,000

121

A $30,000 Budget

For an example, I will use a budget of $30,000 in this book. I will do so on the *'detailed budget'* page, the *'summary budget'* page and in the *'income projections'* page. Thirty thousand dollars is not much money for a film. I have used this figure because it may be useful to filmmakers producing their first film. Please feel free to substitute your own figures on any of the formats within.

The detailed budget format was made using a popular computer *spreadsheet* program on floppy disk called *'Visicalc'* (*'Supercalc'* and *'Multi-Plan'* will also work). Using this program I was able to develop my own budget format which handles my specific needs. The computer program allows me to manipulate the budget in creative ways. I am delighted to not be spending all my time erasing and calculating revisions every time there is a change in the budget. Now, whenever I change one of the variables (such as the shooting ratio) all the other figures that relate to the variables also change instantaneously (film stock, processing, workprint, etc.) because in the budget format I have 'tied' these figures together.

The budget shown here assumes that a 24-minute, 16mm film can be made in three months. It requires a tight shooting script, careful planning, and low salaries. You may be able to make your film with less people than I've included in this budget.

The equipment rentals are calculated at basic rental house prices. You might cut costs by working out a deal with a cameraman or production house. The shooting ratio is very low (1:6). The music will be purchased from a library. Two answer prints and 5 release prints will be made so they may be screened for distributors and program buyers. When you prepare your own budget you will make many of your own assumptions which must happen in reality.

122

In this budget there is an *'overhead expense'* of $3059, (approximately 11% of the budget). It will cover *'overhead and on-going expenses'* that a production company will incur such as taxes, licenses, secretarial, accounting and so forth. A production company will have these expenses whether a film is being produced or not and they must be paid somehow. If you don't have a company to maintain, then the overhead may be used as a *'contingency fund'* for any unforeseen expenses or overruns. If you don't spend it (very unlikely!) you can return it to your investors and be one of the rare few that have brought a film in under budget.

Each budget is very different since it is based on different production needs. What follows are examples of unforeseen budget problems that I encountered during some of the films I produced.

'Hardware Wars'

HARDWARE WARS, a 13-minute parody of *Star Wars*, was budgeted at $5000! *(I went over budget, okay!)* By $3000, because we shot more film than we planned (52 takes of flying steam irons!) and spent several additional days on location and in the studio. Everyone was paid token salaries. The props came from thrift shops. The costumes were made with minimal materials. (4-Q-2's costume was cardboard and sprayed with metallic paint. It photographed like tin.) Some of the *'dazzling special effects'* were close-up shots of sparklers left over from the 4th of July. Every conceivable corner was cut to save money.

Ernie Fosselius, for example, not only conceived the idea, but contributed to every aspect of the production. He wrote the script and directed the film. He animated sequences and the *'wipes'* and scratched the *'lasers'* directly onto the film. He built the mechanical models. He acted in the film as *'The*

123

Wookie Monster' *(puppet)*, as *'Darph Nader'*, and as the *'Debriefing Instructor'* and dubbed the voices of many of the characters. (The film was shot *'silent'* and all the voices were dubbed in later.) Ernie was thoroughly involved with the editing and even did the original promotional poster, postcard and study guide. For all that, he received very little money, taking instead a large share of the profits. Fortunately for him, *HARDWARE WARS* made money which compensated him well for his many contributions.

The crew for the film was very small. John Fante and I did the camerawork and much of the post-production work. Laurel Polanick made some of the costumes. Everyone worked building the sets.

We were willing to work for very little money because the film was essentially a *'portfolio piece'*. We had to make the film for as little as possible because we had no idea whether it had any commercial value. We made it for fun. What a surprise it was when *HARDWARE WARS* became one of the most popular short films of recent years and has earned 35 times its cost to date. (Even the notion of doing a 'portfolio piece' has paid off. Ernie was recently hired to write a feature script for comic Steve Martin. John Fante was a special effects camera operator on *The Right Stuff*.)

'Radiance: The Experience of Light'

The idea for this film came from an *'experience of light'* which artist Dorothy Fadiman had in 1964. She had originally planned to do a book. When I met her she pulled out file boxes of marvelous material about saints, mystics, holy men and the religious experience of light. We decided that the information might better be presented as an *'experience'* through film and be more powerful than a book. Particularly since there was so much we could do photographically with light.

First we developed a 45-minute slide show titled *Do Saints Really Glow?* The slide show used two projectors connected by a dissolve unit, and a 1/4" music and narration tape. I performed the show 'live' at our many bookings for psychic, psychological and religious conferences all around the country. We were quickly able to recoup our $2000 costs (equipment and processing only). Moreover these shows were an excellent testing ground for the show. We learned from our audiences what worked and what didn't and could easily make changes without major expense. Over many months we upgraded our images and rerecorded the music and narration.

The response to *Do Saints Really Glow?* was so good, we decided to raise $25,000 to make a 22-minute film, *RADIANCE: THE EXPERIENCE OF LIGHT.* The investors were friends of Dorothy's and 'fans' of the slide show. It cost $31,000 to complete the film—$6000 over budget.

What happened? We naively thought that since we had already collected the images it would be a simple process to transfer them to film. It wasn't. To make the film interesting, we had to discover ways to make still images 'move'. We found that some of the images (those with subtle color or details) lost resolution and quality in the transfer to 16mm film. Consequently, we had to find new images, with strong graphics, to replace the subtle images. Dissolves, as long as 6 to 8 seconds, are easy to accomplish with slide projectors and a dissolve unit. You get a very magical effect as one image slowly becomes another. That *'in-between'* stage created some very special moments for our audiences. Unfortunately, film laboratory dissolves are much shorter and are 'even'. We couldn't achieve the kind of dissolves we wanted. (This kind of effect can be accomplished now in video production but we were making a film.)

One big job was to secure the rights to all the photos, paintings and music contained in the film. This was enormously time-

125

consuming and expensive. Sometimes we bought the rights to art work and music and then didn't use it. We found that if we had to replace an image or selection of music (either it didn't transfer well or the rights weren't available) often the images or music before and after that section also had to be re-juxtaposed. All these things increased the budget beyond our expectations.

In order to shorten the period between release of the film and our print sales we sent out several thousand flyers to schools and libraries announcing the film's release. We did so before we saw the first answer print. This mailing generated 150 requests for previews. Unfortunately the first answer print did not live up to our expectations. We decided that the film would have to be entirely re-edited because many of the dissolves and camera moves did not work. The *'magic of the slide dissolves'* did not make the transition into film.) Regrettably, I had to send out 150 letters telling people that previews of the film would be delayed.

Dorothy and John Fante spent three more months re-editing the film until the 'magic' of the original slide show was restored. I mention these things, because they could never have been fore-seen when we originally prepared the budget for what we thought would be a simple process.

'Dolphin'

DOLPHIN was originally to be a one-hour television film and was budgeted at $100,000. It cost $165,000 to complete. Why? The main reason is that we did not stick to our initial purpose. After an extraordinary experience with a school of wild dolphins in the Bahamas we were certain we had the makings of a feature-length film. Our increased budget came about through, 1) extra months of editing, 2) lengthening the film to 85 minutes and, 3) *'4-walling'* theaters and promotion.

We premiered the film ourselves at five theaters throughout the San Francisco Bay Area. This expense was not written into our original TV film budget. Although the film did well in its premiere showings ($12,000 gross in six days) it was not enough to interest a theatrical distributor into paying $15,000 or more for a 35mm blow-up. By doing our own theatrical showings in other parts of the country we assessed that there just wasn't enough to be earned with our documentary.

I re-edited the 85-minute film to 58 minutes for non-theatrical distribution and to 52 minutes for the PBS broadcast. Many months later, I edited an 11-minute version for the elementary school market which after 1 year in the educational market outgrossed the 58-minute version! (Schools just don't have the money to buy long films.)

Had we stuck to our original plan and made a TV film we would now be well on our way to breaking even with the film. But hindsight is always clearer. *The Lesson: Determine what you making at the outset, budget for that and stick to it.*

Note: Budgets are exceedingly complex. Small oversights can lead to disasters later. Because budgets are a subject that requires far more than can be covered in this book, I wrote another. *Film and Video Budgets* has 18 sample budgets for a variety of projects including student films, short films, commercials, documentaries, pay television segments, low-budget features and many more. There are budgets for film and video productions and budgets that mix film and video production techniques. The idea is that you locate a production similar in style to your own. The budget format should get you 90% there by reminding you of budget items you may have otherwise left out. See the back of this book for information on how to order *Film and Video Budgets*. I think you'll find it useful.

DISTRIBUTION

Distribution

'If a distributor wants your film, concessions will be made that deviate significantly from the standard contract.'

Finding Distributors

It may take some time to find the right distributor. In the non-theatrical market alone, there are nearly 400 distributors. Some carry only a few titles, others carry hundreds or thousands. In the appendix there is a list of many of the non-theatrical and home video distributors. As you prepare your prospectus you may discuss your film with potential distributors. Even in the development stages, several distributors may be interested. If this is the case, have them write letters expressing their interest in seeing your film upon completion. You may add these letters to your prospectus to show your investors there are potential outlets for the film or tape you propose to make.

Once you've made some films or tapes that are in distribution and have established relationships with distributors this process will be easier. You'll know where to go if you've made films that are successful in a specific market. You can call up your distributor friends and perhaps even negotiate a deal with an advance that can go towards production. This isn't always the case, but if a distributor knows that your films have earned money in the past, he may be willing to help you with new projects.

131

If you don't know distributors, you can ask the end-users of films, (librarians, educators, theater exhibitors, and television program buyers) who may suggest reputable distributors.

If you are making a film for non-theatrical (educational) distribution it is important to know how your film will be used in the classroom. Generally speaking, teachers and film users buy films with lots of information in the narration. They do not like abstract, art or experimental films because they neither understand them nor know how to use them for teaching purposes. It is a very traditional marketplace and not open to much experimentation. They want to know that your film will teach something. In fact, the *HARDWARE WARS* study guide was designed in part to justify its *'educational value'*. Somehow it worked because the film has rented and sold to classes in future studies, sociology, English, creative writing, art, and communications!

Be aware that many classes are only 45 minutes long and that this time must also be used to conduct class business. If you make anything longer than 25 or 30 minutes, your distributor will have trouble selling and renting it to the classroom markets. If you make an hour film, you should break it up into Part I and Part II. When you look through distributors' catalogs you will see most of their films are 10 to 20 minutes long. The magic length, I'm told, is 18 minutes.

Pay attention to the market needs, not your own. If you don't, you will end up with a film that does not find distribution. I have made several films and let them be *'as long as the film wanted to be.'* It was not a very disciplined way of working. So, some are too long for classrooms, others too short for television. I didn't pay attention to the market. I didn't do any market research. I don't receive any royalties. These films now sit in storage where they don't do anyone any good.

Contracts

For many years my films were rejected by distributors (for the reasons I just mentioned). Finally, I got an offer. Boy, was I happy! I was so thrilled that someone actually wanted to distribute one of my films that I paid very little attention to the contract I signed. It was a very expensive mistake.

The pages you are about to read are extremely important and perhaps the most valuable ones in the book. If you are able to make use of this information you may save thousands of dollars.

Negotiations

Once a non-theatrical distributor has screened your film (an interlock or an answer print) he or she will let you know if they want to distribute your film. Do not take the first deal that comes along. Shop around. Remember, the deal you sign will be in effect for many years to come. Make sure you are making the best deal you can with the best distributor for your film.

Get as many offers as you can from reputable distributors. This will speak very highly of your film and will allow you to leverage a better deal. It also demonstrates that several distributors think your film will make money for them.

Most large distributors will not offer you a contract unless they think your film will sell 100 prints or more. It could cost them as much as $30,000 to $50,000 to make prints, promote and distribute your film. They simply will not accept a film unless they think it will sell well.

When you talk to different distributors, you will get a sense of their abilities to promote and sell your film. Be sure to take notes of your discussions because it is easy to forget all the points of the negotiations, especially when you are considering several different deals at the same time.

Take a large sheet of paper and make a series of grids with distributors listed in a row across the top and contract terms (advance, percentage, promotion, budget, markets, etc.) in the left-hand column. The page will fill up as you talk with the various distributors and allow you to keep track of the points of discussion.

To make a wise choice between non-theatrical distributors, get answers to the following questions:

1. Do they already have films similar to mine? How many prints have sold? How many have rented? Over what period of time?

2. Where (or to whom) will they market the film?

3. Will they mail a separate flyer for my film? Will the film be included in their next catalog? When will the catalog be mailed? Will they pay for the printing of a special flyer or poster? Can I design it or supervise its design?

4. Will they enter it in film festivals? Which ones?

5. How many preview prints will they order?

The more they order, the more preview requests they will be able to fill. If they only order a few, then it will take much longer to make sales. A healthy initial order would be 25-50 prints.

6. How many rental prints will they have on hand?

7. What are the purchase and rental prices? In 16mm? In videotape?

134

8. What percentage of their total gross income are sales? Are rentals? Are in videotape?

You may find it very difficult to get them to answer this next question (because it is a direct giveaway of how well they think the film will sell) but somewhere in their minds they have an answer. Ask this, not so you can hold them to it in a contract, but so you can get a sense, in specific terms of how well they think it will do. If they are reluctant to answer, say, *'make something up'*. The truth is, no one really knows how well a non-theatrical film will do until it has been in distribution a year or two.

9. The Big Question: How many film prints and/or videotapes do they think they can sell in the first year? In the second year? In five years? Rental income in the first year, etc.? (With this information you may be able to make more accurate income projections for your investors.)

10. Will they give an advance? How much?

11. What percentage of gross (not net) will I receive? Can we negotiate a sliding scale with my percentage going up with total gross income?

Talking With Other Producers

No one will be more willing to talk to you about his or her experiences with a distributor than another producer. Before making any deal with a distributor, particularly one you've just met, contact other producers whose films are represented by the prospective distributor.

Since you are probably the only one who has ever asked, and because they usually have a lot to say, it can be a very rewarding exchange. If they are happy with the distributor, they will

135

say so and why. If they are displeased, they will be the first to tell you. Don't be shy about making these exploratory calls. What you will learn will be extremely valuable and put you in a better position to make your decision.

Ask these questions:

1. Are you happy with the job the distributor has been doing?

2. Had any specific problems?

3. Do they pay on time?

4. Did you get an advance? How much?

5. What percentage do you receive?

6. Who paid for the internegative? Other costs?

From these discussions you will get a very clear idea of how the distributor operates. (By the way, not everything you hear will be horror stories. Surprisingly enough, you'll hear many good things about distributors.) Sometimes you'll learn awful things and wonder how you got in the film business in the first place. Sometimes you may feel that you are forced to make a choice between the 'lesser of two evils'. But it's better to find out early about a distributor's bad habits, than later when you've signed away your film.

Write down everything you learn in your discussions on that large sheet of paper. Then study the information you've gathered. Ultimately, it may break down to which distributor you can trust. Pick the one which you think will do the best job for you. It may not necessarily be the friendly one or the one you like the most. Sometimes it may be wiser to take a smaller percentage if you feel that through promotion the distributor will generate a higher volume of sales. Sometimes it may be better to forego an advance and have the distributor guarantee a specified amount of money for advertising.

Only sign a distribution contract when you have received answers to all your questions and when you (and your lawyer) feel that you have explored all the options. *Don't be in a hurry because negligence at this stage may result in your losing everything you have worked so hard to gain.* Remember, you are representing your investors in any deal you make. They believed in your making the best film you could and now, with your signature, you can make the difference between a loss and a profit for them.

Once the papers are signed, what was once an adversary relationship becomes a partnership (in the non-legal sense of the word) and it is no longer to your advantage to challenge your distributor. It is time to support him or her because now you are in this thing together.

The Non-Theatrical Distribution Contract

Before describing distribution contracts, I want to make it very clear that you do not *'sell'* your film to a distributor. You don't *'sell'* your film to anyone. You *'license'* it. You always keep ownership of your film and allow others, by means of a *'licensing'* agreement, to do things with the film, such as show it on television, distribute it, or exhibit the film in a theater. *'Selling'* your film, that is your ownership in your work, should never be done.

There is no *'standard contract'*, although that's exactly what a distributor will offer you and lead you to believe. For the distributor, a 'standard contract' is the deal they would like to make. For you, it is a place to begin your negotiations. *Remember: 'Everything is negotiable.'* If a distributor wants your film, concessions will be made that deviate significantly

137

from the initial 'standard contract'. If they are not terribly interested in your film, their 'standard contract' may be the best offer you'll get.

What follows are the standard elements that you will find in most distribution contracts.

1. Exclusive Rights. All distributors will want an *'exclusive'* contract which means that during a specified time and in a specified territory, they will be the only distributor handling your film. Since the market is so small they will be insistent on this point. If the distributor clearly does not promote your film in some specialized markets you may try to retain these rights for yourself or another distributor.

2. Format. The distribution contract is a *'license'*. It allows the distributor to *'rent, sell, lease, exhibit, distribute and in every way exploit'* your film. There are many different formats; 16mm, 8mm, 3/4" videotape, 1/2" videotape, videodisk, etc.

Here's where you must be very careful. Distributors will undoubtedly ask for as many of these format rights as possible. For example, they may ask for the videodisk format rights even though they do not distribute videodisks. What they will do is license these rights to a *'sub-distributor'* (another distributor) who does distribute videodisks. The first distributor will make additional revenues by licensing it to a *'sub-distributor'*. Only grant those *'format'* rights to those distributors who are powerful and successful in distributing in that specific format. This way you can have one distributor for 16mm film, another for videotape, another for videodisk and so forth, and reap higher profits. You'll eliminate some of the middlemen.

You must also be aware when a distributor asks for rights in *'any media now existing or which may exist in the future'*. That

138

means, if any new format (like videodisk, or micro-chip, or whatever) comes along in the future and can be marketed and distributed, then the distributor will have those format rights as well. If you had signed a contract with a distributor that contains this kind of language then you may lose a great deal. Why not delete this line and, if and when another format comes along, find an appropriate distributor at that time? You will, in the long run, earn more money by being very selective in this regard.

3. Exclusions. Some agreements are written in a vague manner. If this is the case with your contract, you could accidentally give away some rights that you really intended to keep. To safeguard yourself from this, be very specific in stating what rights are *'included'* and what rights are *'excluded'*. If you don't want to give the distributor the Pay TV rights be sure to write this in the contract as an 'exclusion'. Other examples might be: PBS, Foreign Television, Canadian non-theatrical, Armed Forces Television, Inflight Services, Airlines and Ships, Pay TV, Videodisk, stock footage rights, etc. On the other hand, if a distributor can prove to you that they are strong in making sales in any of these areas, then you may wish to 'include' some of these areas. Be aware of what rights you are licensing and what you are not.

4. Terms. A distributor will ask for a specific amount of years (usually high) in which to distribute the film. Be very careful about signing a contract for *'perpetuity'*. That means *'forever'*. Most will ask for 5-7 years. If you are unsure about a distributor, give them a year *'trial period'*, with the understanding that if they gross so much money ($ X), then the contract will automatically be renewed for a year. This guarantees some performance on their part. If they don't meet this agreed upon amount, then the film is not tied up for 7 years and you can look for another distributor. Don't make this figure so high that it cannot realistically be obtained by the distributor. Why set up a no-win situation with unrealistic expectations? If the distributor gives you an estimate of what the film might gross in one year, reduce it 25% in your own mind. Allow some leeway because no one really knows what a film will make in a year.

5. Royalties. Royalties are your share of earnings from distribution. The 'standard' these days with non-theatrical distributors ranges from 18-25% of GROSS (not net) income. Gross means from the *'first dollars'* earned. Some distributors will offer a contract with a higher percentage from net income which, if you don't understand the difference between *'net'* and *'gross'*, will look more attractive. *'Net'* is the figure that is left (if any) after first deducting costs, such as prints, advertising, promotion, freight, etc. A 'net' deal is not bad, just more difficult to monitor than a gross deal. With a gross deal you need not be concerned with what the distributor is spending on promotion because it doesn't affect your share. If you do a net deal then specify exactly what expenses can be deducted or you may never see any income from your film, even though it may be earning a large gross income. A 'net deal' gives the distributor an advantage. When questioned he can always say, *'Oh, that was an advertising expense'*.

6. Advance. An *'advance'* is a portion of your royalty, given to you in 'advance' before your film has actually earned it. This can amount to several thousand dollars. Distributors are usually less interested in giving you an advance than you are in receiving one. In some cases an advance will be used to entice a filmmaker to sign a deal. (Even though it is your money paid early.) The advantage in receiving an advance is that you can repay your investors more rapidly.

You may, however, not wish to take an advance because it may deplete the cash a distributor has for promotion. Instead it might be to your advantage to have the distributor put this cash to use in promoting your film and receive your share of income, when it is actually earned. If your film does not earn back its advance it will be the distributor's loss and not yours. You don't have to pay back an advance.

7. Printing Materials. The contract should specify who pays for what. The distributor should pay for the internegative and sound negative because these will be used for making release prints. It costs about $1000 for the master printing negatives for a one-hour film. By the time you are ready to make masters you may very well have spent your budget on production. Sometimes a distributor will 'advance' these costs. What that really means is that the distributor is loaning you the money to pay for it. It is a loan and not a real 'advance'. This is a negotiable point. Be sure that the contract specifies that once the internegatives are made the A & B rolls are returned to you. (They are not only the most valuable things you possess but you may need them to make printing masters for other distributors.)

8. Payment Schedule. Most contracts state that a royalty statement and check be sent 30-45 days following the end of each quarter. Obviously, the more often you receive payment the better. Some distributors report bi-annually. Have the distributor send you a royalty statement that also lists who bought and rented your film. You may not always get it, but without this information all you see are totals which tell you nothing about who your buyers actually are. The distributor may want to keep this information confidential because these customer lists are their bread and butter. On the other hand I'd like to know who the customers are because I can suggest market segments they may not have thought of. It took me more than a year to get this information from one distributor before discovering that several markets had been overlooked. You can

141

also check these reports to see if there have been unauthorized showings. (This happens often with *HARDWARE WARS*. It will be *'loaned'* to a campus theater from a library. I'll hear about the showing but it won't be listed on the distributor's royalty statement because the film was obtained illegally through a library and not through the distributor.)

Libraries *are* allowed to loan the film to individuals for free viewings. Unscrupulous college theater programmers will sometimes check the film out for a supposed private screening. The little sneaks will then show it in the college auditorium and charge admission. No money will go to the distributor or the owner. Follow-up letters to the culprits usually result in an apology and a check.)

9. Advertising. Do you have any approval of advertising? Probably not, but if you have talent and expertise in this area a distributor may be very willing to have you design the advertising and promotion. (It saves the distributor expense and work.) I designed the flyer for *DOLPHIN*. Ernie Fosselius designed the poster for *HARDWARE WARS*. By keeping some control or approval of the promotion and advertising you can be sure that your film is being accurately represented.

The distributor pays for the design and printing of the promotional material. Sometimes it is possible to negotiate an exchange where you will provide the design for the promo material and they will pay for the internegative, which is what you wanted anyway.

10. Credits. Credits may be the only thing you'll get out of making a film so you might as well get all the publicity you can. In the contract, specify that whenever the film is advertised (journals, programs, study guides, posters, flyers, press

142

PYRAMID FILMS Box 1048 Santa Monica, CA 90406 (213) 390-FILM

RADIANCE: THE EXPERIENCE OF LIGHT
By Dorothy Fadiman/Michael Wiese
22 minutes, color
Also available in Spanish

RADIANCE is a journey from the light in nature to the radiant spirit in all life. Using a stunning array of nature footage, kinetic mandalas, video images and religious art, Dorothy Fadiman shares her own encounter with the phenomenon of inner light.

Poetic narration leads magnetically from the personal to the universal. This deeply moving inquiry into unknown and uncharted territory leads us to a deeper understanding of the special qualities of every living thing.

RADIANCE is accompanied by a comprehensive, 20 page discussion guide showing how the film can be used in many ways – in religion, the arts, English and the humanities, women's studies, developing self esteem and body energy.

Special recognition:

"Shows that the ordinary is extraordinary. It is, quite simply, a work of art."
John White, New Realities

GOLD AWARD, Assn. of Media Educators in Religion
GOLD MEDAL, Miami Film Festival
SILVER CINDY, Information Film Producers of America, IFPA

Recommended for: humanities, philosophy, religion, art, film study

Audience: JHCGS

```
Rental $40
Sale $375
```

HARDWARE WARS
By Ernie Fosselius/Michael Wiese
13 minutes, color

This popular parody of *Star Wars* takes on high budget spectaculars and coming attractions trailers, using ordinary household appliances to create its 'special effects.'

HARDWARE WARS will delight all audiences – even those few viewers who have not seen the original.

Special recognition:

"Imaginative, ingenious, fast and funny. Bet you can't show this just once."
Film Library Quarterly

BLUE RIBBON, American Film Festival
SILVER HUGO, MOST POPULAR SHORT FILM OF THE YEAR, Chicago Film Fest.
Recommended for: literature and creative writing, film study, entertainment programming

Audience: IJHCG

```
Rental $30
Sale $275
```

releases and catalogs) credits read, *'A Film by . . . .'* or *'Directed by . . . Written by . . . '* or whatever is appropriate. Do not expect the publishers of this material to credit more than two people because there often isn't enough space. Very often the credits will be dropped anyway as the distributor's art department may not be aware of the contractual agreements. (This is another good reason for designing all promotional material yourself.)

11. Editing. The contract should state that the distributor cannot edit your film without written permission. They can, however, insert their logo at the head or tail of the film. This lets audiences know who distributes the film, which is very important. Some logos are quite nice and add a real snazzy look to your film. Never mind that it will give the impression that the distributor produced the film.

12. Warranties. You must own all the rights in your film and state this in the distribution contract. It will read that you are not infringing on anyone's copyright and that in the event of a suit you will be responsible for all costs incurred. Reasonable enough. On the other hand, I think it is also fair to state that if the distributors don't carry out their responsibilities and a suit is brought about, they pay legal expenses.

By now, we have substantially altered what was once the *'standard contract'*. Since there is probably not room for anything else on the standard contract, I attach a page of my own amendments to be included in the contract. This is labelled *'Exhibit A'*. Above the signatures on the distribution contract, I add: *'By mention of the attached page 'Exhibit A' it shall be part of this agreement.'* (Check with your lawyer for correct wording.)

144

My Amendments

Always try to get all your amendments into the contract. When you negotiate, each side must give up something. My amendments give me something to give up when necessary.

Examples are:

1. Ask for the right to purchase prints and videocassettes at lab cost (plus handling). The cost for prints, if ordered through the distributor's lab, is far less than you can get them for because distributors order hundreds of release prints each year and can buy them at great discounts.

2. Ask to receive a supply of 200 or more flyers, study guides, etc.

3. Ask that the distributor pay all entry fees and shipping to film festivals. Reserve the right to request festivals. The more, the greater visibility. Ask that they use their cassettes and prints. Any cash awards or trophies go directly to you, the filmmaker or videomaker.

4. Reserve the right to rent or sell films when approached directly at the same price as the distributor. (You are not to advertise this right.) This will not amount to many sales but every little bit helps. If you speak or show your film at a college or film festival someone may ask to rent or purchase your film. There is really no reason why a distributor shouldn't allow you to keep all the money from this kind of transaction because you are the one that generated the sale or booking. This is really small potatoes and a distributor should not object.

5. The contract should clearly state who supplies and pays for internegatives, A&B rolls, poster design, printing, study guide, various shipping costs, etc.

145

6. Ask that you receive a royalty report and royalty check (if any) on a quarterly basis. If possible, ask to be supplied with a list of buyers and renters. (Since most distributors have this information on computers, it is not difficult for them to provide. It is really a question of whether they want to or not.)

7. Minimum credit lines are to read: 'A Film By . . .'

8. (Applies to Warranty Section.) In the event the Licensee (distributor) shall default in the agreement, Licensor (that's you) shall enjoy the same privileges. (This simply provides you with the same privileges that the distributor is asking you to provide if someone defaults on the agreement or if a lawsuit arises.)

9. If the company is sold, all rights to distribute should revert back to you. I ask for this because some deals I make are based on who is running the company. If another company buys the distributor out, a new sales policy may place my film on the shelf for the remaining years of the contract.

10. A sliding scale for royalties. For example, if the gross exceeds $100,000 then the royalty percentage is increased. (I figure that if $100,000 is made then the distributor has long paid for promotion costs and is into profits. We should be more equal partners in these profits. Your film may never reach this gross but it doesn't hurt to have this in your contract because one never knows.) You could propose a sliding scale of royalties like this:

Gross	Royalty to You
$ 50,000	20%
75,000	25%
100,000	30%

Since it is a minor accounting hassle and because it diminishes the distributor's profits, they'll only do this for a 'must have' film.

146

Sample Non-Theatrical Distribution Contract

This is a copy of an actual non-theatrical distribution contract. It is a 'standard contract' without many modifications. I am not in any way suggesting that the terms of this sample contract are those which you should agree to. I am not a lawyer and am not providing any legal advice. This contract is provided for your information only.

Non-Theatrical Distribution Contract

This film agreement (herein called the 'Agreement') made this 15th day of August, 1984 by and between MICHAEL WIESE FILMS, having its principal place of business at PO Box 406, Westport, CT, 06881 (herein called 'Licensor') and BEST DISTRIBUTORS, a California Corporation, having its principal place of business at 1234 Money Drive, Beverly Hills, CA, (hereinafter referred to as 'Licensee').

Witnesseth: Whereas, Licensor owns certain rights to a motion picture film or video tape entitled 'THE BIG GROSS', (herein called the 'Film'), and Licensee is willing to distribute the same upon the terms, representations and warranties hereinafter set forth.

Now, therefore, in consideration of the mutual convenants and agreements herein set forth, the parties agree as follows:

1. *RIGHTS*. Licensor grants to Licensee the sole and exclusive right to rent, license, lease, exhibit, sell and otherwise exploit the film in 16mm film gauge, videocassettes in all sizes and gauges, for nontheatrical use only as such term is defined herein. The term 'lease' as used herein includes for the life of the film print or other format material.

2. *TERM*. The term of Licensee's rights under this agreement shall be for a period of five years commencing on August 15th, 1984 and upon receipt of satisfactory preprint material.

3. *TERRITORY*. United States and Canada.

147

4. *NON-THEATRICAL RIGHTS*. The term 'non-theatrical' shall mean the use of the film by direct projection in schools, universities, homes, summer camps, prisons, hospitals, public libraries, airlines, ships, business and industry, museums, film societies, and to all other individuals and groups and in all other places except for regularly established commercial motion picture theaters to which the public is admitted and pays an admission fee. All of these rights are granted unless specifically excluded in part 5 of this agreement.

5. *EXCLUSIONS*. US television, worldwide theatrical, worldwide pay cable, worldwide videodisk, worldwide television.

6. *DELIVERY*. The Licensor shall loan the Licensee the master printing materials by collect freight to Licensee's laboratory. In the case of a videotape, Licensor shall deliver to Licensee a 1' Video Master of the highest quality available. Such master must conform to NTSC standards and must be made on or before September 15, 1984.

7. *OWNERSHIP OF MASTERS*. Master materials are copyrighted by the Licensor and will at all times be the sole possession of Licensor. This agreement provides for the Licensee to use the master printing materials for making release prints and tape copies only and in no way may be construed as being a transfer of property. The master materials, if damaged, will be replaced in full by the Licensee.

8. *ROYALTIES*. Licensee shall pay to the Licensor royalties of 25% of the Gross Receipts derived from the non-theatrical distribution of program. 'Gross Receipts' are defined as the total of all payments received by the Licensee for the sale, lease or rental of the film less: 1) amounts received by Licensee as reimbursement from customers for postage, delivery expenses, handling and insurance and 2) any sales, use or other taxes collected by Licensee from its customers.

9. *ADVANCE*. Licensee will advance to Licensor $2500 to be recouped from royalties.

10. *MATERIALS*.Licensor shall provide Licensee with a 16mm internegative and sound negative and a composite 16mm print. Licensee will deposit said material at a laboratory of its choice. Licensee will pay the cost of internegative and sound printing negatives. All additional negatives and answer prints will be paid for solely by Licensee.

148

11. *ACCOUNTING*. Licensee shall keep full and accurate books of account showing in detail all gross revenue received in respect to said film, which shall be available at all reasonable times and upon reasonable notice to the Licensor or a duly authorized representative of the Licensor or his agent who may examine the same and make excerpts from such portions of Licensee's books as shall be deemed appropriate. Licensee shall render to Licensor no later than 45 days following the end of each calendar quarter an itemized statement showing the sums payable to Licensor hereunder in respect to the preceding quarter, and Licensee shall remit to Licensor the amount shown on such quarterly report. Each statement will show all rental and print sale income and shall list the names of all purchasers and rentors of said film.

12. *ADVERTISING*. Licensee shall have the full discretion to control and determine the nature and extent of advertising and promotion of the film. Licensor shall furnish to Licensee stills, reviews, background information, study guides, and a music cue sheet and a statement that the music is an original composition and other materials as shall be agreed upon between the parties to assist the Licensee in promoting the film.

13. *EDITING*. Licensee agrees not to make any changes or additions to, or eliminations from, the content or continuity of the film. Licensee shall have the right to affix to the film visual and sound head and tail sections identifying Licensee as the distributor of the film.

14. *WARRANTIES*. Licensor represents and warrants that it has the sole and exclusive right to enter into and perform this Agreement and grant all of the rights herein granted to Licensee. Licensor represents, warrants, and agrees to and for the benefit of Licensee, its officers, agents and licensees in and for the Term and Territory; 1) That Licensor owns all necessary rights in and to the literary material upon which the Film is based and the title thereof and in and to all music or lyrics synchronized with the Film necessary to enable Licensor to grant to Licensee the rights, licenses and privileges herein granted to Licensee to make the warranties and representations herein made; 2) That Licensor has affixed to the answer print or video master and negative appropriate notices of copyright protecting the film against unauthorized use or duplication; 3) That with respect to all persons

149

appearing in or rendering services in connection with the film, Licensor has the right to use such persons and to issue and authorize publicity concerning them; 4) That there are and will be no liens, security interests or rights of any nature in or to the film or any part thereof which can or will impair or interfere with or are equal or superior to the rights, liens or licenses of Licensee hereunder; and that the Program and each and every part thereof, including the sound and music synchronized therewith, and the exercise by any party authorized by Licensee of any right herein granted to Licensee, will not infringe upon the copyright, patent, literary, dramatic, music, or property right, right of privacy, the moral rights, or any other rights of any person, and that the film does not contain any unlawful or censorable material; 5) That Licensee shall quietly and peacefully enjoy and possess, during the entire period of its exclusive rights hereunder, all of the distribution rights herein granted and agreed to be granted to Licensee and that Licensor will grant to no other person, firm or organization rights inconsistent with those granted to Licensee herein.

15. INDEMNITY. Licensor shall, at its own expense, indemnify Licensee and its officers, employees, agents, assignees and licensees against and hold them harmless of and from all loss, damage and liability and expense, including attorney's fees, resulting from any breach of Licensor's warranties contained in this agreement.

16. TERMINATION. In the event that Licensor breaches or defaults in any material provision of this Agreement and does not cure such breach within ten (10) days after written notice thereof from Licensee or Licensor, licensee may elect to terminate this agreement and/or all of its obligations hereunder. In the event Licensee shall default in the performance of any term in this Agreement, Licensor's rights, if any, shall be limited to damages in an action at law and in no event shall Licensor be entitled by reason of such to terminate this Agreement or any of the rights granted to the Licensee or to enjoin Licensee from exercising any of the rights granted in this Agreement.

17. NOTICES. All notices or consents required by this Agreement shall be given in writing by registered or certified mail to the parties hereto at their respective addresses as previously set forth in this Agreement and shall be effective when deposited with the United States Post Office properly addressed and with postage prepaid. Each of the parties from time to time may change its address and, if so, will give written notice to the other party to such effect.

18. ASSIGNMENTS. Licensee shall have the right to assign its rights and licenses under this Agreement to sub-distributors, sub-licensees and selling agents.

19. NO PARTNERSHIP. This agreement shall not constitute a partnership or joint venture between the parties hereto.

20. AGREEMENT ENTIRE AND COMPLETE. This Agreement is entire and complete and contains the entire understanding between the parties hereto and no representations, warranties, agreement or covenants expressed or implied of any kind of character whatsoever have been made by either party hereto to the other except as specifically set forth herein in the attached Exhibit A.

This agreement shall be binding upon and shall inure to the respective successors, heir, executors and assigns of the parties hereto.

The parties to this Agreement have affixed their respective authorized signatures on the date and year first written above.

Exhibit A is attached herein and by this reference made a part of this Agreement. Licensee has read such Exhibit A and each term and condition therein and hereby agrees with Licensor's understanding with respect to this Agreement.

BY: Licensor

BY: Licensee

151

A Note About Distributors

I don't want to give the impression that distributors are out to take advantage of you. However, it is a business and the more information you have about dealing with distributors the better. The test of a good distributor is not necessarily how good a deal you make but if you are able to work together in successfully distributing and promoting your film. You want a relationship that is beneficial to everyone.

You may hear horror stories about how a distributor made some huge mistake, but before scratching that distributor off your list I suggest you probe deeper. Distributors, like anyone else, make mistakes. Good distributors are those that take care of their mistakes quickly and responsibly. (That could be said about good filmmakers as well!) Good luck in finding and signing with the best distributor for your work.

There is an extensive list of non-theatrical and home video distributors in the back of the book.

MARKETS

Markets

> *'Think of yourself as a
> 'communicator' and not just a
> 'filmmaker' or 'videomaker'
> and you will significantly
> increase your audience.'*

Introduction To The Marketplace

I have assumed that the non-theatrical market will be the primary market for your film or tape. (Therefore I used the earlier discussion of this market as a springboard for this section. Many of the same distribution principles apply in these other markets.) However, as this market decreases and the overall marketplace changes this may no longer be the case. There are more and more opportunities for distribution. Soon, the number of videotape players in the home will outnumber the subscriber base of HBO and create new and greater distribution possibilities for programs. So, in designing your project you need to be clever about how it will be used. You need to plan to produce one or more products from your single *'concern'* or idea that you can license in various markets. You'll need to do considerable homework to gather the information you need to make the correct choices. But if you take the time now, in the planning stages of your projects, you increase your chances for financial and critical success.

This section should give you some ideas about what markets to explore and how to think of them as exciting new showcases for your work.

The Distribution 'Pie'

The Distribution *'Pie'* gives you just some of the many income producing possibilities for your films and videotapes. (Please refer to the previous section 'Distribution Markets' for descriptions of these markets.) When you think of yourself as a *'communicator'* and not just a *'filmmaker'*, a *'videographer'* or a *'tv producer'* you expand your viewpoint as represented by this diagram. If you are successful in arranging distribution in only a few of these markets you will significantly increase your income and expand the audience for your efforts.

THE DISTRIBUTION PIE

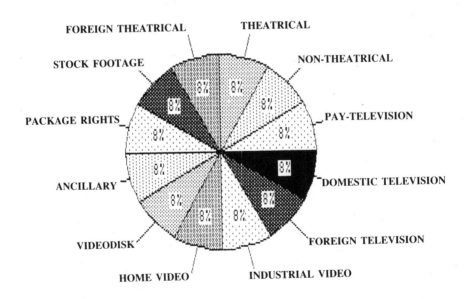

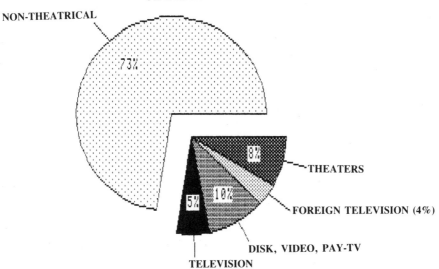

HARDWARE WARS

NON-THEATRICAL
73%

THEATERS
8%

FOREIGN TELEVISION (4%)

DISK, VIDEO, PAY-TV
10%

TELEVISION
5%

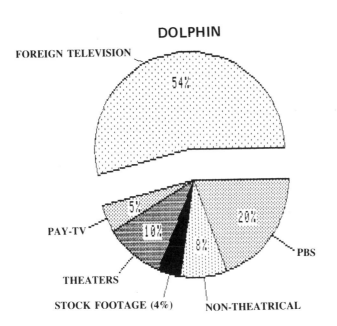

DOLPHIN

FOREIGN TELEVISION
54%

PBS
20%

NON-THEATRICAL
8%

STOCK FOOTAGE (4%)

THEATERS
10%

PAY-TV
5%

These are the *'pie charts'* for the short, *HARDWARE WARS* and the feature documentary, *DOLPHIN*. They show the approximate breakdown for income received in the various markets. Most of the income from *HARDWARE WARS* came from the non-theatrical sale of prints over the last 5 years. (It is possible that in the years to come and with Warner Home Video distributing videocassettes this 'slice of the pie' could expand.) *DOLPHIN's* main income has been from foreign television sales. New sales to pay cable are already increasing this *'slice'*. Again, note how each film has a primary market but is greatly supported by secondary markets.

Contracts in Other Markets

The distribution and licensing agreements for the other markets on the 'pie' charts are similar to the non-theatrical distribution contracts. Some of the same notions and ideas may be carried over in negotiating deals with distributors in these other markets. The percentages and other elements do differ and will be discussed in this section as will the different needs of these markets. Your project may not be suited to all of these markets, but this section will give you an idea of many other possibilities for your work.

Theatrical Shorts

So often I hear filmmakers say that when they finish their short films they are *'going to show them in the theaters'*. Now I don't mean to be rude but *'good luck'*. The realities of this naive notion are startling.

An Exercise

Suppose a theater booked your 10 minute film to play before *The Empire Strikes Back*. It runs for 4 weeks in a 2000 seat theater in Hollywood. There are lines around the block. All of the shows for the entire week are sold out. (This actually happened with *HARDWARE WARS*.)

Question: What weekly rental would you receive?

A.	$10,000
B.	$1,000
C.	$500
D.	$50

Take a guess.

The answer is D; $50 (actually between $25-75 dollars, with $75 being tops.) The $50 is split 50/50 with your distributor. That leaves $25 for you and your investors. If all goes well, and the theater pays the distributor on time, you will get your $25 share three to six months later. But wait. That's not all. It will cost you $2000 or more to make a 35mm blow-up (if you shot in 16mm) and $150 for each release print. After a few months of showings the print will be badly scratched.

'Outrageous', you say? Audiences love to see shorts. Why then, don't we see more of them in theaters?

Simple. Money. Economics. When so little is paid who can afford to produce them? Besides, theater managers like to turn

159

over the audience as many times per day as possible. A short film adds time to the program. I'm told it's a lot of trouble for a projectionist to splice the short film onto the main reel and then after the showing splice it off and ship it to the distributor.

Over the course of a year you may only see a dozen or so shorts play at all in theaters anymore. Out of 18,000 to 20,000 theaters in the United States there are only about 100 theaters that show short independent films on a regular basis. These are mostly smaller art and repertory theaters. (This pattern may be changing with the introduction of 35mm 'music videos' in theaters. See Music Video section.)

Another reason that theatrical shorts are nearly extinct is that distributors simply cannot earn enough money when the rental is so low and expenses are so high. They pay for prints, shipping, advertising, accounting. And they get $25 per week rental in return for their efforts. Big deal.

The only reason a filmmaker might do this at all is exposure. His or her film will be seen and enjoyed on a large screen. Now that's exciting. Any income must be regarded as gravy. You can't count on much. Over time it adds up, but even a successful short like *HARDWARE WARS* didn't make as much as it would seem to outsiders. When the film is booked on an individual, theater-by-theater basis it is hardly worthwhile, but every so often a theater chain will book it in many theaters over many weeks, then it pays off. But a block booking for a short is an exception. Our distributor has about forty 35mm prints, which by feature release standards is very few. Currently only a few are in circulation each month.

Once we made a deal with an Australian distributor. He wanted 50 prints of *HARDWARE WARS* to play with the theatrical release of *The Wilderness Family*. Instead of hassling overseas with the accounting we accepted a flat $2000 rental fee for a year's worth of showings. We didn't get rich

160

but it was another source of income. Keep in mind, however, that as a theatrical short, *HARDWARE WARS* has been an exception. Not many short films are shown theatrically.

To help alleviate this situation, The National Endowment for the Arts has sponsored the Short Film Showcase, a competition for 16mm shorts. The winners receive a $3000 honorarium (which can be thought of as a 'license fee') and distribution in 4500 participating theaters throughout the country. In addition, the winning filmmakers get to supervise the 16mm to 35mm blowup of their work. In 1981, nine new shorts were chosen from over 300 entries. The selected films were released free to the dozens of participating theaters. The exposure was tremendous. That combined with a $3000 honorarium and a 35mm blow-up (worth another $2000 to $3000) was very good. But that alone probably did not pay back anyone's production costs. (Not long ago it was announced that because of government cutbacks NEA has not received sufficient funding to continue the Short Film Showcase in 1984.)

'Four-Walling' Theatrical Documentary Features

Very few theaters book documentary features. Those that do show 35mm prints. To release *DOLPHIN* theatrically we *'four-walled'* a theater (that means that we rented the 'four walls' of the theater). We paid a flat rental fee for the hall ($600 per day, 1300 seats). Ushers, stage lighting, lighting man, projection equipment and projectionist were all extra since the hall was not normally used as a theater.

As a very rough rule, theater rental, including projectionist, for a commercial theater is about $1 per seat per day. But this rate will vary greatly depending on how busy the theater is, the time of year, location and size of the theater. When you 'four-wall', you pay all the costs, theater rental, advertising, etc. When you take this great risk you get all the ticket money. The

161

DOLPHIN

For centuries we have believed we were the only ones on earth
with a mind and soul . . . perhaps there are other such creatures.

Directed by HARDY JONES & MICHAEL WIESE Produced by MICHAEL WIESE Written by HARDY JONES
Music Composed & Conducted by BASIL POLEDOURIS
"Dolphin Song" Performed by MORGAN SMITH • Underwater Piano: STEPHEN GAGNE • With BUCKMINSTER FULLER

SAN FRANCISCO FILM PREMIERE
TUESDAY JUNE 26th • 8 pm
PALACE OF FINE ARTS
3301 Lyon Street, San Francisco
(Next to The Exploratorium)

Premiere & Celebration Party **$6** • Reserve Seating Only
Tickets in advance through all **BASS** Outlets (plus 75¢ service charge)
For information call T-E-L-E-T-I-X or charge tickets by calling 835-4342
Tickets also at the door on the evening of show unless previously sold out.

SHOWINGS CONTINUE AT THE PALACE OF FINE ARTS
WEDNESDAY JUNE 27th — SUNDAY JULY 1st • 7 & 9 pm
SATURDAY & SUNDAY SHOWS • 1, 3, 5, 7 & 9 pm

Tickets $3.75 at the door • Ample Free Parking

BAY AREA SHOWINGS:

PETALUMA	Plaza Theater	JUNE 27
SANTA CRUZ	Sashmill Theater	JUNE 30—JULY 1,2
BERKELEY	UC Theater	JULY 8
SACRAMENTO	J Street Theater	JULY 10, 11, 12

See local papers for show times.

theater keeps the money from the concession stand. (Which can be as much as 30% of the gross ticket sales! Some theaters claim they wouldn't exist at all without this income.)

To 'four-wall' you must be very certain your film will have an audience because it is a very expensive venture with high risk. The first week of advertising could cost $10,000, or much more, although once the film gets going and there is word of mouth the ad budget will be reduced. If you read the theater grosses in *Variety* you will see that when a small theater grosses $5000 per week it is considered quite good.

If you have a film that has an audience you might book a low cost, small theater and run the film for as many weeks as you can, relying on minimum advertising and maximum word of mouth. Spend 6 weeks or more publicizing your film in every way you can, with the reviews, articles and interviews to appear a week before the film opens. If it is a good film and people talk about it, you can build a larger and larger audience.

If you are fortunate enough to find an exhibitor (theater operator) that thinks your film will draw, you may be able to work out a deal.

Repertory Theaters

With repertory theaters that change their films every few days, you may negotiate 35%-50% of the gross receipts. The theater provides the theater, projectionist, and box office person and sometimes minimal advertising (like inclusion of your film on their monthly calendar). You provide any other advertising such as newspaper ads. The more publicity you do, the larger percentage you are entitled to.

College Auditoriums

College auditorium theaters are usually run by student activities departments. The program directors change frequently so it is often difficult to know who you will be doing business with. Gross receipts are difficult to monitor so it is often safer to charge a flat fee (unless you will personally be in attendance to count heads). The flat fee can vary from $100-250 per night which is a guarantee, versus 50% of the gross receipts, whichever is greater. Most of the time the flat fee/guarantee is the best you can hope for. If you have a film that is popular you can negotiate other arrangements. Know that it can take 2 or 3 months for university processed checks to arrive.

The Theatrical Arena

There are a variety of deals that are made in the wonderful world of theatrical films. I cannot pretend to be an expert in this area because other than managing a theater and 'four-walling' *DOLPHIN*, I've had little experience in this area. However, I hope to cover some of the 'nuts and bolts' of this area. It is a peculiar and fascinating system that has evolved from the early days of the film business.

The 'House Nut'

No, this isn't someone who lurks in the dark balconies of theaters. The *'house nut'* is a negotiated sum that represents the exhibitor's cost of keeping his theater open. But it really isn't. It's more than that. It's padded. It has some built-in profit. But everyone knows that so it's okay. It is an agreed upon figure between the exhibitor (theater operator) and the distributor. Here's how it works.

In New York City the weekly *'nut'* could amount to $10,000. It is also not unusual for this 'nut' to vary depending on who the distributor is doing business with. But hang on, there's more.

The 90/10 Deal

One theatrical deal is as follows. Say that a theater in a large city grosses $40,000 in first week. From $40,000, the $10,000 'house nut' is subtracted and the balance divided 90% to the distributor and 10% to the exhibitor. The distributor gets $27,000 and the exhibitor gets $10,000 plus $3,000 for a total of $13,000. In this instance, regardless of how poorly the film does, the exhibitor is guaranteed a profit, since his 'house nut' already includes some profit. (The exhibitor will also receive all the revenue from the concession stand which, on some kiddie pictures, can be as high as 20-30% of the box office gross. With an adult picture, fewer candy bars will be sold.)

Floors

This formula becomes more complicated as we move along. Since the exhibitors had (as perceived by the distributors), more security with the guaranteed house nut, contracts were changed to give the distributors an advantage. The new deal included a *'floor'* which meant, regardless of the 90/10 deal, that the distributor would never take less that a certain percentage of the box office receipts. (This kind of thinking only comes about when box office is low; when it's high everyone makes money.)

The floors are adjustable each week the film plays. So in the first week the floor would be 70%, the second week 60%, then 50%, 40% and so on. Take our first week gross of $40,000 as an example. The distributor is guaranteed 70% of the box office or $28,000 or the 90/10 deal, whichever is greater. In this case, the floor is greater by $1000. Not much. But take, as

165

an example, a first week gross of only $15,000. In the standard 90/10 deal we subtract the $10,000 house nut. The remaining $5,000 is split 90/10. The distributor gets $4,500 and the exhibitor gets $10,000 plus $500 for a total of $10,500. We get one unhappy distributor. He's made considerably less than the exhibitor. Here's where the distributor wants a different deal. With a 'floor', the distributor is protected from a low gross. The 'floor' arrangement would give the distributor 70% of the $15,000 or $10,500. A full $6000 more than the straight 90/10 deal. You can see how the floor gives additional security to the distributor (and producer who is waiting for his money down the line.)

Blind Bidding

Most exhibitors 'blind bid' on Hollywood films before they see them. (And many exhibitors have been burnt on big budgeted pictures with top stars that flopped at the box office. One big flop will cause them to lose enormous guarantees that they have put up on a picture by blind bidding.) In many states, exhibitors have lobbied their state legislatures who in turn have made blind bidding illegal.

If I were an exhibitor I'd want to see the film before deciding to book it, especially if I am required to put up huge sums of money to get the film in the first place. Obviously no one can predict a hit picture, but I'd rather gamble my money on something I've seen than something I haven't.

But on the other hand, as a producer or distributor, this would mean that I'd have to wait to make my deals until the film was finished when I could screen the film for exhibitors. With blind bidding, exhibition deals are made before a film starts shooting. There is no waiting or screening of films for exhibitors. The films can go straight into the theaters after production. Obviously this is what is desired by producers (and dis-

166

tributors) who want to start recouping and avoid the huge interest that is paid out before a film goes into exhibition. They simply want to get their monies back as soon as possible. Therefore, there is a great reluctance to take the time to screen the film for exhibitors. And what if their film turns out to be a real *'dog'*. This problem continues to persist in the film business. Strong arguments can be made for both sides with no solutions in sight.

Guarantees

Once an exhibitor's bid is accepted he is required to put up front money a few weeks before he opens the picture. The exhibitor may then keep all the box office money until his guarantee or front money has been earned back. With a popular Hollywood film this money can be earned back in the first few days. The risk is minimal. If the picture does poorly then the exhibitor has a problem of recoupment.

Majors' Domination Of The Market

For the small, art or documentary feature, breaking in is very, very difficult. The major studio distributors control nearly 90% of the total theatrical market. The best theaters are tied up with Hollywood product. The total box office gross for 1983 will be over $3 billion dollars. Of this amount, about $880 million becomes available for new production. If you count the six major studios (Fox, MGM/UA, Columbia, 20th Century, MCA/Universal, Warner Bros., Paramount Pictures), add Home Box Office's new *'instant major'* Tri-Star as seven, and add one more to cover the smaller companies like Disney, Embassy, and Orion/Filmways, you get 8 major producers. Divide these 8 companies into the $880 million that could be spent on new production and you get $110 million per company. If the average film now costs $13 million each major production entity will make between 6-10 films per year. With more and more films being made, the average dollar gross for each picture diminishes (since there is a limit to the theatrical market) so that when studios calculate what they will spend on production in the future it will be made on the total market available and not on the last successful smash of the summer. By examining the total box office gross and the money available for production a better understanding of the mechanics of the theatrical business can be gained. This is an example of market research that can be valuable to the independent feature producer.

Distribution Fees

The distributor's share of box office receipts is called *'film rental'* or *'distributor's gross'*. From this, the direct costs of marketing and releasing the film such as advertising, prints, shipping, etc. will be deducted. What remains is the *'distributor's net'*. From the 'distributor's net' a *'distribution fee'* of approximately 30% will be deducted. This 'fee' goes to running and maintaining the distribution company. Any profit to the distributor comes from this 'fee'. The remaining 70% of the 'distributor's net' goes to the film's producer. This will pay off production costs and bank interest. If there is anything left after all these deductions, it will be profits to investors and the production company.

Non-Theatrical (Educational & Business)

As mentioned in earlier sections of this book, royalty payments to the producer from non-theatrical distributors range from 18%-25% of gross receipts. Films sell for $15-20 per minute and rent for $1-2 per minute. Total revenues from the entire non-theatrical distribution business is about $100 million. The business and industry market has grown to about $500 million per year.

Basic and Pay Cable Television

Basic cable television reaches nearly 50 million homes and pay cable reaches 38.4 million homes. Advertising revenues have reached about $1.9 billion in 1989 which is about double what it was in 1987. By 1988, in the course of 4 years, broadcast television gave up 8 percentage points of total television households to pay and cable networks (and independent television stations). Clearly, basic and pay television are tremendous buyers of programming reaching more and more people. And now that basic cable penetration has increased to well over 50%, advertisers have found cable to be ideal in reaching highly targeted audiences. The added revenues allow broadcasters to create more original programming.

BASIC CABLE PENETRATION

	Subscribers(million)	% TV Households
1984	37.3	43.7
1985	39.8	46.2
1986	42.3	48.1
1987	44.9	50.5
1988	48.6	53.8

(Source: A. C. Neilsen Company)

These top 20 cable networks—by subscribers—give an idea of the kind of broadcasters whose programming is reaching the widest audiences and garnering higher overall ratings.

169

THE TOP 20 CABLE NETWORKS

1. ESPN
2. CNN
3. SUPERSTATION TBS
4. USA NETWORK
5. MTV
6. NICKELODEAN
7. THE FAMILY CHANNEL (CBN)
8. TNN (The Nashville Network)
9. C-SPAN
10. LIFETIME
11. NICK AT NITE
12. THE DISCOVERY CHANNEL
13. THE WEATHER CHANNEL
14. A & E CABLE NETWORK
15. HEADLINE NEWS
16. FNN
17. VH-1
18. TNT (Turner Network Television)
19. WGN
20. CABLE VALUE NETWORK

Shorts & Documentaries on Pay-Cable Television

When cable began there were not enough programs to fill the enormous amount of air time available. Many broadcasters such as HBO, Showtime and Nickelodean sought out independently produced short films which they used as "interstitial" or filler material. They paid perhaps as much as $100 per minute. And although was not a significant amount of money it did give independents a new source of revenue and exposure. This situation has changed considerably.

In a move to give their networks "their own look" and at the same time save money, almost all of the pay cable systems are now producing their own interstitial or short programming. Therefore, few short films are licensed by basic and pay cable.

The good news is that documentary production is in an upswing period. More broadcasters are scheduling documentaries—either that they acquire themselves or that they finance. HBO has been a leader in documentaries and often pays producers to develop documentary ideas. Turner, A&E and The Discovery Channel are others who frequently schedule documentaries. Payment for these programs can range from a straight one-year acquisition of $10,000 to half a million or more for original productions. Bill Couturie's DEAR AMERICA for HBO was budgeted at $500,000. When the programming executives saw the quality of his work they increased the budget significantly. They were very proud of the production and spent additional sums to promote and publicize the film. In an unprecedented move, they even allowed the film to have a theatrical window (probably to qualify for an Academy Award) after the airing.

There are opportunities for producer-writers who want to create short pieces for television such as working for a broadcaster in their on-air departments. When I worked for Showtime/The Movie Channel, in a year and a half, I oversaw the production of 1200 on-air segment ranging in length from a few seconds to 15 minutes. Most basic and pay services have their own in-house, on-air division that creates original, short programming. This is an excellent place to do a lot of work and learn new skills. What follows is a brief description of The Movie Channel's on-air, original programming as an example of what kind of short programming is produced.

Interstitial Programming on The Move Channel

The Movie Channel broadcasts only movies. Unlike Showtime or HBO there are no sports, music specials, comedy shows or original programs. They show only movies. Never shorts. (The Movie Channel, my former employer, was the only Pay TV service that didn't show *HARDWARE WARS*.)

Instead of purchasing shorts and in order to fill the breaks between the movies (which accumulates to 50-80 hours per month) *'interstitial'* segments are produced. ('Interstitial', a cable industry word, is certainly better than the demeaning *'filler'* although no one ever knows what it means. Movies are not scheduled back-to-back since people are accustomed to tuning in on the hour and half hour. The breaks enable the features to start at conventional times. Add up all these short breaks and you get 50 to 80 hours that must be filled each month! (For example, multiply the average 12 minute break times 13 movie breaks per day times 30 days, which equals 78 hours of accumulated time.) Of course that doesn't mean that 80 hours of programming would be produced. Instead, about 200 spots totalling roughly two hours would be produced each month and then scheduled in innovative ways to fill the time. (That was also my job.)

The Movie Channel's (and other systems') breaks use customized trailers and coming attractions to promote upcoming movies. The channel also promotes itself with *'image'* spots to increase the subscriber's perceived value of the service—the objective being to convince the subscriber that having and retaining The Movie Channel is a good value. (The old *'churn'* problem.) Subscribers' favor is gained by offering exciting, prize-filled contests such as *'The Goin' Hollywood Giveaway'*. The winner and his date got a first-class trip to Hollywood, stayed in a luxury hotel suite, received thousands of dollars for a Beverly Hills shopping spree (though it turned out they didn't spend anything, they wanted to keep the cash), a new wardrobe from a California designer, a helicopter hop to a Palm Springs spa and a brand new sports car (the winner had already bought a new car the week before). It was one of the most

172

popular Movie Channel contests and drew over 250,000 post-card entries. (The Movie Channel had 2.5 million subscribers at the time.)

Since many competing networks have the same movies, special on-air spots are edited to package the films in innovative ways and give viewers the perception that they are receiving something different by subscribing to their particular pay service. It's really a perceptual sleight-of-hand. The Movie Channel's repackaging and scheduling of movies is very successful in promoting difficult movies, increasing tune-in's, and creating an identity for the channel. Special promotions include *'The Saturday Special'* (for the wild and crazy, Saturday Night Live audience), *'Best of . . . The Mysteries'* (every Wednesday night, with a different *'Best Of . . . '* each month) and *'Sundays With Sherlock'* (Sunday afternoon Sherlock Holmes series). Showtime has special promotions like *'The Richard Pryor Double Feature'*. This programming is nothing more than movie promotion with a twist.

The Movie Channel's *'Star Profiles'* are 7 to 10 minutes long. They are exclusive interviews with actors like James Mason, for example, that are edited with biographical stills and movie clips). They air in the breaks between the movies to *'soft sell'* an upcoming movie like *The Verdict* in which Mason also appears. Research shows that the 'Star Profiles' are very popular with viewers and increase their appreciation of the movies (and hence the service). They help establish a *'perceived'* connection to Hollywood even though The Movie Channel is in a Manhattan skyscraper. It's the image that counts. (Style versus content. Since most pay services show the same movies it's the *'look'* of the channel that will differentiate one from the other.)

Unfortunately for independent producers these interstitial segments are produced in-house and not acquired from outside suppliers. Since one of the objectives of the channel is to offer

173

something different from all the other services, it is important to show exclusive interstitial programs that cannot be seen anywhere else. (The breaks are in fact the only place this can be done since the same movies can be seen on other services.) And, by producing everything in-house, the content, the 'look' and editing can all be controlled. The breaks are consistent. Pieces fit together, make sense overall and have an identifiable 'look'. This is not possible when shorts with various production values are strung together.

In summary, the market for shorts on pay cable is shrinking and being replaced by original 1/2 hour programs, free music videos and interstitial promotional segments. Independent producers must look instead to designing original programming for cable if they wish to penetrate this market.

Pay TV Prices For Shorts

Pay TV pays very little for shorts. When *HARDWARE WARS* first came out, the Pay TV services had not yet established prices for shorts, we were able to negotiate higher prices. The fact that it is a very popular short film with Pay TV audiences helps. What follows are some examples of licensing fees received for *HARDWARE WARS* (13 minutes) and *WONDER OF THE DOLPHINS* (11 minutes). Most licenses are for either 6 months or one year and include 12-20 plays.

Pay Service	Licensing Fee
1981	
HBO	1100
ON-TV	125
STV of San Francisco	200
STV of Washington	180
Times-Mirror	250

174

1982

Nickelodeon	900
Select TV (10 plays)	480
SHOWTIME	700

1983

Oak Communications	800
Entertainment Channel	825
SHOWTIME	525
Super TV Washington	175
Times-Mirror	450
Star Channel, Canada	650

I've presented these prices only to give you a general idea of what one can expect to receive for shorts. You may receive more or less today than *HARDWARE WARS*. With some re-licenses to the same systems we receive more as their subscriber base increased. At other times we received less for relicensing. Probably because the short had already played on so many systems.

Pay TV Prices for Features

This is an area shrouded in mystery and intrigue. Licensing fees are calculated by the Pay TV services using very complicated and sophisticated formulas that take into account the film's box office gross, the studio's advertising budget, the film's production budget, the number of Pay TV playdates, whether the airing is exclusive or not, the number of subscribers in the system at the time of the purchase (plus an escalation clause for increased fees as the subscriber base rises), recognizable stars, and the public's awareness of the film. Obviously very subjective elements come into the decision as prices are negotiated. As one Pay TV film buyer once told me, *'It's not a question of whether the studios will sell a film to Pay TV, it's at what price.'* The meaning is clear. Sooner or later the studios will make a deal with Pay TV.

To date, *Star Wars* received the largest amount of money ever paid for a film: $1 per subscriber. All you have to do to determine how much each service paid is multiply its number of subscribers by $1. The film was sold non-exclusively so everyone got the film at the same time. If you didn't show *Star Wars* you took the risk of being perceived as a second-rate service.

Some independent dramatic features have received as little as $10,000 on a one year, 12-play license. On the average, a Hollywood feature with recognizable stars, an average budget and a moderate box office gross will get between $.20 and $.30 per subscriber. But as the Pay TV marketplace begins its shakedown and there are fewer and few Pay TV services, those that survive will be increasingly powerful. And, with increased original production, acquisition prices will drop. (This was one of the reasons The Movie Channel and Showtime merged. The increased bargaining power allows pictures to be licensed for less money for each service.) If a studio wants to sell its pictures to Pay TV it will have fewer and fewer places to go and must ultimately accept what a service offers. (Or start its own.)

One of the reasons the studios have been trying so desperately to get into the Pay TV game themselves is this loss of revenue. When a film is shown at the box office they can receive as much as $1 from each admission. When the same film is shown on Pay TV they receive $.20 or less. Not only that, there is strong evidence that Pay TV cuts into the theatrical market. If a movie isn't a *'must see now'* movie, people know they can wait and see it on Pay TV later. They won't bother going to the theater so a studio begins to loses its *'marginal audience'* to the Pay Television set.

176

Basic and Pay Television Programmers

One of the greatest opportunities for independents are in supplying programming to cable television. There exists nearly 100 operating services. This includes both the basic services and the pay television broadcasters. Many services operate 24 hours a day and use a phenomenal amount of programming which they license from both domestic and foreign producers. The more financially successful broadcasters produce original programming. Producers may look to cable television as an "after window" (once they've exploited theatrical and home video) or they may look to cable as a co-production partner, supplying a portion of the production financing for cable broadcast rights.

What follows are thumb-nail sketches of both basic and pay television broadcasters. The cable world is still growing so both the number of subscribers, program mix and telephone numbers may be somewhat out of date by the time you read this. Nevertheless it should give you an overview of the industry from which you can cull your personal "hit list" for the type of programming you produce.

For an updated report of cable operators and systems you may wish to contact the National Cable Television Association, 1724 Massachusetts Avenue, NW, Washington, DC 20036 (202) 775-3550.

A & E Cable Network

They operate 24 hours a day and show a wide variety of quality programming including comedy, drama, documentaries and the performing arts. They reach 35.6 million subscribers. They are a basic service and accept advertising. 555 Fifth Avenue, New York, NY 10017, (212) 661-4500.

ACTS Satellite Network (American Christian Television System)

A 24-hours-a-day faith and family programmers targeted to mainline Christian demographics. They reach 9.5 million subscribers. 6350 West Freeway, Fort Worth, TX 76150, (817) 737-3241.

Alternate View Network

This small network reaches 4 million subscribers on Sunday mornings between 7:30 am and 1 pm. They show family, moral and ethical programming. 500 Common St., Shreveport, LA 71101, (318) 226-8776.

American Movie Classic

This channel is devoted exclusively to showing Hollywood's classic films and entertainment. They reach 15.5 subscribers. Rainbow Program Enterprises, Inc., 150 Crossways Park West, Woodbury, NY 11797, (516) 364-2222.

America's Value Network

A new broad-based home shopping network with 300,000 subscribers. Rt. 2, Eau Claire, WI 54703, (715) 874-4522.

BET (Black Entertainment Television)

A full day service oriented toward black audiences with news, feature films, music specials, sports, public affairs and music video shows. They reach 21.7 subscribers and accept advertising. 1232 31st Street, NW, Washington, DC 20007, (202) 337-5260.

Bravo Cable Network

A cultural channel which runs 8 pm to 6 am Mondays through Fridays and 5 pm through 6 am on the weekends. They feature award-winning American and international films and performing arts which reach 2 million subscribers. They are a pay TV service. Rainbow Program Enterprises, Inc., 150 Crossways Park West, Woodbury, NY 11797, (516) 364-2222.

The CBN Family Channel

A full day service with original and off-network programming ranging from docs to dramas, comedy classics, westerns and shows for women. Health, homemaking and children's programming. Special and inspirational programs. They reach 44.1 subscribers and accept advertising. 1000 Centerville Turnpike, Virginia Beach, VA 23463, (804) 424-7777.

CNBC

A 24-hour per day network with consumer, financial and market information. They reach 13 million subscribers and accept advertising. 2200 Fletcher Avenue, Fort Lee, NJ 07024, (201) 585-6425.

CNN

Turner's 24-hour news service covering major-breaking stories and summaries, weather, sports and special interest reports. They reach a whopping 50.1 million viewers. 1 CNN Center, Atlanta, GA 30303, (404) 827-1895.

C-SPAN (Cable Satellite Public Affairs Network)

A full day news and events service from Washington, DC and around the country offered without commentary or analysis.

179

Includes live House of Representatives debates, daily viewer call-in programs, National Press Club speeches, Congressional hearings and specials. Reaches 43.3 million subscribers. 444 North Capitol St., NW, Suite 412, Washington, DC 20001, (202) 737-3220.

C-SPAN II

A full day service with live coverage of US Senate and other public affairs programming which reaches 17.3 million subscribers. 444 North Capitol St., NW, Suite 412, Washington, DC 20001, (202) 737-3220.

Cable Value Network

The largest cable exclusive, 24-hour per day, shopping network with 22 million subscribers. 1405 N. Xenium Lane, Minneapolis, MN 55441, (612) 557-5195.

Cable Video Store

A full day pay-per-view service which offers 30 to 40 new and older film releases and special event programming to 700,000 viewers. 2200 Byberry Road, Hatboro, PA 19040, (215) 674-4800.

Cinemax

HBO's sister pay tv service which mixes select and broad appeal films, documentaries, original music and comedy programming. Reaches 6 million viewers. HBO Building, 1100 Avenue of the Americas, New York, NY 10036, (212) 512-1659.

Country Music Television

A full day service featuring country music video clips in stereo and interviews of the hottest country artists. Monthly music

180

specials. Reaches 9 million viewers and accept advertising. 704 18th Avenue South, Nashville, TN 37203, (615) 255-8836.

The Discovery Channel

Operates from 9 am to 3 am and offers non-fiction entertainment programming in nature, science, technology, world exploration, history and human adventure. Have just begun to produce their own original programs. Reaches 43 million subscribers and accepts advertising. 8201 Corporate Drive, Suite 1200, Landover, MD 20785, (301) 577-1999.

The Disney Channel

A pay television service reaching 4.3 million subscribers with programming for children in the morning and afternoon, families in the early evening and adults in the late evening. 3800 West Alameda, Burbank, CA 91505, (818) 569-7500 or (213) 566-8970.

ESPN

A full day service of sports coverage and business every weekday morning. Reaches 50.6 million subscribers and accepts advertising. ESPN Plaza, Bristol, CT 06010, (203) 585-2000.

EWTN (Eternal Word Television Network)

A full day service reaching 12 million subscribers with Catholic religious and family programming. 5817 Old Leeds Road, Birmingham, AL 35210, (205) 956-9537.

Family Guide Network

An "infomercial" system that operates from 1 am to 3 pm as an audience response programming service that emphasizes entertaining, self-improvement and business opportunity. The programmer pays the operator 10-20% commission. Suite A1 Fox Pavilion, Jenkintown, PA 19046, (215) 887-7010.

FamilyNet

A full day family entertainment network that offers original programming, sports and movies. Reaches 3.2 viewers and accepts advertising. PO Box 196, Forest, VA 24551, (804) 845-4146.

The Fashion Channel

A full day exclusive shopping network for fashion, merchandise and accessories. Reaches 10 million subscribers. 1405 N. Xeium Lane, Minneapolis, MN 55441, (612) 557-5195.

FNN (Financial News Network)

Operates from 6 am to midnight, Mondays through Fridays with practical business news from around the world and personal money management. Continuous ticker coverage of the major stock exchanges. Reaches 33 million subscribers and accepts advertising. 320 Park Avenue, 3rd Floor, New York, NY 10022, (212) 891-7300.

FNN/SCORE

Operates from 5 pm to 3 am on Saturdays and Sundays with live sports news, highlights, updates and recaps. Programming also includes live events and sports specialty shows. Reaches 20 million subscribers and accepts advertising. 6701 Center Drive West, Los Angeles, CA 90045, (213) 670-1100.

FNN: TelShop

Operates Midnight to 6 am, Mondays through Fridays and 3 am to 5 pm, Saturday and Sunday with brand-name merchandise offered with on-air comparison shopping. Reachers 15 million subscribers. 320 Park Avenue, 3rd Floor, New York, NY 10022, (212) 891-7300.

GalaVision/ECO Inc.

A full day service with Spanish-language programming such as films, novellas, live soccer, boxing, wrestling, and news and entertainment live from Mexico City. Reaches 3.3 million subscribers and accepts advertising. 2121 Avenue of the Stars, Suite #2300, Los Angeles, CA 90067 (213) 286-0122.

HBO

The giant in pay television with 17 million subscribers, 24 hours a day. Offers motion pictures, exclusive news entertainment specials, music, comedy, original drama, documentary, series, sports, special events, family programs, specials and original movies. Is a major producer of original programs. HBO Building, 1100 Avenue of the Americas, New York, NY 10036, (212) 512-1659.

Headline News

A full day service with update, half-hour newscasts with time for local news inserts. Reaches 35.3 million subscribers and accepts advertising. 1 CNN Center, Atlanta, GA 30303, (404) 827-1547.

Hit Video USA

Operates from midnight to 10 am and shows contemporary hit videos. 1000 Louisiana Street, Suite 3500, Houston, TX, 77002, (713) 650-0055.

183

Home Shopping Network I

A twenty-four hours a day reaching 19.9 million subscribers with original, live, discount shop-at-home services. The broadcasters receive a commission on sales. PO Box 9090, Clearwater, FL 34618-9090, (813) 530-9455.

The Information Channel

A full day service that provides "news you can use" programming to 2.5 million subscribers in 6 program categories: The Cable Video Guide (channel listings), news, weather, sports, home, money and lifestyle information. Creates an editorial environment for the sale of photo advertisements. NuCable Resources Corp., 3050 K Street, NW, Suite 370, Washington, DC 20007, (202) 944-4110.

The Inspirational Network

A full day service reaching 9.5 million subscribers with inspirational programming with talk, variety, children's, drama, music and family specials. Box 240319, Charlotte, NC 28224, (704) 542-6000.

International Television Network (ITN)

Operates 12:30 am to 8:30 am and reaches 22.8 million subscribers with international programming including world and business news, movies, interviews, talk shows, children's shows, drama, adventure, fashion news, sporting events, and "Broadway" magazine. Accepts advertising. 919 Third Avenue, 6th Floor, New York, NY 10022, (212) 223-2635.

KTLA

A full day service from the Los Angeles independent station which reaches 4.9 million subscribers and accepts advertising.

184

Programming mix includes movies, sports, news and specials. United Video, 3801 S. Sheridan Road, Tulsa, OK 74145, (800) 331-4806.

KTVT

A full day service from the Dallas-Fort Worth independent station which reaches 3.6 million subscribers with movies, sports, news and specials. Accepts advertising. United Video, 3801 S. Sheridan Road, Tulsa, OK 74145, (800) 331-4806.

The Learning Channel

Operates 6 am to 2 am and reaches 16 million subscribers with educational series, high school equivalency degree preparation, college level telecourses, public affairs specials and the INDEPENDENTS; a series featuring the works of independent video and film producers. Accepts advertising. 1525 Wilson Blvd., Rosslyn, VA 22209, (703) 276-0881.

Lifetime

A full service broadcaster which reaches 42 million subscribers. Monday through Saturday LIFETIME offers contemporary programming of special interest to women and all day Sunday, LIFETIME Medical Television, which is the world's largest producer of programming for physicians and provides programming for the health care community. Accepts advertising. 36-12 35th Avenue, Astoria, NY 11106, (718) 482-4000.

Mind Extension University

A full day service offering college level telecourses for college credits including an MBA program, also self-help, informative educational programs such as GED and English as a second language. Reaches 4 million subscribers. 9697 East Mineral Avenue, Englewood, CO 80112, (800) 525-7002.

185

MTV (Music Television)

The innovative, 24 hour, all stereo video music channel which features music videos and music specials. Reaches 45.7 million subscribers and accepts advertising. MTV Networks, Inc., 1775 Broadway, New York, NY 10019, (212) 713-6400).

The Movie Channel

A pay TV service which offers movies all day long and reaches 2.7 million subscribers. Shows movie classics, film festivals, and movie-related original programming. 1633 Broadway, New York, NY 10019.

Movietime

A full day service reaching 12.1 million subscribers which covers the world of entertainment. It is the first and only 24-hour cable service network devoted exclusively to coming attractions of new films, celebrity interviews cable television previews, Hollywood premieres, late-breaking entertainment news, behind-the-scenes reports, sound-track videos, exciting contests and prizes. Accepts advertising. 1800 N. Vine Street, Hollywood, CA 90028, (213) 960-5823.

NCTV (National College Television)

A six hour per day service which provides entertainment and informational programming for college students. Includes movie reviews, campus news shorts, music videos, comedy, cartoons, soap operas and game shows. Has 6.1 million subscribers and accepts advertising. 114 5th Avenue, New York, NY 10011, (212) 206-1953.

NJT (National Jewish Television)

Operates from 1 pm to 4 pm on Sundays and reaches 7.2 million subscribers with cultural, religious and public affairs programming for the Jewish community. PO Box 480, Wilton, CT 06897, (203) 834-3799.

Nickelodean

Operates 7 am to 8 pm daily and reaches 45.5 million subscribers with programming devoted entirely to kids and families. Accepts advertising. MTV Networks, Inc., 1775 Broadway, New York, NY 10019, (212) 713-6400).

Nick at Nite

Operates in Nickelodean's off-hours (8 pm to 7 am) with entertainment programming for "the people who grew up with television". Accepts advertising. MTV Networks, Inc., 1775 Broadway, New York, NY 10019, (212) 713-6400).

The Nostalgia Channel

A full day service which reaches 5 million subscribers and targets the 45+ viewer with variety programming, lifestyle information and today's active adults who are looking for "new choices". 71 W. 23rd Street, Suite 502, New York, NY 10010, (212) 463-7740.

The Playboy Channel

Operates 8 pm to 6 am as both a pay service and a pay per view ("Playboy on Demand") service reaching 448,000 viewers with original programming and acquired R-rated and comedy films. 8560 Sunset Blvd., West Hollywood, CA 90069, (213) 659-4080.

187

QVC Network Inc.

A full day service reaching 14 million subscribers which offers consumer band name products, including Sears merchandise at discounts. A live, shop-at-home network with games and sweepstakes. Goshen Corporate Park, West Chester, PA 19380, (215) 430-1022.

Request Television and Request Television 2

Operates from 9 am to 5 am as a pay per view service reaching 4.5 million subscribers with approximately 10 movies per month. Designed to offer maximum exposure of hit films over both channels. Some special events. 1 Dag Hammarskjold Plaza, New York, NY 10017, (212) 984-5900.

Shop Television Network

A full day home shopping service with 5.1 million subscribers. 5842 Sunset Blvd., Los Angeles, CA 90028, (213) 871-8170.

Showtime

A full day, pay service reaching 6.7 million subscribers with a wide range of broad appeal programming including hit films, original movies, comedy specials, dramas, musical concert events, children and family programs, original series, foreign and classic films, and championship boxing. 1633 Broadway, New York, NY 10019, (212) 708-1638).

The Silent Network

Operates 9:30 am to 11:30 am on Saturdays reaching 11 million subscribers with originally produced, exclusive programming for the deaf, hearing-impaired and hearing viewers including sign, voice (full-sound) and open captions. Series

188

include: oil painting instruction, a celebrity and issue-oriented interview program, a dog series, and a sign language instruction program. Accepts advertising. 6363 Sunset Blvd., Suite 930B, Hollywood, CA 90028, (213) 464-7446.

SportsChannel America

A full day service with 8.5 million subscribers that offers live major sporting events. Accepts advertising. 150 Crossways Park West, Woodbury, NY 11797, (516) 364-2222.

SuperStation TBS

A full day service reaching 47.1 million viewers that features movies, sports, original programming and syndicated shows. Accepts advertising. 1 CNN Center, Box 105366, Atlanta, GA 30348, (404) 827-1792.

TBN (Trinity Broadcasting Network)

A 24-hour Christian broadcasting service that reaches 9.9 million subscribers with broad denominational programming. 9020 Yates, Westminster, CO 80030, (303) 650-5515.

TNN (The Nashville Network)

Operates 9 am to 3 am and reaches 44 million viewers with concert specials, exclusive sports coverage, entertainment, news, interviews, information, live variety and classic western movies. Accepts advertising. Group W Satellite Communications, 90 Park Avenue, New York, NY 10016 (212) 557-6532.

TNT

A full service broadcaster which reaches 26 million subscribers with movies, made-for-cable movies, sports, comedy and

189

drama. 1 CNN Center, Box 105366, Atlanta, GA 30348, (404) 827-1792.

The Travel Channel

A full service broadcaster that reaches 10.5 million subscribers with a unique blend of exciting destination shows, up-to-date business and leisure travel news, global weather forecasts and a world-wide calendar of cultural events. Includes shows devoted to the best current travel values available to customers. Accepts advertising. 1370 Avenue of the Americas, New York, NY 10019, (212) 603-4500.

UNIVISION

A full service broadcaster and advertiser-supported service that reaches major Hispanic markets through the UHF and low-power TV stations and cable systems across the U.S. Shows a full range of Spanish language programming produced domestically and throughout the Spanish-speaking world. Features movies, novellas, sports and news. Reaches 5.2 million viewers or 84% of all Hispanic households. 767 Fifth Avenue, 12th Floor, New York, NY 10153, (212) 826-5200.

USA Network

A 24-hour per day network reaching 47 million viewers with entertainment, series, movies and specials with programming for women, children, teens and adults. Accepts advertising. 1230 Avenue of the Americas, New York, NY 10020, (212) 408-9100.

VH-1

A full day music video channel targeted to the 25-54 age group. Reaches 31.8 viewers and accepts advertising. MTV Networks, Inc., 1775 Broadway, New York, NY 10019 (212) 713-6462.

190

Viewer's Choice and Viewer's Choice 2

A full day, pay-per-view network offering the latest in Hollywood films, live sports events and music specials. Both networks reach a total of 7 million viewers. 909 Third Avenue, 21st Floor, New York, NY 10022, (212) 486-6600).

VISN

Operates from 10:30 am to 2 am Mondays through Fridays, and 8 am to 2 am on Saturdays and Sundays with mainline religious and values-based programming. Reaches 5.5 million viewers and accepts advertising. 8500 Menaol NE, Ste. B284, Albuquerque, NM 87112, (800) 522-5131.

WGN

The Chicago independent station full day service with 24.8 million viewers offering movies, sports, news and specials. Accepts advertising. United Video, 3801 S. Sheridan Rd., Tulsa, OK 74145, (800) 331-4806.

WPIX

The full day service from the independent station in New York which reaches 9.7 million viewers with movies, sports, news and specials. Accepts advertising. United Video, 3801 S. Sheridan Rd., Tulsa, OK 74145, (800) 331-4806.

WSBK

A full day service from the independent station in Boston which reaches 2 million subscribers with movies, specials, business reports, variety programming, children's programming and live sporting events. Accepts advertising. Eastern Microwave, 112 Northern Concourse, PO Box 4872, Syracuse,

191

NY 13221 (315) 455-5955 (in NY) and (800) 448-3322 (out of state).

WWOR

The full day service from New York independent station which reaches 12.5 million viewers with movies, news, specials, children's programming and 350 live sporting events a year. Accepts advertising. Eastern Microwave, 112 Northern Concourse, PO Box 4872, Syracuse, NY 13221 (315) 455-5955 (in NY) and (800) 448-3322 (out of state).

The Weather Channel

A full day service reaching 38.5 million viewers with current local, regional, national and international weather information. Includes forecasts for travellers, sports fans, and pilots. Accepts advertising. 2600 Cumberland Parkway, Atlanta, GA 30339, (404) 434-6800.

ZAP Movies

Operates from 3 pm to 2 am with pay-per-view programming that reaches 200,000 viewers with 12-18 movies each month and a full-time promotional preview channel. 2029 Century Park East, Suite 920, Los Angeles, CA 90067 (213) 556-5650.

NEW, PLANNED SERVICES

ATV

An all-advertising basic network featuring theme hours such as auto, fashion, travel, computer, beauty, etc. The hours will consist of 5 and 10 minute "infomercials" produced by national sponsors. 420 Pompton Avenue, Cedar Grove, NJ 07009, (201) 857-3500.

192

Holiday! TV Network

A full day service with leisure and recreation, travel and tourism programming. 5438 Thunder Hill Road, Columbia, MD 21045, (301) 997-1056.

Kids Information Network

The first national television network dedicated to locating missing children. Will operate 24 hours per day and reach 1.5 million viewers. 6201 Sunset Blvd., Suite 30, Hollywood, CA 90028 (714) 998-0573.

Laugh TV

A full day service with comedy programming, featuring videos, stand-up performances taped around the country, sketches and specials. PO Box 52331, Tulsa, OK 74152. (918) 747-6000.

Main Street

A full day service with consumer interactive programming including shopping, travel, entertainment and financial services. GTE—One Stamford Forum, Stamford, CT 06904, (203) 965-4302.

MEN (Maximum Entertainment Network)

Will operate from 6 pm to 2 am with all original programming geared for men, featuring documentaries, drama, action, adventure, finance, science and technology. Full Circle Entertainment, 1901 Avenue of the Stars, Suite 1774, Los Angeles, CA 90067 (213) 556-2450.

QVC Network II

A home shopping service. Goshen Corporate Park, West Chester, PA 19350, (215) 430-1022.

STNN (Spanish Television News Network)

A full day service with news, sports, special reports and coverage of Latin American/Hispanic American affairs. GPO Box 2556, San Juan, PR 00936, (809) 345-0215.

Talk Television

A 24-hour, all-talk show. 351 Nod Hill Road, Wilton, CT 06897, (203) 762-2277 or (301) 983-4291.

Pay TV & Cable TV Distributors

One route to selling your films and videos to pay or basic cable is to locate the acquisition director and send in your programs. Before calling, study the network's scheduling to see if your program is really appropriate to the channel before you call. Plan to spend some time at this. Although there are only a few program buyers, it make take many months to get an answer after submitting your program. Also—do some research so you get a realistic idea of the license fees being paid. This will help you sort out which pay TV networks to go to first.

You might be better off finding a pay TV agent or distributor who knows both the buyers and the prices they pay. The standard split with a pay TV distributor is about 25%-45% distributor, 75%-55% to you. Outside of duplication, postage, telephone and overhead, a distributor's costs are low. Another advantage in using a distributor is that since they supply more programs to the cable services, they can leverage more monies from buyers than you probably can. *Coe Film Associates*, 65 East 96th Street, New York, NY, 10028, (212) 831-5355 and Fox/Lorber Associates in New York City are both reputable pay TV distributors. Others may be found in the Video Distributors section in the back of the book. (*New Video*, 276 3rd Avenue, New York, NY, 10010, (212) 473-6000, is a retail store that rents and sells independent videos too specialized for pay TV.)

Many traditional non-theatrical distributors have hired specialists to distribute their films to the pay television markets. If, after talking to the non-theatrical distributors, you feel they will do a good job, then you may grant them pay TV rights. Be careful though, many will want the rights but may have no more clout than you. Negotiate a reasonable fee which will be different than your royalty. (See paragraph above for an acceptable range.)

Pay Cable Program Buyers

In the appendix you will find a list of pay cable program buyers and a list of cable distributors.

Whether or not you find a distributor, you should always try to license your program to pay-cable on a *'non-exclusive basis'* so that you can sell your show to the many other pay TV systems simultaneously. Often you won't be able to. Most systems will want to air your program first and demand *'blocking rights'* and *'holdbacks'*, which means you must keep your program off other services for a specified period of time.

Videocassette Marketplace

Over 30 million video cassette recorders have been sold in the United States alone and more than 100 million world-wide. For independents there are two seperate markets for video. The first is the educational, non-theatrical market where tapes are sold for relatively high prices to schools, libraries, business and industry. The second is the traditional video rental store which primarily rents feature films.

Note: Since the first publication of this book in 1981 the video market has prospered significantly. So much so, that in the summer of 1986 I completed a new book about the opportunities for independents in this new market. *HOME VIDEO: PRODUCING FOR THE HOME MARKET* covers the development of ideas specifically for home video, financing and marketing techniques, video budgets, video distribution agreements, packaging, various program genres and formats and other information specifically written for the producers of home video programs. The scope of this information far exceeds what could be realistically be covered in this book. (To order, please see the last page in the book.)

Videocassettes (home video market)

Most video cassette recorders have been sold for home use. Avid owners rent approximately 3 tapes per week or 150 per year! Of those who purchase videos, they may buy up to 5 tapes per year. As prices drop, more tapes will be sold to consumers. Tapes sell at retail from $9.95 (public domain movies, children's half-hour programs) to $89.95 (recently released Hollywood movies). Blank tapes sell for as little as $4.50. A made-for-home video program (non-feature) that sells more than 25,000 units (or $1 million at wholesale) is deemed a best-seller by the RIAA (Recording Industry

Association of America). Consumers prefer the *VHS* format (85%) over *BETA* (15%). Some video retail stores are only stocking VHS. A new format, 8mm, has been introduced by Sony and is expected to grow.

We got lucky with *HARDWARE WARS* when Warner Home Video packaged it with other short films. That simply doesn't happen much today with the plethora of tapes in the market. Back in 1980, our deal with Warner Home Video, was for a comedy package of shorts titled *HARDWARE WARS AND OTHER FILM FARCES*, we received a $10,000 advance and 12% of the gross receipts (wholesale price) which was shared among the other producers. If the advance wasn't paid back in 2 years then the agreement becomes non-exclusive and we may use other distributors. Feature films get much larger advances of up to 20% or more of the wholesale price. Since our film was released early on in the home video business there was a small VCR population and fewer rental stores than there are today (20,000 or more). To date, our video has sold about 4500 units at $39 retail, which is actually quite good, considering there are now 500 new videos released each month!

Few of the major distributors like Paramount, CBS/Fox, RCA/Columbia and Warners are interested in acquiring non-feature product from independents. They already have a steady flow of movies available from their film divisions. Independent video distributors who cannot get studio films are hungry for independently product. Here's where a great opportunity lies. Distributors like Vestron, Karl/Lorimar, Media Home, Active and others are good places to start.

Videocassettes (business and industry market)

Videocassettes in 3/4', VHS and Beta formats are sold by about a dozen distributors to the business and industry markets. This has become a very lucrative business for some. Hour

197

programs, such as business training tapes are sold for $750 to $1500. A program that only sells a few hundred copies can recoup its production cost and a profit. Corporations are willing to pay what seems like high prices for this media until you consider that it would cost $10,000 or more to bring in a live speaker on the same subject.

Producers receive about 25% of gross revenues from these distributors. There are more than 90 smaller distributors of health, training and business tapes, some of which you will find in the section Video Distributors at the back of the book.

Videocassette (specialized)

There are many small videotape distributors that distribute experimental, documentary and personal videotapes of independent producers. There is Electronic Arts Intermix, Portable Channel, Synapse, all located in New York State. In San Francisco there is BAVC (Bay Area Video Coalition). In Minneapolis, University Community Video. Many independent videotape producers self-distribute their own tapes through specialized mailings and by advertising in video magazines.

Videodisks

The videodisk player (CED) were discontinued by RCA. There are only about 700,000 in use. (Fewer each year. They wear out.) Only the more popular feature films are released on CED disk. Laser disk, however, continues to be a small but popular format. Some expect this to gain in popularity in future years. There are only 20,000 to 30,000 interactive videodisk players in use. These are owned by business and industry and used for training purposes. An interactive consumer machine has yet to hit the market.

PBS Television

PBS is complex and mysterious. Since it is large and decentralized it is extremely difficult to know where you stand when you do business with PBS. Furthermore, they often change internal policies, so what I have to say about dealing with PBS may be antiquated by the time you read this. But I doubt it.

The shame of it is that I often hear filmmakers say how they are going to *'sell their film to PBS'*. They say this naively, not knowing how difficult and complex it is. You simply don't walk in with a finished film under your arm and someone hands you some money. If you have the idea that PBS is a benevolent network serving public and educational interests, a renewed study is suggested. Read on.

There are several ways to approach PBS, and not necessarily in this order.

Acquisitions

There is an acquisition department in Washington, DC, that licenses programs for the entire system.

Station Program Cooperative (SPC)

The SPC (the Station Program Cooperative) is, in the words of PBS, *'a marketing system employed by the nation's public television stations to cooperatively select and finance national programming distributed by the Public Broadcasting Service. Administered by PBS, the SPC has, since 1974, enabled the public television stations to pool their resources in funding a substantial part of PBS' National Program Service.'*

The way the cooperative works is that each station is free to

199

select and help finance national programs it is interested in broadcasting locally. Most of the major series shown on PBS are funded by the SPC. Very few specials have been funded by it.

Proposals and finished programs are presented each winter at the SPC 'market', which means they are prepared for presentation in the fall by the stations and independent producers. Through a process of elimination, programs for acquisition or funding are selected. The average SPC cost for an hour of programming is less than $35,000. Most SPC-funded programs are partially underwritten by non-SPC or corporate sources.

Further information about the SPC can be provided by any local PBS station or through the PBS Program Business Affairs office at (202) 488-5000 or by writing PBS and requesting its SPC fact sheet.

Corporate Underwriting

PBS 'stations of entry' (many of which are larger stations located in major cities) will try to raise corporate underwriting for one of the following: 1) a grant for research and development, 2) full production underwriting, or 3) underwriting for the acquisition license fee for your finished film.

However, you must understand something about PBS and its corporate sponsors. A report by James Roman, titled *Programming for Public Television* that appeared in 'The Independent' (Volume 3, Number 10, published by the Foundation for Independent Video and Film, 625 Broadway, 9th Floor, New York, NY 10012) reveals some surprising facts about PBS programming. Here are some samples:

'In 1977, 75% of prime-time PBS corporate underwriting went

to only four stations; WNET (New York), WGBH (Boston), WETA (Washington, DC) and KCET (Los Angeles).'

Corporate sponsors desire foreign-produced programs chiefly because of their relative inexpensiveness. For example, $3 million might be spent by a corporation to purchase a series already produced and televised in Britain. If that same series were produced in America, the cost could be as high as $37 million. (According to a PBS fact sheet, the cost of producing a top quality program domestically can exceed $300,000 per hour compared to the average foreign purchase price of $8,500. An independent can expect about the same monies as this foreign price or about $8,000 per hour for a flat-buy acquisition.

Stations (SPC) tend to prefer inexpensive cost-efficient series, non-controversial programs, and series or programs that have previously appeared on foreign or domestic television.

'In 1977, oil companies accounted for the bulk of prime-time PBS corporate hours, underwriting 314 hours (72.5%) of all such programming.'

Proposals to PBS

If your program has not been completed and is in proposal form, you can send it to:

PBS Program Offerings, 475 L'Enfant Plaza, Washington, DC, 20024, and Television Activities Office, CPB, 111 16th Street, NW, Washington, DC, 20036.

Since both offices work together on national programming, it is a good idea to keep tabs on your project with both offices. Call for procedural requirements and the name of the current director before sending anything, to be sure it lands in the right hands.

The Story of DOLPHIN & PBS

The path to getting *DOLPHIN* on PBS was extremely long and fraught with frustration. I share this story with you to alert you to what you may expect. While you may have a different journey, I bet you will encounter some of the same difficulties. Notice the date headings as you read through this section to discover the time periods that have elapsed.

June 1978

We took a 20-minute pilot videocassette of *DOLPHIN* (which we used in our investor presentations) to WNET in New York. (Naive as it was at the time, we had the feeling that somehow our show would have more credibility if it came through an East Coast PBS station. It really doesn't make any difference.) A few days earlier we had been in the Bahamas where we had filmed spectacular sequences with wild dolphins by attracting them with our underwater piano. Enthusiastically, we described this aquatic breakthrough in interspecies communication which we had captured for the first time on film and was still awaiting processing. We described how this new footage would complete our *'pilot'*. The WNET executive liked the progress and direction of our work but warned us that *'things could take forever'* and advised us in a friendly manner to go elsewhere. This was not a rejection of our show but a hint of the bureaucracy and politics that lay in our path. We took the advice and returned to San Francisco to edit our new footage.

July 1978

We sent a copy of our 'pilot' to one of the public relations directors at Xerox Corporation. He expressed an interest in *DOLPHIN*, particularly if we would use WGBH (Boston) as our *'station of entry'*. When we took it to WGBH, they felt our

202

asking price of $100,000 was too high. (It had cost $165,000 to make *DOLPHIN* and we wanted to at least come close to breaking even!) Furthermore, we didn't think $100,000 was too much because we knew that WQED (Pittsburgh) had received $250,000 underwriting for the *National Geographic Whale Special*. (We learned later that this money was raised before the program was produced and on National Geographic's good name. Independent filmmakers cannot expect to receive similar compensation regardless of the quality of their programs. PBS and the underwriters are looking for built-in publicity which will attract an audience. (Many shows are bought because they can be readily promoted and attract a large pledge audience who may give money to the local stations. More on this later.)

August 1978-May 1979

We edited an 80-minute, theatrical version of *DOLPHIN* for the premiere and a 58-minute version for PBS although a sale had not yet been made. A cassette was sent to WQED in Pittsburgh, another station-of-entry.

June 1979

WQED liked *DOLPHIN* but also felt our asking price was too high. We lowered it to $80,000. We were told their executive committee would have to make the final decision on whether they would attempt to raise the underwriting for us. Many weeks and telephone calls later the committee still had not decided. Finally, three months later a WQED executive told me that the committee decided not to underwrite *DOLPHIN* because it was *'too similar to the National Geographic shows'* that they were already underwriting with Mobil Oil. They said they were sorry but there was *'an unwritten agreement between them and Mobil Oil (a very large and powerful sponsor)*

203

not to take on anything similar for underwriting.' They didn't want to offend their primary underwriter. Having spent over a year looking for a 'station of entry', we returned somewhat defeated to the West Coast to continue our search.

June 1979

DOLPHIN premiered at theaters in San Francisco, Berkeley, Santa Rosa, Santa Cruz, Sacramento, Los Angeles, Pasadena, and Long Beach, and received some 50 reviews and press notices. Most were very favorable. KQED (San Francisco) was given a screening cassette and a stack of promotion materials.

September 1979

Nearly three months later KQED agreed to do a local *'test broadcast'* of *DOLPHIN* during their pledge week. If it received favorable ratings and high pledge dollars they agreed to seek underwriting for it.

December 1979

DOLPHIN's broadcast was very successful. The program received high ratings and earned over $8000 in pledge dollars for KQED. We received an $800 license fee for the one-time only broadcast. *(Note that the PBS station had already received a profit and considerable good will from our efforts.)*

January 1980

Because the test broadcast received top ratings (5.0) and good reviews, KQED agreed to look for underwriting for *DOL-*

PHIN. At last, we were happy. We felt that we were close to a national broadcast. But this was just the beginning.

March 1980

A proposal was written by KQED's underwriting department and sent out to 30 major corporations. No one was interested. When I read the proposal I learned that it did a poor job in representing *DOLPHIN*. I asked if I could rewrite it. I did and also enclosed a personal letter and a plea for support. Another 50 proposals were sent out. Not much happened. But this was not surprising. KQED's underwriting department consisted of two people. A director and an assistant. Two people were trying to raise money for more than 40 KQED projects! Ours had the lowest asking price (now $50,000), was a finished program and had already earned good reviews and ratings. Given that, it seemed incredible to me that there were no corporate takers.

DOLPHIN was shown at the SPC 'market place', where the independent PBS stations cast their votes and pooled monies to acquire programs. SPC liked *DOLPHIN* and had agreed to give us $25,000, towards a total license fee of $50,000 for 4 plays in 2 years. The disbursement of this fee looked like this:

$ 30,000	*DOLPHIN* license fee (4 plays in 2 years)
+ 20,000	KQED Overhead, Promo & Distribution
$ 50,000	TOTAL Underwriting Sought
− 25,000	From SPC
$ 25,000	Corporate Underwriting Sought

205

June 1980

Six months have passed since the successful San Francisco broadcast. We still needed $25,000. There were some nibbles but no real underwriters. It was difficult to understand. We believed we had a first-class program. Was competition that stiff? Were there that few underwriters? ('Yes' to both questions.)

PBS was making up its national broadcast schedule for August. We had a few days left to find underwriting if we wanted to make the August schedule and be shown.

At the last possible moment *Atlantic Richfield* agreed to underwrite the program. Fantastic! *'But wait'*, said a KQED station executive, *'SPC no longer has the $25,000 they promised. They spent it on something else.'*

What a blow! After all this time, all these months, monies that had been promised by SPC were no longer there. Since the SPC transactions were being handled by the underwriting department, I had just assumed that a contract for these monies had been signed and the promised monies were secure. But they weren't. (*'Michael, you're beginning to learn about the movie business.'*) (To the reader: if you find yourself in a similar situation, get a signed agreement from SPC that stipulates how long the offer is good for or have a clear understanding with the local program executives.)

I find it very curious that the SPC disappearing money was never mentioned until the Atlantic Richfield money was committed. *Was this a surprise to the local executives? Did they sense our desperation and think they could strike a cheaper deal given the time pressures?* These are things I'll never know.

What remained was Atlantic Richfield's $25,000, half of what we had requested.

206

We had a difficult decision to make. Should we accept half of what we wanted (take the money and run) or should we wait, let the August broadcast date slip by and send out more proposals for that seemingly illusive $25,000?

August 1980

It troubled me greatly. I knew that our program was worth $30,000 or much more to PBS. But I also knew that I wanted to begin paying back some of the $165,000 to my investors. It had been over a year since the premiere of the film. The investors had expected some money by now.

I took the money. But, since it was only half of what we wanted, I reduced the license *'window'* to one year instead of two (this was contractual) with the verbal understanding that KQED would attempt to raise the underwriting for an additional year (this was not contractual). This way we could proceed with the August broadcast and take the money at hand. The split of Atlantic Richfield's $25,000 would give us $17,500, KQED would receive $7,500 for *'overhead and promotional costs'*.

Over the years we had reduced our price from $250,000 (WNET) to asking for an 'unrealistic' $100,000 (WQED) to actually receiving $17,500 (KQED). At the same time we were told we were *'paid one of the highest fees ever for a straight acquisition'*. How did we feel? Bitter, disappointed, angry, frustrated and simply worn out. Years of hard work. Investors, friends and crew. High expectations, culminating in a lousy PBS deal.

The fact that PBS will pay more to develop, script and produce a program from scratch than they will to acquire a tested, completed program like *DOLPHIN* is still one of the great mysteries of the PBS.

207

/August 16, 1980.

208

DOLPHIN aired nationally in August, 1980. Atlantic Richfield spent an additional $25,000 or more on ads for *DOLPHIN* in *'TV Guide'* in 12 cities. *DOLPHIN* set ratings records in Chicago (6.3), New York (4.5), and Los Angeles (5.1). In New York City, in the 15 minute 'break' following *DOLPHIN's* broadcast, there were over 500 pledge calls received, resulting in $15,000. In Sacramento, a man sent his local PBS station a $1000 gift because he *'loved the show'*. *DOLPHIN* received excellent reviews in major newspapers throughout the country.

When you look at the *TV GUIDE* ad it looks like *DOLPHIN* was made by *PBS* and *ARCO*. There is no mention of the producers or the people who put up the money. But that's part of the game. The underwriters in any program are 'paying' for exposure. They want to enhance their image.

By my estimates, *DOLPHIN* directly raised $80,000 or more for PBS stations during the national pledge week. That's a profit of $60,000! In essence, it was the *DOLPHIN* investors that *'made this broadcast possible'*!

To the world it looked as if *DOLPHIN* was a smash success. Everyone was congratulating me. But I knew the truth. The investors received only a sliver of their investment. There was no more work to do on the film. I'd been out of a job for some time. And although I had some new projects I wanted to do, given *DOLPHIN's* financial success (or rather lack of it), raising money from new investors seemed out of the question.

What filmmakers should realize is that a sale to PBS will not necessarily pay back your production costs. If you are expecting that, you'll be greatly disappointed. It's a bad deal. Now that you know that, go to PBS and make the best of a bad deal.

DOLPHIN's second PBS broadcast was in March 1981. The license agreement expired a year after the first broadcast in August 1981. But that fact did not stop the Tucson PBS station (and perhaps others) from broadcasting DOLPHIN anyway, out of license. I would not have learned of this unauthorized broadcast had a friend not sent me a newspaper clipping. I called the Executive Producer of the station, who didn't realize PBS no longer had the rights. (This really makes me question PBS internal accounting procedures. Did other PBS stations also make this mistake? I may never know.) We settled on a 'fee' of $400 for the broadcast, which I received a month later. (Note: PBS member stations keep master tapes of their programs in their libraries. Your contract should stipulate that these tapes be erased at the end of the license period and that PBS should provide a *'proof of erasure'* document. Since most PBS programs are licensed for the 'standard' 4 plays in 3 years the stations 'assume' that this is so for all programs.)

KQED offered *DOLPHIN* to the PBS stations for another year but was refused. KQED suggested that they try again in December 1981. I believe they did, but given their attention on many other underwriting projects I can't believe a whole-hearted effort was made. (I was on the other side of the country and couldn't really oversee this process.) The answer came back, *'no thanks'*. The program director implied that the PBS stations were not interested in *'old shows'*. (In one short year, *DOLPHIN* became an aging starlet.) Besides, by this time, KQED was were developing some 'new nature shows' for its own production and national distribution.

Meanwhile our television distributor in Los Angeles offered *DOLPHIN* to commercial television stations without any success. As I mentioned before, there simply is not much interest in a single documentary. No one watches them. They are too

210

difficult to promote. When my agreement expired with the LA distributor I took the rights back.

January 1982–December 1982

In 1982 I was looking for field producers to hire for various political campaign shoots. I met one producer, who had worked for WNET, (the PBS station in New York we had originally taken *DOLPHIN* to). The producer showed me her reel. On it was a WNET promo spot she'd cut, which had several shots from *DOLPHIN*. What an unwelcome surprise. There was no agreement with any PBS station that *DOLPHIN* footage could be used in any way. But WNET felt they could just go ahead, have a spot cut, and no one would notice or care. I called the Executive Producer and after many phone calls and letters they settled by sending a *'letter of apology'* and a $40 license fee and agreed that this would not happen again.

(Note to producers: Once your film is out there it's out. You cannot ever hope to control how it will be used and reused by others. At best you'll be lucky enough to catch a few of the perpetrators and gain some satisfaction. I've only told you of a few of my 'pirate' stories. You'd be too depressed if I told you more.)

January 1983–November 1983

In the two years that have passed since the original PBS license expired (August 1981) I tried several times to interest the national office in Washington to re-broadcast *DOLPHIN* on the PBS network. (I knew that KQED had lost all interest.) But I was not successful. An 'old' show has little appeal. I then began making the rounds of the pay cable systems again. I got

211

'no thank you's' from *SHOWTIME*, *HBO*, *Select-TV*, *First Choice* and *The Star Channel* which are both in Canada, *Spotlight*, *WTBS*, and *Oak Communications*.

December 1983

Other than some outstanding foreign monies that had yet to be collected from the sale of *DOLPHIN* (to 30 foreign television networks), it was very clear to everyone that any future income from *DOLPHIN* would be extremely limited. By the signed consent of 70% of the partnership, we legally dissolved the partnership. The partners took their remaining losses in 1983. I will continue to act as agent for the film and disburse any new income to the former investors.

Then several days after the partnership was officially dissolved, there was a sudden burst of activity on *DOLPHIN*. I think there is a message in here somewhere. Just when we'd given up all hope, things were happening again. Could our collective consciousness (holding to our old expectations of high returns) have kept deals away? Did we just have to give up completely to allow something to happen? Or is it all just a strange coincidence?

The new deals are for two more license periods, first on *The Disney Channel* (for a year window beginning in January 1984) and then on *Nickelodeon* when the Disney license expires.

A few days later, an unexpected check for $325 arrived from *ASCAP* for music licensing royalties from a Holland television broadcast in 1980. It just goes to show that you can never assume that the activity on a film is over.

212

Commercial Television Syndication

Most television stations, whether they are affiliated with a major network or not, buy programs from syndicators (distributors). These are most always series (e.g. game shows, soap operas, music specials) and not single shows. This is not a market open to most independents unless a syndicator repackages your film in the context of some ongoing series. Since this is doubtful, don't get too excited by the following figures. I was never able to interest a commercial syndicator in *DOLPHIN*.

The purchase price per hour television special per market area is approximately:

10	Top Markets	$28,000-10,000
40	Major Markets	23,000- 5,000
162	Minor Markets	21,000- 3,000

There are 212 total markets in the United States. A top-selling show will air in approximately half of these markets.

There are distributors or syndicators that will make sales for you. For a network sale they will take 15% of the gross as their commission. If they sell to the syndicated markets the distribution fee is 35%.

Foreign Television

Making sales to foreign television is time consuming and frustrating. Many foreign television networks are government owned. It is difficult to find out who the buyers are. Once you write or call it may take months to get a reply, a signed contract or final payment. In short, *'it's a real pain.'*

213

I sold *DOLPHIN* to Japan, Hong Kong, Australia and New Zealand before getting a foreign television distributor. It was very difficult making deals overseas because each country has its own way of doing business and the market prices were often unknown to me.

Since the distributor took over, *DOLPHIN* was sold to another 26 countries in about 4 years. It has been a best-seller because *'animal shows are very popular overseas'*.

The Foreign Television Prices chart provides some idea of what a producer can expect from the sale of a one-hour television documentary. These figures are based on the actual sale prices received for *DOLPHIN* (in the countries where it was sold) and on extrapolations based on the prices which *Variety* publishes every year. But since the *Variety* prices are usually inflated and pertain to half-hour television series and feature films, educated 'estimates' have been made. Furthermore, since sale prices are always open to negotiation and are based on rather illusive factors, these prices may be high or low. Try to get as much as you can. Do not base your asking price on what someone else was able to get. That has little to do with it. I think you will be surprised by how little is actually paid for documentaries. Remember, most of the world still watches *Kojak*.

In addition to the license fees quoted on the Foreign Television Prices chart, each buyer will also pay the lab cost of a 16mm print, '*M and E track*', and shipping. (They will make their own film to tape transfer of the 16mm print. Why this is still the standard I don't know. For quality control I would much rather send a 1″ videotape in the appropriate format. But that is not the way it's done. I'd hate to see Burma's video transfer of *DOLPHIN*.) You will provide the distributor an English-language script of the film and promotional materials. The distributor will send these items free to the buyer.

When *DOLPHIN* was sold to the BBC they requested an 'M & E' track. This seemed like an error because after all *DOLPHIN* has an English narration track. When I inquired if they really did want an 'M & E' track they said *'yes, of course'*. Little did I know that in England, the way we speak *'English'* is just not acceptable. Well, excuuuuse me!. (Of course, it will seem like a BBC-produced film, but perhaps that's the point.)

Rebroadcast rights are sometime negotiable. Usually they are written into the original contract and payment is 50% of the original broadcast fee.

The foreign television distributors receive 45% (or as little as 25%) of the 'net'. That means that some costs are deducted before the split. You get 55). Costs deducted from the 'gross' to get the 'net figure' are shipping, duties, custom, insurance, telephone, promotion and cassette duplication. *With a 'net' deal be sure to specify limits on the expenditures that can be deducted.* ($2,000 for a documentary hour should allow the distributor enough cash to make prints, cassettes, etc.) If you don't limit what can be spent on *'expenses'* then an un-scrupulous distributor can add all kinds of promotional costs and you may never see any money.

In addition to the license fees that the distributor will collect, they will also receive small payments for 16mm print costs (sometimes over the actual lab cost). You should share in these profits, if any, as they are part of the deducted costs before the 'net'.

The advantage of dealing with a distributor is that they have sub-distributors and agents throughout the world who know the buyers. And they know the current buyer's prices for films. Because a distributor has many new films that the buyers will want, they have more power than you to collect payment from a slow-paying client. *If you make a deal with a foreign buyer*

215

who won't pay you, what can you do? A distributor, on the other hand, can withhold new product.

A distributor will also go to the international television festivals like Cannes and MIFED (and NAPTE for the US market) where they will show new programs to buyers. If you did this yourself you'd pay foreign airfare, hotel, food, telephone, and booth rental. You still may not make any deals because you won't know the right people to talk to and could return home having spent $5,000 or more.

The most frustrating part of foreign distribution is getting your money. Even when deal memos are signed rarely will a foreign buyer pay on time. Another quirk of the film business. They all feel it's okay to agree to one thing and then slide. And then, if your distributor receives any money at all, it could be 3 to 6 months before you receive it from the distributor. (Some distributors, because of cash flow problems, will try to keep your money as long as possible and use it to keep their business afloat.) The foreign buyers also stall on their payments and make them when the foreign exchange rate is to their advantage. A deal signed today at an exchange rate of $10,000 could be worth only $6,000 a few months later. With *DOLPHIN* there is about $9,000 outstanding from foreign deals that were made two years ago. While I've been told a variety of reasons why, I still have no confidence that I will ever see this money. If you deal with the foreign buyers yourself it may only relieve you of *some* of the problems.

Discuss your project with foreign television distributors prior to production so that they can advise you on its marketability. Many programs that are of interest to US audiences are not popular with foreign audiences. Foreign television best-sellers have *'a lot of action and not much dialogue'*.

Music and Effects Tracks

Important note to producers: Keep all your sound elements (music, effects, dialogue, narration) on separate sound rolls. Foreign sales require that you have a music and effects ('M and E') track and an English-language script. This script has camera shots in the left-hand column that correspond exactly to the narration in the right-hand column. The narration (and dialogue if any) will be translated and rerecorded in the native language. If you want this to be done with accuracy then be sure that your script is very clear. Even then you have no assurance that *'creative translating, creative voicing, and creative juxtaposition'* won't entirely change the interpretation of your work.

If you do not keep your sound tracks separate you are looking for one big hassle and expense. If not now, two years later when you are deeply involved with something else. The fear of having to re-edit your old movie's sound tracks and separate the rolls for a 'music and effects' track should be great enough to motivate you to do it right the first time.

For example:

1. Keep all sound tracks separate as you assemble them. For example, the different rolls are labelled:

A	Narration
B	Music
C	Music
D	Effects
E	Effects
F	Effects
G	Sync Sounds
H	Sync Sounds

217

2. At a *pre-mix* you can mix down dialogue, music and effects on their own rolls. (*DOLPHIN* had 8 different sound effects rolls that were mixed down to one.) You'll then relabel these pre-mixed rolls:

A   Narration Mix
B   Music Mix
C   Effects Mix
D   Sync Mix

3. You now have a manageable number of rolls to mix. This will not only make your final mix easier but your tracks are now separate.

4. Before or after your full mix, you can make your 'music and effects track'. Simply take track 'B' and 'C' (and possibly 'D' if it doesn't have too much English in it) and mix these down to one track which becomes your 'M and E track'. This is what you need for foreign sales. A sync point at the head of the 'M and E track' corresponds with a similar mark on the 16mm print's Academy leader.

5. If you think your film has foreign sale possibilities, it's better to prepare your 'music and effects track' at the same time as your full regular mix because your mixer will be more familiar with the track and save time.)

You cannot make a foreign television sale without an 'M and E' track.

Foreign Television Gross Prices
For A One-Hour Documentary

ARMED FORCES OUTLETS OUTSIDE USA (1)	1,000
CANADA-CBC	20,000
CTV	6,500
CBC (French)	3,500
LATIN AMERICA (All)	12,500
WEST GERMANY (4)	9,500
FRANCE	8,500
HOLLAND (1)	2,060
BELGIUM (1)	1,380
IRELAND (1)	500
ITALY (Unlimited)	1,400
SWEDEN	800
SWITZERLAND (German, Italian) (2)	1,500
SWITZERLAND (French, Swiss) (1)	1,400
ENGLAND-BBC	14,500
GREECE	1,000
SOUTH AFRICA (2)	1,800
PUERTO RICO	1,000
MEXICO	1,000
AUSTRALIA (1)	3,500
HONG KONG	700
JAPAN (2)	4,500
TAIWAN (1)	400
MALAYSIA	175
BURMA	100
SINGAPORE (1)	240
PAKISTAN (1)	280
NEW ZEALAND	1,200
YUGOSLAVIA	525

In countries where there is more than one network, usually only one sale can be made. Brackets indicate the number of plays per license fee. The time window is generally 1-3 years.

Stock Footage

Another source of income comes from licensing film footage to other productions. *DOLPHIN* footage ('ins' and 'outs') have been licensed to *Those Amazing Animals, Mysteries Of The Sea, Evening (PM) Magazine* and *National Geographic.* Clips from *HARDWARE WARS* were licensed to the television special, *Special Effects: The Making Of The Empire Strikes Back,* and the German TV special, *The Star Wars Trilogy.*

All of these sales have come about because producers have seen our films on television or in the theaters. If allowing other producers to use our film footage doesn't diminish or compete with our own work then I have no problem in making such deals.

To find the shots a producer requests I often must look through thousands of feet of *'outs'*. Because of this, a *'search fee'* ($100 to $200 depending on the complexity of the search) is charged up front whether anything is used or not. Before a producer will give the go-ahead he/she must be fairly certain that I will have the shots they need. To minimize their risk I allow the 'search fee' to be deducted from the license fee, if a purchase is subsequently made.

I ask for a $2,000 minimum license fee for any material used and, depending on usage and the rights they want, charge $25-$50 per foot ($900-$1,800 per minute) thereafter. At these rates, it is to the producer's advantage to use at least a minute of my material. If they use a sufficient amount then I also request a title credit.

The minimum is charged because it really is not worth the trouble to engage in negotiations, make long distance phone calls, look for footage, have it mastered and then have a client change their mind. This happens all the time. The $2,000 minimum scares away clients who are not serious about the footage in the first place.

220

In addition to the license fee, the client pays all lab charges (mastering, sound dubbing, workprinting and freight). Have an agreement that you will be credited, either in the end titles or verbally in a voice-over, in the program. This will help other producers find you. Without such credits it will look like the purchaser shot your film.

For television commercials different rates apply. A minimum of $2,000 for up to 10 seconds of material is a good place to start. Or $300 per shot per spot commercial. Sometimes many commercials are made using the same film footage. Each spot would command another $300. For example, if the client wanted to use one shot in 4 commercials that would be $1,200. If they didn't know how many commercials they would eventually produce you could charge $1,000 per shot (or $800 per second): 'total buyout' for an unlimited number of spots.

To determine a fair price calculate how much it would cost for the producer to rephotograph your subject. Pricing is determined by how difficult it is to reproduce your material. Footage of wild dolphins underwater is difficult to redo so it can command top dollar. With one-time only news events, like assassinations, riots or hotel fires, you can set your own price, particularly if you are the only one with the film or video footage.

Many nature photographers will shoot high film ratios (1:30, 1:100) knowing that they will sell their rare footage of soon-to-be-extinct wild animals to other productions worldwide. There are also stock footage houses that you may contact to represent your material. You may find them in any motion picture production directory. (For example, *The Motion Picture TV and Theater Directory*, $5.95 from Motion Picture Enterprises Publications, Inc., Tarrytown, NY, 10591.

PROMOTION

Promotion

> *'Although it may be distasteful to many filmmakers, it is a job that needs to be done and done well.'*

Promotion

So finally, you've completed your masterpiece. You've raised money from strangers. You've had the pleasure of fine-tuning each minute detail of the project. You've done your best to come in on budget and to keep the project on schedule. You've made thousands of decisions during the shoot, in the editing room, and during the sound mix. And then you've researched what feels like every distributor on earth and maybe even have a signed contract. Is that it? Is your job over? Nope. Sorry. You still must promote the film. You must let your intended audience know that it exists and that they should run out and plunk down money to see it. (Now if you've got a distributor they will do much of the work. But because you want your film to have the best promotion, you'll still be involved.) If you don't have a distributor or you will self-distribute your film then you're at the threshold of yet another big job.

Promotion can make the difference between your film's being successful or not. It's not enough to have made an absolutely brilliant film. People must know that it exists. Without promotion, your film may not find its audience. And although it may be distasteful to many filmmakers, it is a job that must be done and done well. No promotion, no audience.

There are several ways to create an audience for your film. They include paid advertising, publicity, promotion and market research. You'll need to use every one to get the word out.

225

Paid Advertising

Paid advertising applies primarily to newspaper ads which you place in local papers during your showings. Some marketing strategists buy larger ads to get the reader's attention when the movie first opens. Once the public is aware of the film the ads can be reduced in size in the following weeks. Unfortunately, without a good-size opening ad the public will presume it's small potatoes. (Studio advertising has set the precedent: big is better.)

When we premiered *DOLPHIN* we were competing with full-page ads for James Bond in *Moonraker*. And, even our 1/4 page ad in the Sunday entertainment section cost about $600! (When audiences came to the theater we handed out our own market research cards. Through a simple poll we discovered that about 70% of the audience learned of the film through the newspaper. Obviously this type of paid advertising is crucial.)

Teenagers, for example, do not get their movie information from newspapers. Consequently, teenage movie promos air on radio and TV when young people are tuning in. Your media advertising must be designed to reach specific audiences. There is no such thing as the *'general public'*. Every film has its own audience and marketing plan based on the most promotable aspects of the film. A film can have a very broad or a very narrow market. Theaters are selected by audience demographics. Fellini would never play in the ghetto and *Super Fly* would not play in Beverly Hills.

It's a good idea to study the marketing campaign, ads and publicity, for films similar to yours. Build on their successes and failures. Read through old issues of *Variety* to see the theaters that have been selected for similar films. Then see if the box office was strong or weak. You will see that marketing films is a very calculated business. The more precise you can be in your marketing the better chance you have of attracting

226

an audience that will enjoy your film. If you attract the wrong audience or build expectations that cannot be met, you will create a *'negative word of mouth'* that will endanger your film's future.

Posters are also a form of paid advertising that, when well placed, will bring out an audience for your film.

When designing either posters or newspaper ads it's important to select one image and one line of copy that best represents your film. The graphics should be powerful and immediately recognizable. The copy should be inviting, exciting, and tease an audience into wanting to see the movie. (*'HARDWARE WARS, a spectacular space saga of romance, rebellion and household appliances.'*) If you have a sufficient advertising budget you can make several different versions of ads and test them out. Market researchers use *'focus groups'*, a group of 12 people who represent the target audience in age, income, education, sex, neighborhood, etc. The focus groups help determine which design to use for theatre trailers, posters, ad copy, and even titles. You can do successful market research on a smaller scale and produce results that will benefit your film's marketing strategy.

You are looking for a strong reason for people to want to see your film. You are then trying to find the best way to communicate this reason to your audience. All forms of media, radio and television spots, theater trailers, posters or newspaper ads have this objective. They must give the audience a reason for seeing the film.

Radio spots increase awareness but they are not effective for all films. We bought many radio spots when we opened *DOLPHIN*. We made a *trade* with a rock radio station. We traded free premiere tickets, which they gave away on air, for announcements. So every time tickets were given away, the movie was promoted. We also produced a radio spot. You can do this in a variety of styles appropriate to the film. For example, if you're promoting a horror film you can use a scary, gravel-voiced announcer and mix with blood-curdling screams. For a family film you can use a warm voice with a smile in it. For a comedy you might use actual dialogue 'bites' from the film itself. Once the music for a film is known (like *Chariots of Fire* or *Flashdance*) you can use the music to promote the film. Whatever you do must appeal to your target audience. Our audience poll revealed that very few people came to see *DOLPHIN* because of the radio spots. But that's probably because rock and rollers didn't have any interest in a film about dolphins. At the same time, for some, hearing the radio ads reinforced the fact that *DOLPHIN* was in town.

Some films design different campaigns for different audiences. A worthwhile exercise might be to take some big films, like *On Golden Pond*, *E.T.*, *An Officer and A Gentleman*, *Risky Business*, *National Lampoon's Vacation*, and see how they were marketed to different segments of the market. Then look at *Gallipoli*, *Fanny and Alexander*, and *Return of the Secaucus Seven* for other approaches.

A well-coordinated advertising and promotion campaign will take on an energy of its own. Add good 'word-of-mouth' (which is impossible to buy) and you've got a successful campaign. As the 'word-of-mouth' increases the expensive forms of paid advertising may be reduced to increase profits.

Publicity

Publicity is equally as important as paid advertising. Publicity is another way of getting the public's attention. But unlike advertising, publicity is not paid for directly. That doesn't mean it's free, because it takes a very skilled person to help create publicity for a film. It doesn't just happen by itself. It requires an orchestrated plan. Your publicist is being paid for his or her creative ideas and contacts with radio and TV stations, magazines and newspapers. The publicist creates interest in the film several weeks before its opening with a crescendo of media attention coming at the time the film opens. The publicity and public interest will hopefully continue as the film plays and further increase the public's interest in wanting to see it.

This publicity can begin while the film is in preproduction. News and feature stories can come out announcing the film, the story, stars, director, producer, location, and so forth. It is the publicist's job to come up with every conceivable angle on the film. Press releases are then sent to the press on a regular basis. If successful, news articles will appear in local and national newspapers. Radio and TV personalities will talk about it. Interest will grow among distributors, exhibitors and film buyers.

By the time the film actually comes out people should be dying to see it. A publicist's (and producer's) dream is to see people lined up around the block when a film opens.

During production, the publicist can arrange magazine and TV interviews with the stars. This should not disrupt the filming. Directors and producers have little patience as they are occupied with the real business at hand: making the movie. At the same time, they all realize the value of on-going publicity.

Most interviews will occur while the film is being edited. Since there is really not much news on the film at this time the publicist can send out stills, bios and press releases. Once the release date of the film has been set, the publicist can schedule TV and radio interviews, and magazine articles for specific times.

A studio will spend an enormous amount of money on thousands of press kits. These slick packages contain a dozen or more stills, bios, feature stories, and story synopses. 'Video press kits' (3/4″ cassettes) are sent to television shows and contain clips from the movie and behind-the-scenes interviews. Some studios even produce 'Making Of . . . ' featurettes that either play in their entirety on television or are edited by the TV shows to fit their own programming needs.

For both *DOLPHIN* and *HARDWARE WARS* we prepared clip reels in both 16mm film and 3/4″ tape. This was very inexpensive to do and opened many TV talk show doors and gained much free publicity. However, our poll revealed that while some people had seen *DOLPHIN* promoted on TV it wasn't what got them into the theater. (Once again, the talk show audience was not *DOLPHIN's* audience.) But then again, it all helps. Paid advertising and free publicity have a synergetic effect. The more ways someone learns about your film, the more reasons they may have for wanting to see it. More information creates more interest.

Press screenings allow movie reviewers to see the film and hopefully write a good review the day before it officially opens. Obviously you will want the very best screening room you can find with excellent projection and sound and comfortable seating. (Most cities have them for rent.) Publicity kits are handed out to the attending press. This screening should be the most pleasant showcase possible for your film. It certainly doesn't hurt to provide the press with good coffee and Danish for a morning screening, and wine and cheese for an evening screening). Sometimes several screenings must be scheduled. It's best to call the most important reviewers and arrange a convenient screening time for them and then invite the 'lesser' radio and TV critics, rather than book a time and then find the 'heavies' cannot come.

There are many, many ways to bring attention to your project. A brainstorming session with a publicist would supply you with many good ideas. So would a study of the promotion of other movies. The earlier you start this process, the better. (I've heard of producers who have raised financing on the basis of a strong title and a newspaper ad!)

Your goal is to find all the positive points of your film and bring them to the public's attention. Create a desire for people to see your film. It is not something that just happens but, like the production of your film, is a carefully choreographed plan. Maybe a few big stories break and you get lucky. But most films will need all the help they can get in the very competitive marketplace.The more prepared you can be, the better your chances for success.

SELF-DISTRIBUTION

Self-Distribution

'Producers complain about how distributors handle their films. Well, if you want something done . . .'

Self-Distribution

So often producers complain about how distributors promote their films. Or that no distributor will even take their films. As they say, 'If you want something done, then do it yourself'.

Self-distribution means that you distribute the film yourself. You order prints from the lab, place advertising, do promotion, invoice customers, ship print orders, maintain records and so forth. In short, run a distribution business. If you are also trying to make films, then you've got a lot on your plate. But, if you can't find a distributor it may be the only way to go.

My approach to distribution has been to find the best distributor for each market and then let the distributor do the job he knows best. And rather than give all rights to one distributor (which you unknowingly could do) I have suggested that you find the most powerful distributor for each of the rights in the *'pie'*. I have suggested ways to do this. While it is a lot of work, it is not really self-distribution because you are not handling direct sales to each customer. You are putting together your own *'consortium of distributors'* that will market your film. They do the actual distribution.

235

Many independent filmmakers self-distribute their films and tapes. Either out of desire or necessity.

Why Self-Distribute?

Many independent films will not sell enough prints to interest a traditional distributor. There may be many reasons for this ranging from the subject matter being *'too specialized'* (e.g. feminist films were once a very small market) to the film being inappropriately designed for a distributor's target audience.

I have made several films that did not find distributors. Since I wanted the films to be seen I had to self-distribute them. It was a lot of work. And every time I'd sit down to work on a new film I'd be interrupted by an order or preview request. You should understand that for most documentaries and experimental works, very little money is to be made through self-distribution. You'll be lucky enough to cover your expenses, let alone make enough money for new films. But there is a certain amount of satisfaction from knowing who is watching your film throughout the country. And it feels good when you hear an audience liked your film.

Another reason for self-distributing may be that you know you have a 'large audience'. You know who they are and how to get to them. And even though many distributors want to distribute your film you've decided you want to go after the market yourself. Therefore, if 1) you want to expend the energy it will take, and 2) you think you could do a better job than a distributor, and 3) you want to make more than 20-25% royalty, then self-distribution might be the way to go.

Information on Self-Distribution

There are already two excellent books on the mechanics of non-theatrical self-distribution. I suggest you read these books

236

MICHAEL WIESE FILM PRODUCTIONS

EXTRAORDINARY POWERS

A film that explores mind-body connections with some of the fastest men and women runners in the world.

"A fine short film about athletics. . .Wiese's footage of track and field events is impressive, his use of stop-action sequences is perfect for clinically examining the incredible energy flow of the shot-puts or the sprints."

Michael Johnson
Daily Californian
University of California

"A homage to the grace and discipline of track and field athletes . . . primarily concerned with the spiritual and philosophical values of sports."

Kevin Thomas
Los Angeles Times

"Optimism reigns full force . . . a film fusing positive mental attitude with sports."

Helen Raece
Daily Illini
University of Illinois

EXTRAORDINARY POWERS
A film by Michael Wiese
1976 / Color / 12 minutes
Rental $ 30 Sale $190

I MOVE

"Bodies in motion are beautiful to experience. They reflect a vitality common to any living form which is moving through space. You can see this surging life force in every body, particularly when the motion is an outflow of positive mental energy."

Dorothy Fadiman
Do Saints Really Glow?

I **Move** explores new developments in the body arts emphasizing Americans' growing concern for their mental and physical health and well-being."

Library of Congress

"There's nothing new about the concept of a 'sound mind in a sound body' but I **Move** shows the renewed appreciation for what that all means."

Judy Stone
San Francisco Chronicle

I **Move** is a synthesis of what is happening in sports, dance and the martial arts.

I MOVE
A film by Michael Wiese
1976 / Color / 24 minutes
Rental $50 Sale $360

237

from cover to cover. I don't have the space to cover in detail the *'nuts and bolts'* of this complex business. And these books do a great job in describing every step.

They are: *Doing it Yourself* written by Julia Reichert, a member of New Day Films. Copies may be ordered from AIVF, 99 Prince Street, New York, NY, 10012, for $5.00.

16mm Distribution, compiled by Judith Trojan and Nadine Covert may be ordered from EFLA, 43 West 61st Street, New York, NY 10023 for $6.00. This book is an anthology of articles by filmmakers, distributors, and exhibitors.

If you have a feature-length film and wish to distribute it yourself to theaters I suggest you obtain the *Commercial and Non-Commercial Exhibitor's Survey* prepared by Joy Pereths for The Independent Feature Project, 80 East 11th Street, New York, NY, 10003, (212) 674-6655. This lists more than 100 theaters that show independent films.

If you have short films or a collection of short films and you wish to set up your own tour you should obtain a copy of *The Film and Videomaker's Directory* from The Film Section, Museum of Art, Carnegie Institute, 4400 Forbes Avenue, Pittsburgh, PA, 15213. It lists not only hundreds of US independent filmmakers but also many museums, schools and theaters that book films and tapes and personal appearances by independents. Don't plan to get rich by such a tour, but if it's well planned, you should be able to pay for all your expenses as you travel the breadth of the United States.

Mailing Lists

The best place to research potential film print buyers is through mailing lists. You will get many ideas about markets just by studying these lists. Each list will be totalled so you can determine how many potential buyers you may have. Even if you don't self-distribute your film, these lists will give you a sense of whether or not your film is marketable. It is a good idea to do this research prior to production and include it in your prospectus. The market potential (based on mailing list totals) for film on the handicapped might look like this:

Non-Theatrical Markets

Users/Teachers

Medical College Teachers-Senior College	3,672
Physical Therapy	751
Occupational Therapy	410
Nursing-Senior College-Dept Heads	423
Nursing-Junior College-Dept Heads	472
Special Education-Dept Heads	2,399
Intro to Learning Disabilities	2,067
The Disadvantaged Child	1,596
Introduction to Audiology	909
Speech Pathology	1,151
Speech & Hearing in Public Schools	796
Teacher Aid Education	296
Computers in Education	792
Total	15,734

Buyers

Libraries-Colleges	2,948
Audio-visual	164
Business	947
Medicine	2,344
Public Libraries	8,798
Elementary Institutions with 16mm Film Collections	6,392
Regional Media Centers	853
Public Elementary Schools w/Media Centers	51,005
Junior Highs w/Media Centers	9,996
High Schools w/Media Centers	14,631
Hospitals	7,015
Medical Schools	53
Total	105,146

Some lists will look like better possibilities than others. These will be your *'A list'* and you will mail to this group first. Test mailings could sample various lists to determine which would yield the best results. This approach will save money because you can avoid large mailings where there have been weak results.

Mailing List Sources

There are mailing list companies which sell every kind of list imaginable. For film and tape sales, business, health and educational mailing lists are the most appropriate.

For high school and college lists write:

The Educational Directory, One Park Avenue, NYC, 10016 or the West Coast Offices at 131 Camino Alto, Suite D, Mill Valley, CA 94941.

For organizations and individuals write:

Zeller Letica, 15 East 26th St, New York, NY, 10010.

Dunhill International List, 444 Park Avenue South, New York, NY, 10016.

For libraries and film collections write:

The Educational Film Library Association (EFLA), 43 West 61st Street, New York, NY, 10023.

Some mailing list firms will also sell subscriber lists from magazines and journals. Some of these magazines will take advertising.

Self-Distribution Budget

The best way to get an idea of what is involved is to play some '*what if*' games with budgets and projections. On any new project, I always list my anticipated expenses and income before proceeding. Although I am enthusiastic about my projects they do not always have a large enough audience to pay back the costs involved. Sometimes the numbers simply don't make sense and I am forced to abandon the project. Many times I discover ways of slimming down costs or increasing the potential market by adding some element to the project. It is valuable to do your own '*paper study*' before leaping in.

To self-distribute you will need capital over and above your production costs. If you are planning from the outset to self-distribute you may revise the sample self-distribution budget provided and include it in your prospectus as part of a master plan for production and distribution.

You will promote your film through direct mailings to potential buyers and by placing ads in journals and magazines. Travel may also be necessary. 16mm preview prints (one of the largest costs) are sent to the prospective buyer, free of charge, who may keep them for 1-3 months before returning them. Rarely is a film bought sight unseen. (If you are distributing in videotape then you'll want to make this change in the budget. The sample budget is for expensive 16mm film prints and not video.)

SELF-DISTRIBUTION BUDGET   One Year Projected Costs

A. PROMOTION

Flyer Design	1	FEE	250	250
Printing	10000	EACH	.35	3500
Stamps	10000	EACH	.09	900
Stuffing	10000	EACH	.008	80
				4730

B. PREVIEW PRINTS

Prints	20	PRINTS	69	1382
Cases	20	CASES	9	180
				1562

C. ON-GOING EXPENSES

Ads	12	ADS	50	600
Travel	2	TRIPS	300	600
Phone	12	MONTHS	200	2400
Bookkeeping	12	MONTHS	100	1200
Postage	500	EACH	.20	100
				4900

D. STAFF

Part-time	12	MONTHS	500	6000	6000
		TOTAL	$17192		17192

My hypothetical *Self-Distribution Budget* gives you an idea of some of the things involved. This is a very *'bare bones'* budget and assumes that you already have a typewriter, an office, office furniture and so forth. You may, of course, approach distribution in a very different way. This budget is an example of the decisions and assumptions when planning a budget.

My small-scale budget to distribute a 24-minute film includes the following expenses:

1. Mailing 5000 flyers per year.

2. Twenty preview prints.

3. A minimum of ad, travel, and phone expenses.

4. A $500 per month salary for one person.

This budget ties in with the cash flow chart on the following pages.

Cash Flow Distribution Chart

The Cash Flow Distribution Chart requires a detailed explanation. It is based on a hypothetical model in which I have made many assumptions about how the distribution business will be conducted. It is for demonstration purposes only. The income and expenses have been projected over a 10-year period (the anticipated *'life'* of the film. What follows are the details for each line item. Please keep in mind that this chart is for the non-theatrical distribution only (the sale of prints to colleges, libraries, institutions, hospitals, etc.). For the sake of simplicity, rentals are not included in this chart, but if you like you can add 15% to 35% onto your total income to account for this additional income.

243

CASH FLOW DISTRIBUTION CHART

	1982	1983	1984	1985	1986
PROMOTION MAIL 5000	2790	2790	2790	1395	500
PREVIEW PRINT COSTS	1550	1550	0	0	0
ON-GOING EXPENSES	2360	2360	1180	1000	1000
STAFF	6000	5000	5000	3000	3000
PREVIEWS (4%)	200	200	200	150	100
PREVIEW COSTS $7 ea.	1400	1400	1400	1050	700
PRINT COSTS	3090	3090	3090	2287	1545
PRINT SALES (1:4)	50	50	50	37	25
INCOME $400 ea.	20000	20000	20000	14800	10000
TOTAL EXPENSES	17190	16190	13460	8732	6745
TOTAL NET INCOME	2810	3810	6540	6068	3255

1987	1988	1989	1990	1991	1992	TOTALS
500	200	200	200	200	0	11565
0	0	0	0	0	0	3100
1000	1000	1000	500	500	500	12400
3000	3000	3000	3000	3000	3000	40000
100	100	100	100	100	100	1450
700	700	700	700	700	700	10150
1545	1545	1545	1545	1545	1545	22372
25	25	25	25	25	25	362
10000	10000	10000	10000	10000	10000	144800
6745	6445	6445	5945	5945	5745	99587
3255	3555	3555	4055	4055	4255	45213

Promotion Mailing

The distribution business relies almost entirely on mailings. It is therefore important to do mailings several times a year. Hiqh-quality printing and design is imperative. In my model 5000 flyers are sent out twice a year. (Probably should send more.) This continues for 3 years. It will take a year to get the film into the marketplace. If you get a good (3% or more) return, a second follow-up mailing to the same list might be worthwhile. The first mailing should get a 2-3% response rate. A second mailing might add another 1%. Wait to see how well the first mailing does before remailing to the same list.

You will not want to generate more preview requests than you can handle with 20 prints because your reputation will depend on your delivering preview prints upon request. By 1985, the mailings are reduced considerably (unless you've made other films you wish to distribute.) If you find a mailing list that is productive, then follow up with more mailings and promotion. If a market is not productive, drop it. You can sample various markets with your first mailing, then re-mail to the ones that receive the best response.

Preview Prints

Twenty are ordered the first year and another twenty the next year. Public libraries will keep the film 2-4 weeks, public schools take much longer. Figuring that it takes roughly one month to turn a print around, you can service (12 months $\times$ 20 prints) 240 previews per year. By the second year, you add another 20 preview prints (if the business justifies it and you can afford it) and can handle 480 previews. I assume that a total of 40 prints will be enough to handle your requests. The previews should be scheduled for maximum efficiency.

246

DOLPHIN

A documentary on these intelligent, graceful sea-going mammals. DOLPHIN traces the history of dolphin lore from antiquity to present times and gives a sense of respect and affection for this friendly sea creature with as yet untapped intelligence.

A crew sets off on a remarkable adventure to meet and make friends with wild dolphins in the crystal blue waters of the Bahamas. An underwater piano is used to attract a school of wild dolphins who join their human companions in an exquisite underwater ballet.

"AN ABSORBING WORK ABOUT DOLPHINS . . . WELL-WORTH SEEING."
Jeanne Miller. **San Francisco Examiner**

"A MIXTURE OF SCIENTIFIC DREAMING AND HEART-WARMING NATURE STORY . . . INFORMATIVE AND ABOVE-ALL ENTERTAINING."
Madelaine Shellaby. **Sacramento Union**

"AN EXCELLENT FILM . . . THE WHISTLES OF THE DOLPHIN MIGHT INDEED BE YET ANOTHER MIRACULOUS VOICE."
G. Varney & M. Ventura. **Los Angeles Weekly**

"EXCITING EXPERIMENT WITH UNDERWATER SOUNDS . . . A SEQUENCE OF BREATH-TAKING BEAUTY."
Win Murphy. **Greenpeace Chronicles**

"THE DOLPHINS ARE THE STARS." San Jose News

DOLPHIN (1979) Directed by Michael Wiese & Hardy Jones

58 minutes 16mm Color

$660 Purchase $495 Videocassette

FILMS INCORPORATED
733 Green Bay Road
Wilmette, Illinois 60091

(800) 323-4222
Illinois call collect
(312) 256-3200

For Rental (312) 256-4730

On-Going Expenses

The business is run on a shoestring budget and has a minimum of advertising the first two years. If you find that the advertising is effective then increase it. The present budget would only allow for a half-dozen very small ads a year in magazines. You will also send preview prints to magazines that review films. This will help generate previews in addition to those you get by direct mail.

Staff

The first year will require the most work. You'll cull and order mailing lists, design brochures, and do major mailings. You will set up the procedures for a smooth and efficient office and handle preview requests, shipping, inspection, invoicing, record keeping, promotion and advertising. Costs will be greater for the first year than in the following years assuming the same activity. Start-up will take at least one year. In my model, salaries are cut back each year and the business is run on a part-time basis. If things pick up and you find good markets for your film(s) and tape(s) then you may in fact increase your staff. You may also take on other films to distribute which will change this model significantly.

Previews

A 4% (very high) return on your mailing would generate 200 preview requests each year for 3 years. On the average that would require that you ship 4 prints a week. (Perhaps you'll need fewer preview prints to start.)

Preview Costs

It will cost about $7 per preview for the shipping, insurance and record keeping. Perhaps less if you do all this work yourself. (It costs large distributors about $17 per preview because of their higher overheads.) Once you get your business running you will have a much more accurate idea of what your cost per preview will be and you can budget accordingly.

Print Costs

If you order many prints at the same time you can get a volume discount from your film laboratory. I have used $0.08 per foot to calculate these costs. (Check current prices as increases occur yearly.) Large distributors can get even lower prices because they order millions of feet of release prints per year.

Print Sales

Many distributors consider a 1:4, sales-to-preview ratio to be 'good'. I have used this ratio to estimate how many sales there will be per preview.

Income

Prints are sold at $400 each. One sale is made for every 4 previews sent out.

Total Expenses

This is the total cost of being a distributor in this limited way. Of course if you have a larger library and can consolidate expenses then your profits will be higher. (It costs virtually the same to advertise one film as it does to advertise 4 films.)

249

Total Net Income

In the first few years, in my model, profit is only a few thousand dollars. Even so, you may find it necessary to plow this (and more) back into the business. (I haven't included office costs like rent and equipment. I've assumed you'll use your home as an office and rent a post office box.) Promotion and advertising are important to survive, but also costly. You'll need to let people know you exist and be visible to your buyers through advertising. It may take several ads before some buyers request a preview. The first 3-4 years, distribution of a film will be the strongest. The first year may be weak because it takes a very long time to send the mailing, get preview requests, fill these requests and receive purchase orders. Once the preview print is mailed it can take another 90 days or more to get an order. And then another 90 days to receive payment. (If you have a distributor and are waiting for royalties, you'll need to add yet another 90 days for the money to go through their accounting systems and for the mailing of quarterly reports.) One advantage to self-distribution is that you can speed up the process of collection. You're not waiting on the distributor to send your royalties. But still, assuming you take three months to get your mailing out, it may be a year before you see money from your sales.

Actual Sales

The overall assumption in this chart is that you have a film with a total sales potential of 362 prints in ten years.

Some of my films (by non-theatrical distributors) have sold both more and less than my hypothetical sample. *RADIANCE* has sold only 130 prints in 5 years but rents well. *HARDWARE WARS* has sold over 1000 prints in 6 years and has an extraordinary high *'sale-to-preview ratio'*. *DOLPHIN* (60 mi-

250

nutes), which sells for a whooping $770 in 16mm, has sold only 30 prints in 4 years. It is obviously too expensive for this market. By comparison, the 11-minute children's version, THE WONDER OF DOLPHINS, has sold 136 prints in 3 1/2 years. The self-distributed experimental film BEAUTY has sold about 20 prints and cassettes in 3 1/2 years with virtually no money spent on advertising or mailings. It has an extremely low sale-to-preview ratio. So low in fact, we've discontinued its distribution.

For a film to be successful it must be timely and fit in with the market's needs. Besides being a well-made film it will require sufficient and appropriately placed advertising. Everyone expects their films to be hits. The fact is, it will take nearly 2 years of distribution to really know how well a film will do. Market research will improve your chances tremendously but few filmmakers, even with this knowledge, will take the time to do so. They would rather start shooting and hope for the best. *Films are sold because they fill the user's, not the filmmaker's, needs.* This requires the filmmaker to take on the role of market researcher and business manager. And while fewer films would probably be made, they would stand a better chance of supporting the filmmakers (and their investors).

MUSIC VIDEOS

Music Videos

'*Every teenager with cable television quickly found MTV on their dial and left it on day and night.*'

Background

Music videos began as short, 3-minute promotional clips that were produced by record companies. They generally featured new songs by existing artists. Early music videos were little more than filmed performances. Bob Pittman, a former rock radio program director (and founder of *MTV, Music Television*), was the first to recognize and sell Warner-Amex Satellite Entertainment Company on the idea that these promo clips could be strung together and programmed like rock radio. He added a half dozen '*VJ's*' ('*video jocks*') and MTV was born. To the surprise of many, MTV took off like a rocket. Every teenager with a cable television quickly found MTV on their dial and left it on day and night. MTV was an '*electronic environment*' for teenagers everywhere. (Fifty-four percent of MTV's audience are 18-34 year olds, 23% are 12 to 17 and 23% are 35 and over.) Newspapers were filled with MTV articles. National magazines printed stories on the lifestyles of MTV's video jocks. A wave of MTV imitations followed.

When MTV went on the air, record companies saw a dramatic rise (5% to 35%) in record sales among artists whose videos were seen on MTV. Kids went to their local record stores and tried to buy songs by New Wave MTV groups whose songs were neither on the charts nor the stores' shelves. The power of

255

MTV was evident and the record companies were quick to exploit the value of music videos and began committing more dollars for video production. No longer did they have to risk hundreds of thousands on national tours at a time when few tours made money. All they needed was one or two music videos of each group to expose their new releases to the masses. And one video cost an average of $25,000 which they would provide free to MTV and others who, hopefully, would air it. With luck, MTV might play it in *'heavy rotation'* or many times each day. In a matter of days, millions of kids would see the video and maybe buy the album.

Previously unknown groups in the US like Duran Duran, A Flock of Seagulls, and many others became overnight sensations because of MTV-aired music videos. The album by Men At Work went platinum after its MTV launch. The success of The Police must in part be credited to their tremendous exposure on MTV.

This symbiotic relationship not only led to the phenomenal growth of MTV (who received all the music videos free) but more significantly fueled the revival of the music industry.

The music videos became more experimental. *'Performance'* pieces were replaced by a plethora of *'concept videos'*, heavily-laden with costuming, special effects and fast-paced editing. And now, of the 30 or more new videos that MTV receives each week, only 2 or 3 are *'performance'* videos. Most feel that the videos that are the most successful are those that can stand the test of repeatability, the *'concept'* or *'story'* video. A young audience prefers fast-moving, visually-loaded videos, where new things can be discovered with each viewing.

Once a training ground for young directors and producers, this new media has attracted *'name'* commercial and feature film directors.

256

Tobe Hooper directed Billy Idol's *'Dancing With Myself'* on a $70,000 budget. To improve its production value Hooper brought special effect technicians and props from his features *Texas Chainsaw Massacre* and *Poltergeist* to enhance the look of the futuristic video.

New and established directors, art directors, cameramen and editors have lined up at record company doors for the opportunity to produce music video for their reels. Not only do they work for little or no money, but some have even contributed money to a video they've really wanted to do. The new directors bring a raw and exciting energy to their often New Wave or punk rock videos. The feature directors utilize production techniques used in films like *Poltergeist* and *Twilight Zone*. The commercial directors draw on their experience in producing in *Dr. Pepper* and *McDonald's* spots. MTV recently saw the premiere of a *'long form'* music video of Michael Jackson's *'Thriller'*, a short film in itself which was directed by *Animal House* director John Landis.

In the early years, many English commercial directors with avant-garde tastes pioneered the way, but now American directors have picked up the slack. Bob Giraldi, best known for his Michael Jackson *'Beat It'* video and his *Dr. Pepper, Miller Lite Beer* and *McDonald's* commercials. *'Beat It'* played for months on MTV in heavy rotation. Since it was shot in 35mm it has also played in foreign theaters. This $150,000 production was choreographed by Tony-Award winning Michael Peters who is also featured as one of the dancing gang leaders. This production has helped produce record-setting sales: Michael Jackson's album sold 10 million copies in 1983.

Music Video Showcases

Unlike most other program forms, music videos are generally supplied free to commercial and pay television networks.

MTV and VH-1, are both 24-hour-per-day services, and broadcast more videos than any other system. NBC's *'Friday Night Videos'* premieres music videos. NBC pays the record company an *'administrative fee'* for the airing and the exclusive right to premiere the video first. MTV also pays fees to a number of record companies for the privilege of broadcasting the videos exclusively, thereby gaining an edge on the competition.

Other showcases for music videos include, ABC's *'Goodnight LA: Videos'* seen on KABC in Los Angeles, CBS's, *'MV Network'* on KNXT in Los Angeles, Superstation WTBS' *'Night Tracks'* and *'Night Tracks Chartbusters'* from Atlanta which features six hours of uninterrupted videos on Friday and Saturday nights. *'Deja Vu'*, *'Putting on the Hit'*, *'Video Soul'*, which is on Black Entertainment Television, *'Mundo Music'* with Spanish-language clips on KSCI in Los Angeles. *'Night Flight'* on the USA Network shows features, concert footage, shorts, cult movie classics and music videos. The USA Network also has *'Radio 1990'* and *'FM-TV'*, a syndicated music program. Both HBO and SHOWTIME (*'Take Five'*) program music videos during their interstitial breaks.

Yet another showcase for videos which have replaced discos are videotheques which project videos on large screens adjacent to nightclub dance floors.

Music Videos on Home Video

Music videos are often repackaged and released in home video by the record companies' home video branches. Some record companies use their existing distribution companies to sell the music videos to record retailers. This offers the record companies an opportunity to recoup music video production costs and in some instances earn a profit—which is terrific given the videos are actually promotion pieces for records. Producers and directors generally do not share in home video profits as they are hired by the record companies. The music artists however do share in profits.

Although music videos have received tremendous trade and consumer attention—especially Vestron Video's *'Michael Jackson's Thriller'*, a mega-hit which sold over 1 million video tapes worldwide—the overall music video sales have been well below expectations.

Combined sales of the 26 all-time top-selling videos (all had major stars) totaled 2.4 million units with estimated wholesale revenues of $45 million.

Major hits included Prince's *'Purple Rain'*; 475,000, *'We Are The World'*; 175,000, *'Lionel Ritchie'*; 125,000, *'Band Aid'*; 120,000, and *'Rolling Stones Video Rewind'*; 110,000. These six titles, including *'Thriller'* accounted for 67% of all sales. The next twenty titles on the best-selling list have sold between 25,000 and 80,000 units with prices ranging from $16.95 to $39.95. The average sales of all other releases are between 5000-10,0000 units each.

These low numbers are because the market for music videos are the record-buying youth between the ages of 12-18. VCR owners are between 25 and 45 years old. Music videos appeal to an audience that does not own a VCR! This will change however as VCR prices drop and second machines come into teenagers rooms. Also, most videos are released in home video after the 'heat' is off the record, this diminishes the appeal of ownership. Vestron Video released Pete Townshend's *'White City'* video simultaneously with the record. The cross promotion paid off as the album and home video hit the charts at the same time.

259

Creative Trends

What can audiences look forward to? Are there new emerging styles and formats for music videos?

As mentioned earlier, music videos have have taken a dramatic move away from straight performance pieces. Bands can still be seen performing their songs but usually in fantasy and action-oriented, futuristic settings. Rather than lip-sync an entire song, the music videos are half-enacted and half-lip synched. This enables the visuals greater freedom and less dependency on the song, so much so, that mini-movies with loose story lines are being produced. Some videos are stretched into a 'long form' where several music pieces are woven thematically together within the context of a 'story'. The musical artist may or may not play a lead role in the long form music video.

A video director first listens to the song and suggests various approaches to the record company and artist. The music video can be a 'concept' piece where the imagery has little or nothing to do with the song. Or, it may be a 'story' video where the song and imagery are very closely related. Most artists and producers feel that the song is the most important element and that a bad video can ruin a good song.

The groups themselves now face a new dilemma. A few years ago they were only called upon to be good songwriters and musicians. Now they are asked to be script writers and actors. Many are not up to the task. Nor should they be. But the pressures on musicians to do music videos are great. Without them, there a loss of exposure and record sales. This coercion has led the non-visual musicians into a dilemma. They need the music video television exposure to boost sales and concert attendance but they also risk turning off an audience unless the visual element is strong and professionally executed.

Some question whether the artists should be in the videos at all. Their opponents feel the audience is cheated unless you show the group. Most agree that there has been an overkill of visual effects and that as the video-music vocabulary matures, there will be less of a dependency on technological glitz and special effects and a return to basic 'story-telling'.

Recently the content of music videos has been under attack by educators and psychologists alike who are worried about the excessive use of sex, violence and drug references in the tapes. A voluntary 'x' rating system has come into play by some record companies to counter the public ill-will. Since rock music roots began in a counter-culture environment, it isn't surprising that rebellious images reoccur. Regardless, whatever your taste, it's clear that music video is here to stay.

Production Budgets

Music videos are shot in 16mm film or 1' video. The film is transferred to videotape so that all the post-production work can be done in video with a heavy helping of video effects.

The average clips take 10 to 14 days to develop and execute. Budgets range from $20,000 to $100,000. MTV's Basement Tapes demonstrate that original work can be created for as little as $5000.

Record companies put up $30,000 to $50,000 for new video music artists. Budgets increase for big names and complex productions. Rarely is more than $100,000 spent except for superstars like Michael Jackson, Billy Joel, Paul McCartney, Madonna, Prince, and Lionel Ritchie where costs can be recouped from home video profits.

The 'live' performances can cost as little as $30,000 and use

261

multiple cameras. This requires careful choreography of the performance and its photography.

Independents should be encouraged by the fact that MTV receives dozens of new tapes each week, or nearly 1500 a year. With average budgets of $25,000 each, a total of $37.5 million per year is spent on music video. This does not include music video commercials from everyone from Levi's to Campbell's Soup. There are music videos for soft drinks, candy bars, computers, perfume, and clothing.

Because there are more than 100 television outlets for music videos, producers can take advantage of this opportunity by designing *other forms of programming* (tv programs, features or home video programs) that include a music video within them. When the program is finished the music video can be pulled out of the program. Not every tv program will broadcast the music video but some will. It's free programming for them, free publicity for the producers.

At Vestron Video, I've encouraged producers to include a music video within their home video programs. Often the music video can be part of the opening or close title sequence so that no money is spent on editing a seperate music video. Vestron has released music videos from *non-music* original home video programs such as *'New Wave Comedy'*, *'Amazing Masters of the Martial Arts'*, *'Father Guido Sarducci Goes to College'*, *'Shock It, To Me'*, *'The Joe Piscopo Special'*, *'Pro Wrestling Illustrated's: Lords of the Ring'* and *'Lisa Sliwa's Common Sense Defense'*. When the music videos are broadcast the home video title is promoted. Music videos are an excellent low-cost, promotional device for non-music programs.

The Future of Music Video

There is little doubt that music video production will continue to expand. Low cost VCRs are finding their way into teenager's rooms. The price of video software is dropping as low as $9.99. New formats (like 8mm and disk) and high speed duplication techniques are bringing the price of music videos down so they approach those of albums and hardcover books. It wouldn't be suprising if high-fidelity videos replaced albums in the future.

Only about 1100 record stores sell video product. This is only 10% of the number of stores that could carry it. Many still do not believe that music video is a viable retail product. Mass merchandisers, bookstores and convenience stores have, in just the last year, begun to sell music videos. As distribution channels improve, greater numbers of videos will be sold, generating more production. Portable mini-VCRs will begin to appear in cars and on beaches during the next few years. More and more video programs will be played and collected.

It may however be frustrating for independents who work outside the major record companies to put together big name music video deals. The music *rights* for records and videotapes are controlled by the record companies. Without music licenses and clearances from the record companies (not the music artists!), music videos cannot be made. Producers can turn to new music acts (on small labels) but since these groups are unknown, their music videos will be extremely difficult to market.

Top music artists, like Sting, Prince, and Madonna see themselves as music and film/video stars and will continue to look for new film and video vehicles. The success of *'Purple Rain'* points the way to a new long-form music-movie format. *'Miami Vice* has also brought music video conventions to network television. There will be other successful permutations of form and style. Innovative, creative producers will lead the way.

MUSIC VIDEO CONTACTS

These are some of the major decision-makers and producers in music video. Most music videos are commissioned by record companies. It is best to call first to confirm who currently holds these positions, because people move frequently.

A & M RECORDS INC, 1416 N. La Brea Avenue, Los Angeles, CA, 90028, (213) 469-2411, Sherry Marsh; Director of Video, Rich Frankel; Director Creative Services, Martin Kirkup; VP Artists Development, Laura Reitman; Director, Video Programming, Z. Zimmermann; Manager Home Video.

ARISTA RECORDS, 6 W. 57th Street, New York, NY, 10019, (212) 489-7400, Abbey Konowitch; VP, Artists Development, Peter Baron; Manager, Video Services, Kenneth Reynolds; Director R & B Product Management.

ATLANTIC RECORDS, 75 Rockefeller Plaza, New York, NY, 10019, (212) 484-6000, Perry Cooper; VP, Artists Relations/Media Development, Gila Lewis; Director, Advertising/Media Development and 9229 Sunset Blvd., Los Angeles, CA, 90069, (213) 278-9230, Tony Mandich; West Coast Director, Artists Relations/TV.

CAPITOL RECORDS, 1750 N. Vine Street, Los Angeles, CA, 90028, (213) 462-6252, Mark Levinson; President, Picture Music International, Inc., Bob Hart; Vice President, Production and Marketing, Michelle Peacock; National Director of Press and Artists Development, Peter Blachley; Manager of Marketing and Promotion, Marc Rodriguez; Video Coordinator, Victor Rappoport; Director of Business Affairs, Jim Yukich; Director of Production, Mick Kleber; Manager of Creative Services, Cynthia Biedermann; Manager of Production and Administration and Graybar Building, 420 Lexington Avenue, New York, NY, 10017, (212) 867-1325, John Diaz; Director of East Coast Operations, Michael Pillot; Director of East Coast Sales; Lynn-Alain Dalton; Staff Producer.

264

CBS-COLUMBIA RECORDS, 51 W. 52nd Street, New York, NY, 10019, (212) 975-5275, Debbie Samuelson; Associate Director of Video Placement and 1801 Century Park West, Los Angeles, CA, 90067, (213) 556-47600, Debbie Newman; Director, Artists Development/Video, Jeanne Mattiussi; Manager, Artists Development/Video.

CBS/EPIC/PORTRAIT/ASSOCIATED LABELS, 1801 Century Park West, Los Angeles, CA, 90067, (213) 556-4700, Glen Brunman; Director, Media Relations/Video, West Coast, Larry Stessel; Director, West Coast Marketing, and 51 W. 52nd Street, New York, NY, 10019, (212) 975-4321, Harvey Leeds; Director, National Video Promotion, Dan Beck; Director, East Coast Merchandizing.

EMI/AMERICA/LIBERTY/A SUBSIDIARY OF CAPITOL RECORDS, 6920 Sunset Blvd., Los Angeles, CA, 90028, (213) 461-9141, Clay Baxter; Manager Of Video and Artists Development, Marsha Groff; Coordinator of Artists Development.

CHRYSALIS MUSIC GROUP, 9255 Sunset Blvd., Suite 319, Los Angeles, CA, 90069, (212) 550-0171, Fran Musso; Director of Merchandising, West Coast and 645 Madison Avenue, New York, NY, 10022, Daniel Glass; Director of New Music Marketing.

DISNEYLAND/VISTA RECORDS, 350 S. Buena Vista Street, Burbank, CA, 91521, (213) 840-1665, Glynn Magon; Product Manager, Sandy Spector; Ad/Sales Dept.

ELECTRA/ASYLUM/NONESUCH RECORDS, 665 5th Avenue, New York, NY, 10022, (212) 355-7610, Robin Sloane; National Director of Video Promotion.

DAVID GEFFEN CO., 3300 Warner Blvd., Burbank, CA 91501, (213) 846-9090, David Geffen; President.

265

IRS RECORDS, 100 Universal City Plaza, Building 422, Universal City, CA 91608, (818) 508-4730).

MCA RECORDS, 70 Universal City Plaza, 3rd Floor, Universal City, CA, 91608, (213) 508-4550, Larry Solters; VP, Artist Development, Liz Heller; Manager, Video Services.

MOTOWN RECORDS, 6255 Sunset Blvd., Los Angeles, CA, 90028, (213) 468-3500, Bob Jones; Executive Director, Press/Artist Relations, Phil Kaston; Director, International.

POLYGRAM RECORDS, 810 7th Avenue, New York, NY, 10019, (212) 399-7069, Len Epand; VP, Video Music Division, France Harper; Video Manager and 8333 Sunset Blvd., Los Angeles, CA, 90069, (213) 656-3003, Dan Pine; Video Communications.

RCA RECORDS, 1133 6th Avenue, New York, NY, 10036, (212) 930-4000, Michael Vallone; Director, Video/Promotion, Pat Kelleher; Director, Video, Janice Daidone; Video Manager.

SOLAR RECORDS/GALAXY PICTURES, 9044 Melrose Avenue, Los Angeles, CA 90069, (213) 859-1717, Karolyn Ali; Director, Film/Video Division.

WARNER BROS., 3300 Warner Blvd., Burbank, CA, 91501, (213) 846-9090, Jo Bergman; VP, Video, Sally Piper; Manager, Video.

APPENDIX

Income Projections

'It's too easy to be optimistic and make the figures come out looking like the next 'Raider's'. Don't do it.

Expectations

This is what you've waited for. It's the one page where everything you discovered through market research and distribution comes together. It's the grand tally that most investors look at first. It's *'the bottom line'*. Since it's so important, be as accurate as you can in projecting your program's potential. *'It's too easy to be optimistic and make the figures come out looking like the next 'Raiders.'* Don't do it. Be conservative. It's easy to fool yourself. Beware of your own unfounded expectations. Do not raise your investor's expectations. If your project doesn't return the money you fantasized, everyone will suffer. I know. I've been there. If you have a good project, do your homework, do market research, then do some more. *Then* produce the best film you can. You'll do fine. Don't gloss over what you may have learned in order to make your income projections look good. I can't overemphasize this point because 9 out of 10 producers overvalue their projects. If you recoup more than you projected, terrific. Everyone will love you. If you recoup *anything less* than what you promise, someone will feel mislead. Be realistic.

Income Projections From All Markets

The *Income Projections* table on the following page is an over-

269

INCOME PROJECTIONS

10 YEAR LIFE OF A 85 MINUTE DOCUMENTARY

BUDGET: $150,000

MARKETS	1986	1987	1988	1989	1990
THEATRICAL	40000	5000	0	0	0
HOME VIDEO	35000	10500	4000	3000	1000
PAY-TV	140000	0	0	0	0
NON-THEATRICAL	0	3000	7000	5000	1000
FOREIGN THEATRICAL	0	0	0	0	0
FOREIGN HOME VIDEO	10000	0	0	0	0
FOREIGN TELEVISION	0	20000	15000	0	0
TOTAL GROSS	225000	38500	26000	8000	2000
ONGOING EXPENSES	5000	3000	2000	1000	750
INVESTOR RECOUPS	150000	0	0	0	0
TOTAL NET	70000	35500	24000	7000	1250
INVESTOR'S 50%	35000	17750	12000	3500	625
% EARNINGS	23.33	11.83	8.00	2.33	0.42

270

1991	1992	1993	1994	1995	TOTALS
0	0	0	0	0	45000
500	400	400	400	400	55600
0	0	0	0	0	140000
500	200	200	200	200	17300
0	0	0	0	0	0
0	0	0	0	0	10000
10000	4000	0	0	0	49000
11000	4600	600	600	600	316900
500	500	500	500	500	750
0	0	0	0	0	0
10500	4100	100	100	100	316150
5250	2050	50	50	50	158075
3.50	1.37	0.03	0.03	0.03	105.38

view of the expected income from distribution of an 85 minute film in all markets over 10 years. (The figures represent the *'net'* income that the producer actually receives from distributors or direct sales. The program will earn significantly more money, but will go to exhibitors, distributors, network overhead, and marketing before the producer receives his share.

Potential investors will study this page in depth. If the projections are not thought out and not supported by your market research, you will lose their confidence and rightfully so. Do your homework so you can back up your projections. Anyone can project gold at the end of the rainbow. Few come through with the real McCoy.

These projections are *purely hypothetical* and only for purposes of illustration. There is no such film. It's pure fiction. Your income projections will be different. Not every 85 minute, $150,000 program will perform like this. It's an example, okay?

Some filmmakers think that if they copy this page it is a short cut to monetary nirvana. They think this chart, as is, will work for their film. It won't. Don't use it. Research your own numbers. If you don't and you go broke, it's your own fault. This a guide, a format for presenting financial information.

This 10-year income projection chart assumes that the markets listed actually produce income for the program.

Theatrical

Let's assume the film has limited appeal. Ten prints circulate and play 50 one-week engagements in a dozen or more cities. The average weekly gross is $7500. The total gross is $375,000. (The film also grosses $63,000 from repertory cinema playdates.) The total gross after one year is $438,000. (A better performance than most foreign films!) The exhibitors contribute only $20,000 to the ad campaign, half of which they deduct *off-the-top* before sending the distributor his 35% share of $150,000. The distributor then deducts $30,000 which he has spent on advertising. His net is $120,000. He agrees to split income 50/50 (after costs) with the producer and sends him $60,000. The producer however has agreed to pay for the $15,000 print cost (10 prints, $1500 each), and after doing so has $45,000 left. It takes many months to receive his money. He collects $40,000 the first year, and $5000 the second year. Even though the film *earned* $438,000, only $45,000 dribbled back to the producer. And in reality, that's not bad! (There are no foreign theatrical opportunities.)

Home Video

The film is not a exploitation film but rather a documentary. However it has highly promotable subject matter (prostitution, the Mafia, AIDS, Japanese business) so the producer can make a home video deal for a $35,000 advance and a $15% royalty of gross receipts for the US and Canada territories. He gets the advance right away. The tape isn't released until 6 months after the theatrical window. Assuming a $59 retail price, and a $36 wholesale price, the producer receives 15% or $5.40 per tape sold; 6480 are sold the first year, the advance is recouped and additional royalties are received in subsequent years. Sales fall off after two or three years.

Pay-TV

The subject matter of the documentary is so hot that HBO licenses the film for a year for $140,000. It is released around the time of the home video release. If HBO doesn't buy it, let's assume that PBS does with underwriting of $200,000; $140,000 license fee, $50,000 PBS overhead. Or, let's assume that PBS and many smaller cable and pay services together make up $140,000 in the first year. No sales occur thereafter. Most documentary filmmakers would be very happy with this kind of money!

Non-Theatrical

A year later a 24-minute version of the film is released to schools, libraries, and institutions. The producer receives a $3000 advance from a distributor. Prints sell for $480, royalty is 20% or $96 each. The advance is recouped in the first year afer 31 prints are sold. Because of the traditionally slow sales curve, more prints are sold during the second year bringing in $7000 in royalties. Sales drop off after a few years.

Foreign Home Video

The program is licensed for international home video distribution is Germany, Japan, England and Australia. A total advance of $10,000 is received in the first year. The advance is never recouped. There are no other royalties in future years.

Foreign Television

Sales are made directly to Japan, Germany, New Zealand and Australia through a sales agent who only takes a 20% fee (cheap!). The producer nets $20,000 but has to wait nearly a year to receive his money. The next year sales to the BBC and a few other networks bring in $15,000. Three years later the program is relicensed by some of the previous foreign broadcasters and nets $10,000 and $4000.

Total Gross

These are the monies from all sources after the appropriate distributor fees and expenses are deducted. The monies are deposited in the partnership's account and at appropriate times are disbursed to the investors.

Investor Recoups/Total Net

Miracle of miracles! After paying $5000 for on-going expenses (bookkeeping, accounting, legal, phone, dubs, shipping, etc.) the $150,000 investment is recouped by investors. There is a total net of $70,000 which is split 50/50 between the producer (general partner) and investors (limited partners).

Investor's Share/Profits

At the end of the first year the investors make $35,000 profit or receive a 23% return on their investment. The second year sees additional profits for the investors. Over 10 years they receive 105% over their initial investment. Given inflation and the fact this is a *film investment* its not bad. They took a risk on the producer's ability to complete the film and find distribution and on the film's ability to attract an audience. It worked!

Even a small return might be enough incentive for many investors to try again. The producer demonstrated his or her ability, was successful during production, distribution and marketing. The investor's confidence was renewed. They received some money. If the producer's projections were realistic, and he delivered, then he's more successful than most.

'Rent a small theater and have lines around the block.'

Your Film Premiere

Many people, myself included, like to premiere their own films, regardless of the length, in their hometowns. The advantage is that you will be launching your film to a (hopefully) sympathetic audience. You have the opportunity to test the film before a real audience. You can also collect film reviews that will assist you in marketing the film later. The sample budget that follows should only be used for study purposes. Your opening may cost much more or much less. (You may be able to find a college auditorium or VFW Hall for free.) It is very expensive to showcase a film. The promotion alone can gobble up thousands. *My advice: Rent a small theater and have lines around the block.*

Sample Budget

	Week 1	Week 2
Theater Rental (300 seats)	3,000	3,000
Printing Flyers/Posters	500	0
Distributing Posters	150	0
Postage	180	0
Newspaper Advertisements	2,000	1,000
Press Screening Costs	200	0
Still Photos	50	0
Publicist's Fee	1,200	0
Press Releases	50	0
TOTAL	$7,330	4,000

277

To break even you must have 1,832 people at $4 each for the first week or make $1,047 per day (261 people) or fill roughly half of the theater for each show. Can your film do it?

If you are able to 'holdover' for a second week your expenses drop in half. Subsequent weeks will bring down the cost of newspaper ads. To break even on the second week you need to bring in $571 per day, or draw 142 people per day (or fill roughly 1/4 of the theater for each show). Is that possible? If it is, or if you can do better, then you can make a profit.

To spend less money on a premiere in any major city would probably not create enough attention for the film to attract the necessary audience. (Unless you are in your hometown and have a built-in audience.) You will have to spend a good deal of money on advertising and promotion.

Perhaps you can strike a deal with an exhibitor where you split the receipts after expenses. That would certainly reduce your up-front risk and cash outlay. At the same time, if the film was successful it would reduce your profits. You take the risk, you get the money.

Also it will cost nearly as much to do a one-evening show as it will to play your film for a whole week. The advertising, promotion and theater costs are substantial expenses so you can try to run your film as long as possible. You can reduce your risks by booking an even smaller theater with lower rent. Perhaps a 100- or 200-seat theater would yield greater returns than a large theater. These are the kinds of things to consider when producing your own 'four-wall' premiere.

Another approach, if your film is strong enough, is to rent several theaters in the same general area (not so close that they would compete with each other) at the same time so that you can use the same newspaper ad and promotional campaign to publicize all the showings. By amortizing your costs over

MICHAEL WIESE FILM PRODUCTIONS ANNOUNCE

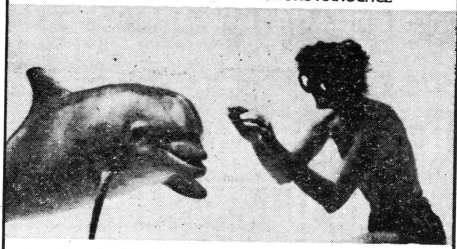

For centuries we have believed we were the only ones on earth
with a mind and soul. . .perhaps there are other such creatures.

DOLPHIN

Directed by HARDY JONES & MICHAEL WIESE Produced by MICHAEL WIESE Written by HARDY JONES
Music Composed & Conducted by BASIL POLEDOURIS
Editor: JOHN V. FANTE Cinematography: JOHN KNOOP Underwater Cinematography: JAMES HUDNALL & JACK MC KENNEY
"Dolphin Song" Performed by MORGAN SMITH • Underwater Piano: STEPHEN GAGNE • With BUCKMINSTER FULLER

PALACE OF FINE ARTS

3301 Lyon Street, San Francisco
(Next to The Exploratorium)

WEDNESDAY JUNE 27th — SUNDAY JULY 1st • 7 & 9 pm
SATURDAY & SUNDAY SHOWS · 1, 3, 5, 7 & 9 pm

$3.75 Adults/$2.25 Children • Tickets at the door.

Premiere & Celebration Party
TUESD' 'INE 26th · 8 pm
Tickets $~ ough all **BASS** Outlets
For ~ ~ation call **T·E·L·E·T·I·X**
~kets also at the door

SOLD OUT

BAY AREA SHOWINGS:

PETALUMA	Plaza Theater	JUNE 27
SANTA CRUZ	Sashmill Theater	JUNE 30 — JULY 4
BERKELEY	UC Theater	JULY 8
SACRAMENTO	J Street Theater	JULY 10, 11, 12

See local papers for show times.

several theaters you reduce the risk of having *'all your eggs in one basket'*. *DOLPHIN* played at five theaters in the San Francisco Bay area at roughly the same time. One poster and one newspaper ad promoted all the showings.

It is exciting to put together a premiere of your film(s) but plan to start work about 6 weeks or more before the opening day. This requires careful planning, perseverance and inspiration to compete with Hollywood's movies. Good luck, should you give it a try.

Posters

Posters come in a variety of sizes and can be used for different purposes. A large poster is used in theater display cases to advertise the current (or coming) film. Independent films usually are not theatrical films so do not require a poster of this size.

Smaller posters can serve as both posters for screenings and as advertisements to possible buyers or renters These posters are usually no larger than 8″ × 11 1/2″. It is possible to have inexpensive, large black-and-white blowups of the small posters made for theater display cases, should you ever have an exhibition.

The graphic used on the poster is extremely important as it is the sole image that represents your film.

The *HARDWARE WARS* poster is very successful. It is an oversized poster measuring 8 1/2″ × 22″ so when folded it can be either mailed 'as is' (the back side is white with a return address) or inserted in a regular 8″ × 11″ envelope. The poster is in 4 colors, is predominantly red, and is funny. The poster is consistent with the humor of the film. It too is a parody. Ernie Fosselius, the director, supervised the production of the poster.

HARDWARE WARS

A SPECTACULAR SPACE SAGA OF ROMANCE, REBELLION, AND HOUSEHOLD APPLIANCES.

HARDWARE WARS
13 minutes, color

"Here's one *Star Wars* spinoff George Lucas wasn't counting on
Hardware Wars, a thirteen-minute parody that is becoming
the hottest short subject to hit the screen"
ROLLING STONE Magazine

A spectacular space saga of romance, rebellion, and household appliances

Created by Ernie Fosselius   Produced by Michael Wiese

Available from: PYRAMID FILMS, P.O. Box 1048 Santa Monica, CA 90406 (213) 390-FILM

The Award-winning Television Special as seen on PBS and BBC Television

DOLPHIN

This is the amazing story of a small band of dolphin enthusiasts who set off on a remarkable adventure to meet and make friends with wild dolphins in the open seas of the Bahamas. Music from a specially-designed underwater piano is used to attract a school of sixty wild dolphins who join their human companions in an exquisite underwater ballet.

An innovative and engrossing film that combines superb underwater photography of wild dolphins with a narrative describing the dolphins' behavior, intelligence, sonar and communication abilities and gives the viewer a sense of respect and affection for these friendly sea creatures.

Directed by Michael Wiese & Hardy Jones
58 minutes/Color
16mm:
Sale $730/Rent $65
Videocassette:
Sale $365/Rent $65

Special Prize: The Cup of the Prime Minister of Italy at the Milan Maritime Film Festival.

CINE Golden Eagle

"Ambitious, spectacular underwater photography, carefully researched, well-paced, informative, entertaining—as fine as anything going in the documentary field."
—The Independent

"Exciting experiment with underwater music . . . an underwater sequence of breathtaking beauty."
—Greenpeace Chronicle

"The filmmakers have succeeded in revealing to us a world that seems fantastic, dreamlike, and yet is utterly real and within reach."
—New Age Journal

"A mixture of scientific dreaming and heartwarming nature story . . . informative and, above all, entertaining."
—Sacramento Union

"An unique and honest record of a novel—and successful—experiment in interspecies communications . . . It is easily the best movie on the subject to date."
—Future Life

FILMS INCORPORATED
733 Green Bay Road Wilmette, IL 60091
(800)323-4222 (in Illinois, call collect (312)256-3200)

283

It uses a *'Rolling Stone'* magazine review quote, our credits, and gives the non-theatrical distributor, Pyramid Films. They paid for the poster and gave us an ample supply for our purposes. By adding a simple stick-on banner, showings can be announced using the same poster.

DOLPHIN had three posters. One for the theatrical premieres and two others for promoting non-theatrical sales and rentals. These posters were also used to advertise the film to foreign buyers. The third poster was printed after the film played on PBS and the BBC and we'd acquired new reviews that we wanted to use. Next to the film itself, posters are the major tool used to sell and promote a film.

Study Guides

Study guides are printed by distributors to accompany the film. They assist the teacher in using the film to its best advantage. The study guide is also an effective sales tool as it shows the film buyer that the film has an educational value (and thereby justifies the purchase.)

The study guides for *HARDWARE WARS, RADIANCE, DOLPHIN* and *WONDER OF THE DOLPHINS* follow.

The *HARDWARE WARS* study guide was written by Ernie Fosselius, the film's creator, and Dorothy Fadiman upon request by the distributor.

'The purpose of the study guide,' says Ernie Fosselius, 'is to satisfy the use of the film in the schools. Comedy is useless for schools because it does not fit into the school curricula. The study guide satisfies the needs of the distributor and the school and is itself a kind of parody. Satire is by its nature critical of the very forms that are a standard way of teaching or presenting things. HARDWARE WARS really doesn't require a study

284

guide, it should be self-explanatory. The film asks not to be taken seriously and a study guide by its nature is serious. The whole point is to learn how to not take things seriously. You can't really break down comedy and teach why something is funny. Comedy is a mystery.'

The *RADIANCE* and *DOLPHIN* study guides give the viewer additional information about their subject matter. They provide questions and exercises that may be used after the film is shown. You can see by the thought that went into the study guides, particularily *RADIANCE*, that every conceivable use of the film was explored. The more educators discover how to use the film, the more they will use it.

By Ernie Fosselius and Michael Wiese
13 minutes, color   (16mm or Videocassette)

STUDY GUIDE
Written by
Ernie Fosselius and
Dorothy Fadiman

Where does humor come from and how do we use it?

Humor is everywhere in latent form. It is all around us every day. All it takes to bring it out is for someone to recognize it. Comedy writers and humorists are actually reporters. Their job is to observe the humor that exists in our everyday life and faithfully report it back to us. Sometimes they must exaggerate or take a description to a ridiculous extreme before we can see it the same way. But this is something we can all do, it is just a matter of how we look at things, or perspective. That perspective is called sense of humor. We all have it, developed to different degrees. Sense of humor does not just mean the ability to laugh at a joke or something that is presented to us in a funny way, but it is also the ability to "sense" or recognize the humor in situations that are not necessarily funny on the surface. When tragic or sad events sometimes make us laugh or giggle, it is the sense of humor at work to help relieve the tension. Tension can create the mood that brings on the humor of relief.

A sense of humor can help us deal with the emotional heaviness of a serious, unhappy, uncomfortable, frustrating, or even just boring situation. It may not change the situation itself, but it will change the way we look at it and also the effect it has on us. We are not laughing at the thing that brings on the uncomfortable feelings, but at ourselves for being so serious.

This helps to take away the strong emotional weight connected with the situation, and may even help us deal more directly with a problem that, without this fresh perspective, would be too difficult to face.

Humor can make the heavy light and the pretentious silly. In *Hardware Wars,* when Augie "Ben" Doggie grasps his forehead in apparent reaction to suffering a great inner pain, Fluke asks him, in seriousness: "What is it? Did you feel a great disturbance in the Force like thousands of souls crying out in terror and suddenly silenced?" Augie responds in a way that makes fun of the pretentions: "No, it's just a little headache."

Humor can also be a very important and useful means of making a statement. Some things you feel strongly about may be difficult to talk about in a serious way. Through the use of humor and satire these things you want to expose can be easily pointed out to people. By exaggerating the aspects of a subject you wish to focus on, people can be shown the absurdity, pretentiousness, silliness, etc., of things that they normally take seriously and for granted. Through humor you can tell people the truth about how you feel in an entertaining way. That may make them listen more readily and be more willing to deal with an otherwise upsetting subject.

humor (hyōō'mer) a comic quality causing amusement

amuse (e myōōz') to hold the attention agreeable; to entertain or divert in a pleasant, cheerful manner

parody (par'e dē) a humorous or satirical imitation of a serious piece of work

satire (sat'ier) the use of irony, sarcasm, ridicule or the like, in exposing, denouncing or deriding folly, vice, etc.

Hardware Wars is a **parody.** It uses **humor** to **amuse** as it proceeds to imitate *Star Wars,* satirically. The good-natured, light-hearted approach of *Hardware Wars* clearly opens the space for people to laugh freely, without feeling guilty at being unkind to something sacred.

Hardware Wars satirizes not only *Star Wars,* the movie, but also the film industry's approach to advertising their own product via the "coming attractions" trailer. *Hardware Wars* is actually a preview of a film that does not, in reality, exist. It reveals key highlights of this mythic film and promises much more. However, as is very often the case, the preview probably contains all of the action scenes, and more excitement than the film it represents. It promises more than the film can deliver.

Its main thrust, however, is a funny takeoff on *Star Wars.* As a takeoff on *Star Wars, Hardware Wars* also takes on several subjects:

■ SCIENCE FICTION/
SCIENTIFIC ELITISM

For many people, the bigger-than-lifeness of a science fiction thriller is inspiring and satisfying. For others, and at subtler levels for some, a sense of separateness and alienation is also there. A feeling of personal inadequacy can accompany the admiration for the vast, heroic realities of science fiction drama. We are presented with inconceivable distances, super sophisticated technology, and adventures normal mortals can only dream about.

Hardware Wars makes real the unreal. When an iron flies through space, you recognize it as a familiar object from your own reality. You can work an iron. When a waffle maker opens its great jaws in outer space, you think of waffles and syrup rather than the technical magnificence of beings whose intelligence must be far more developed than your own. Humor results from unlikely juxtaposition of two normally unrelated objects or a familiar object in unusual surroundings. *Hardware Wars* playfully looks at the kind of scientific elitism in which science fiction trades heavily, i.e., the wise technical expert gives his profound briefing in double talk. People are invited to have fun with what's usually placed out of their grasp.

■ SPECIAL EFFECTS

Hardware Wars aims to give away the secrets. Instead of being mys-

288

tified, we are shown the gimmicks, led "behind the scenes." For instance, the wires controlling the household appliances in outer space are deliberately filmed. Instead of the secret power of special effects, the viewer can have fun with knowing the truth and seeing the mechanics. The spoof is capsulized when the announcer says "Thrill to the expensive spine-tingling special effects," and we are shown a dinky sparkler. The film juxtaposes hi-tone hype with cheapness to dramatize the ways in which glamor is used in an advertisement to seduce you into thinking that the movie it advertises contains much more than you can imagine. *Hardware Wars* makes fun of and laughs at its own pretentions of being a spectacular film.

- ■ THE FILM INDUSTRY'S COMMERCIALISM

"Coming soon to a theater near you . . . get in line now!" The high-pressure announcer is trying to make you believe that the film will be so successful that you'll have to get in line very early — in fact, even before the movie begins playing — in order to get a seat. This is an exaggeration of the type of attitude we often experience when we are being sold something. *Hardware Wars* expresses an opinion about how annoying this can be by accentuating the ridiculousness of it. There is often comic relief in hearing someone else express an opinion about something that annoys or disturbs us but that we might not have con-

sciously expressed ourselves. In this way, humor exposes our common likes and dislikes and shared feelings.

EXERCISES

The following exercises may facilitate further exploration of certain aspects of *Hardware Wars*.

1. Experiencing the Creation of Parody

A parody must look as much as possible like the original, with selected elements or details changed, exaggerated, or "sillified" for humorous effect. For example, the princess's hair buns become similar looking cinnamon rolls. In *Hardware Wars* some of the parody names are:

Luke Skywalker ⇒ Fluke Starbucker
R2D2 ⇒ Artie Deco
Darth Vader ⇒ Darph Nader
Obie-Wan "Ben" Kenobie ⇒ Augie "Ben" Doggie
Star Wars ⇒ *Hardware Wars*

Parody a Name:

a. Think of a name, of a famous person, or TV show, or film. Briefly describe the original.

b. Change a characteristic or two of the original, making it funny or silly.

c. Change the name to describe the new character or title, e.g., Jimmy Carter becomes a volcano expert called Jimmy Crater.

E.g., *Star Wars* uses household appliances and tools for space gear, and thus becomes *Hardware Wars*.

Parody a Product:

Hardware Wars is the parody of the advertising approach to a certain product, in this case a science fiction thriller. In order to see the ways in which commercial presentations lend themselves so well to parody, try this:

a. Choose a product which you've seen advertised in the media.

b. Write humorous commercial copy describing a different product which you create by using the same style, a parody name, etc. The new product will resemble the original as it usually appears, but the name and feature change will make fun of it.

2. Developing a Sense for the Humorous Potential of Ordinary Objects

a. Make a list of six items around your house (tools, food, furniture, etc.).

b. See what completely different things they bring to mind. For example, in *Hardware Wars*, drills and egg beaters become sophisticated weaponry; a vacuum cleaner becomes a robot; flashlights become laser swords.

3. Seeing that Alienation or a Feeling of Being on the Outside Can Be Overcome with Humor

Hardware Wars can be viewed as an appreciative and humorous statement arising out of discomfort with the disproportionate reality created around *Star Wars*.

a. Select a situation or person that makes you feel uncomfortable with a feeling of alienation, powerlessness, or inadequacy.

b. Begin to play with that image. Let your mind wander, allowing any absurd aspects or exaggerations to arise. Try to look at it from a detached perspective.

c. Make notes as you continue to be open to any ridiculous notions that come up.

d. Make a stick figure cartoon strip bringing this serious subject into the light of humor.

4. Understanding the Challenge and Process of Editing a Production for Humor

a. Two to four people improvise a short, funny skit while others watch and take notes.

b. Everyone (actors and observers) writes an individual critique, based only on what and where to cut. The goal is to become sensitive to how timing effects humor. Generally, the more succinct and concise, the funnier.

c. The actors read and discuss the input among themselves, then perform again, applying the feedback.

d. A general discussion of editing as a tool follows.

5. Having Fun with So-Called "Special Effects"

a. Choose a magic trick.

b. Learn how to do it skillfully.

c. After you can perform it correctly, do it in front of a goup in a way that makes it a joke instead of a clever deception. Your goal is simply to make people laugh.

6. Exploring the Dimensions of Archetypes

Hardware Wars, true to its parody of *Star Wars,* represents major archetypes, including:

Fluke — the Hero
Darph Nader — Evil
Augie Ben Doggie — Good
Artie Deco and 4Q2 — Loyal
   Comrades
Ham Salad — Swashbuckling
   Knight Errant

a. Choose one archetype from the film.

b. Give examples of its appearance in a particular area, e.g., *the hero* — in mythology or in comic books or in romantic literature, etc.

c. Discuss the similarities of a certain archetype as it appears in a variety of settings, e.g., Superman, Spiderman, Cap-

tain Marvel, etc. All have certain characteristics in common. What are they? List several distinguishing characteristics of each one

or

Choose one archetype from the film. Trace its appearance through time, e.g., the *evil force* from primitive through modern times

or

Discuss the appearances of a certain archetype cross-culturally, e.g., *the heroine* in mythology — Greek, Nordic, African, American Indian, etc.

RADIANCE
The Experience of Light

Discussion Leader's Guide

The Film

More than ten years ago, Dorothy Fadiman, the writer and director of *Radiance,* had an experience of dazzling light. Realizing that the "light" of saints and mystics was not just a metaphor, she wanted to share this insight. Her career had been one of communication, through freelance writing, leading workshops, and as an exhibiting artist. In 1976 she and Michael Wiese, the producer, co-created a slide presentation titled *Do Saints Really Glow?* which communicated the power of that illumination to thousands of people throughout the United States.

The following year, work began on a film based on the slide presentation. The film captures the essence of the original experience with its new title, *Radiance.* Featured are the cinematography and editing of John Fante and the photography of Steven Mangold.

The film offers a stunning array of nature footage, religious art, video images, kinetic mandalas, and a narration which leads magnetically from the personal to the universal.

As an Art Film it is Unique and Elegant . . . It can be viewed as a visual poem, with the narration and music serving simply as sound and rhythm.

As a Dramatic Moment it is Deeply Moving . . . It can be viewed as a liquid voyage through a range of feelings, after which one is safely brought to shore.

As a Documentary it is Informative and Intriguing . . . It can be viewed as an inquiry into realms of human potential which are uncharted and full of wonder.

Suggestions For Viewing

1. That the room be very dark. Some of the effects are subtle, so we suggest blacking out as much ambient light as possible.

2. That no discussion happen before viewing the film. A few introductory remarks followed by a moment of silence, with eyes closed will provide a receptive atmosphere.

3. That no discussion immediately follow the film. A moment of quiet will allow people to be with their own experience.

Background

Particularly for those times when it will be viewed as a documentary, we offer the following discussion of the ideas behind *Radiance*.

The Inner Experience of Light. The concepts presented in this film will be inspiring to some, challenging to others, and simply affirming to people who already feel aligned with certain experience of light. To the filmmaker, the original experience of being filled with brilliant energy was vivid. But was it real?

That question opens many doors.

The experience of inner light is unquestionably real to the people who see it. For those who have only read or heard about luminous states, this light is often treated as an illusion or hallucination occurring during a period of high suggestibility. Recent scientific studies are beginning to provide evidence that certain mystical visions may not be just symbolic.

It's a provocative phenomenon. Some see it, some don't! For those who do, the whole world sparkles like diamonds, light floods the body, some see a radiant messenger.

Universality of Light. Whether treated as a metaphor or an actual physical reality, brilliant light *is* associated with intense spiritual events. Aldous Huxley, a lifetime student of consciousness, reviewed a number of visionary experiences. He concluded that light is *the* most common factor. Mircea Eliade, from the perspective of comparative religion, and Maurice Bucke, in his classic, *Cosmic Consciousness*, both find, as did Huxley, that light is one of the major factors in almost every mystical encounter. Illumination appears universally, whether the experience is spontaneous, from a psychedelic drug, or during meditation, chanting, dancing, fasting, etc.

Light is also a recurrent theme in religious ceremonies and rituals throughout the world.

Holy People and Spiritual Exercises. Certain Eskimo Indians link the key step in a holy man's initiation with the presence of a mysterious light which the shaman can feel in his body. Thousands of miles away, Australian medicine men are initiated by a mythic magician whose eyes are said to shine with light. He sprinkles the candidates with sacred water, described as liquified quartz, their bodies then become filled with crystals, manifestations of celestial light. Not only for shamans and holy people, religious guidance for any individual who seeks God-experience may involve working with light. Actualism, a contemporary Western system, teaches people to direct light through their bodies from a radiant star visualization above the head. The desired effect is a release of physical tension and elevation of spirit. From the Indian, *Rig Veda*, discovering "the god of gods" is attained by contemplating "Very High Light." A Chinese source, *The Secret of the Golden Flower*, describes a method of meditation, "circulation of the light," which leads to conscious realization of the light of heaven which then blazes forth from within. With few exceptions, when saints and holy people have been described or painted, they are emanating an aura of light. Christ, Buddha, and Moses are among those who have been described as visibly radiant.

In Western philosophy, the theme of light linked with divinity is not well recognized, but is definitely present in the works of thinkers like Plato, Plotinus, Paracelsus, Goethe, and Descartes. There are hundreds of cross-cultural examples of spiritual light, but the link between enlightenment and physical light has stood virtually unexplored until recently.

Recording and Measuring Energy. The possibility of observing and understanding human energy systems is a subject of growing interest. We are now finding out that the metaphysical concept of an energy body may refer to a measurable phenomena. There are several methods of recording energy fields around bodies. One of these, Kirlian photography, is based on producing photographs from the interaction of high frequency currents with matter. With Kirlian photography we may

have a scientific way to measure changes in this "energy field" which some systems have referred to as the "aura."

The results are controversial. Some of the color effects have been shown to be an artifact of the film, and there is a question about the extent to which moisture affects the results. It remains, however, that the patterns of radiant emission which the photographs show are at least reflections of the changes a body goes through. According to the research of Thelma Moss at U.C.L.A., the energy surrounding the object (e.g., a fingertip) is recorded by the photographic film. The visual image thereby produced has been shown to contract, expand, or even send out flares, depending on the physiological and/or emotional state of the subject.

Another kind of measurement being done involves the detection of direct-current electrical characteristics at the acupuncture points. Russian research has shown that the eyes emanate a measurable radiation.

Energy Input. Not only are we establishing the validity of energy emanating from the body, but also the extent to which energy input affects the organism. Several years ago, it was shown that energy applied to an amputated stump caused a rat to partially regrow its limb. Energy input affects mental states as well. Several studies show that psychiatric hospital admissions correlate with changes in the earth's magnetic field, stages of the moon, and solar flares.

Many cultures have accepted the body as a vibrant organism which has measurable, chartable, changeable patterns. Much Eastern medicine is based on diagnoses and treatment in relation to these patterns. East Indian, Arabic, Tibetan, and Oriental countries have archives full of medical charts showing various patterns of energy flowing through the body. Western medicine is hesitant to accept these ideas, but curious. Experimental acupuncture programs are appearing in selected settings, like alternative wholistic centers, which are being created throughout the United States.

It is crucial to be stimulated and challenged. Not only can we conceive of the possible, but consider the unheard of, the ridiculous, the wonderful mysterious questions of the unknown. In *Radiance* we proceed from the known to the unproven in sequences that flow visually, and open speculation without demanding any belief. By making unlikely connections, new relationships are suggested, and new, exciting questions take shape.

Religion

When *Radiance* was shown for the first time to an art history class, the professor pointed out that it was a living icon.

To the extent that this work communicates the energy of the author's original experience, we have an actual phenomenon. A popular understanding of "icon" is simply a symbolic likeness of a religious figure or scene. However, the metaphysics of iconography reveal that the object itself has the power to communicate energy.

Not only does *Radiance* provide an opportunity to share in the expression of a spiritual experience, it also invites an exploration of "holy light" from several perspectives: that holy light and everyday light are not separate forces, but connected on a continuum; that holy light exists universally, from ancient rites to sophisticated theologies; that holy light is not limited to the experiences and appearances of saints and mystics.

Exercises

Communicating Religious Experience. This film is an artistic statement of a religious experience. Think about your own moments of connectedness with the universe.

Write a poem, a descriptive paragraph, or draw a picture which communicates the feeling of one of those moments. Perhaps a series will work even better for you. Continue until you feel satisfied. Share with others in the group.

Linking Light With Divinity. Light appears in conjunction with Divinity in the Old and New Testaments of the Bible, the Koran, and Kabbalah, the Upanishads, the Teachings of the Buddha — essentially every major religion incorporates that link.

Choose a source of religious teaching. Give examples of the "light" — descriptive, explanatory, naming of God(s), metaphors, prayers, etc., as it appears in these writings.

Physical Light. Discuss some of the ways physical light (fire, candles, sunlight, shiny gold, etc.) is used in religious ceremonies. Give specific examples.

Halos. What do you think a halo actually is? An artist's interpretation? a symbol? an actual observed radiance? Discuss different types of halos — mandala, nimbus, aureole, etc.

Sun Worship. The sun was worshipped in Egypt for centuries as one of many Gods. However, under the reign of Akhanaten, a unique dimension of sun worship evolved. Discuss this particular period.

There are many sun gods. Select two from different times and geographical locations. Discuss their functions for the people who worshipped them.

The Power of Prayer on Plants. Recent research has proven, and has replicated, that positive attention stimulates plant growth. One of the descriptions of the work is "the power of prayer on plants." (See *The Secret Life of Plants*, by Chris Bird and Peter Tompkins.)

Set up an experiment: take two boxes of seeds or seedlings. Give equal water, nutrients, and light to both boxes. Praise, admire, and love one group. Simply care physically for the others. Notice the results. If there is a difference in the two groups at the end of several weeks, what inferences can be drawn?

Inner Light Meditation. Close your eyes. Relax comfortably. Visualize a star above your head. Let a shower of light pour down from the star, through your body. Open the soles of your feet with your imagination. Let the light carry tension and negativity out the bottoms of your feet. When you feel clear, close the soles of your feet with your mind, filling with light. When full to overflowing, enjoy the feeling!

Some Helpful Readings

Bucke, Richard. *Cosmic Consciousness.* Descriptive discussion of individuals who had classic transcendental experiences, many with an experience of light. Causeway Books, New York, 1900, 326pp.

Eliade, Mircea. *The Two and the One.* Scholarly discussion of the mystic light with many examples from worldwide cultures. Harper & Row, New York, 1962, 223 pp.

Huxley, Aldous. *The Perennial Philosophy.* Exposition of the one essential Reality, and its many forms. Harper & Row, New York, 1944, 306 pp.

James William. *The Varieties of Religious Experience.* The classic text for understanding higher states of consciousness. McMillan Co., New York, 1961, 416 pp.

Shah, Idries. Any of the many books of Sufi stories published by Dutton and Penguin.

Stapledon, Olaf. *The Starmaker.* Penguin, New York, 1973.

Sturgeon, Theodore. *More Than Human.* Ballentine, New York, 1975.

Tagore, Rabindranath (Chakravarty, Amiya, ed.). *A Tagore Reader.* Beacon Press, Boston, MA, 1966.

Thoreau, Henry David (Shepard, Odell, ed.). *The Heart of Thoreau's Journals.* Dover, New York, 1960.

Whitman, Walt (Kouwenhoven, John, ed.). *Leaves of Grass and Selected Prose.* Modern Library, New York, 1950.

Yeats, William Butler (Crossley-Holland, Kevin, ed). *Running to Paradise: Poems by W.B. Yeats.* MacMillan, New York, 1968.

Zimmer, Heinrich (Campbell, Joseph, ed.). *The King and the Corpse.* Princeton University Press, Princeton, N.J., 1971.

The Arts

From the perspective of the arts, this film can be regarded within at least three contexts: as a personal statement; as a living design; as a stimulus to creativity through the presentation of a spectrum of "seed" images which can be used to generate new works. Through all of these, there is a feeling which runs like a theme throughout, which affirms the light in everything.

Exercises

The Statement. In making a personal statement, the artist may be asking the viewer to agree with the view. Did you feel pressured? or free to experience your own feelings? In your own work, do you want agreement? How do you communicate this?

Juxtaposition. *Radiance* uses contrasts for effect — classical music vs. electronic synthesizer, simple nature images vs. video art, real people vs. painted saints.

Discuss juxtaposition as a tool in creating art.

Give other examples of contrasts in the arts which intensity a desired effect.

Religious Art.

Halos: The light surrounding holy beings appears in many religions. Find examples from various cultures in which light or energy is drawn around special people. In addition to Christian, Buddhist and Islamic, consider shamanistic art and children's work.

Icons: Radiance has been referred to as a contemporary icon. What is an icon? Why is the icon itself considered sacred? Create an icon centered on someone you hold in high regard.

Light in religious architecture: Light is an integral force in creating a religious feeling within Mosques, Temples, Cathedrals, Synagogues, etc. Design examples of at least three different ways in which light could enter a place of worship and have an emotional, spiritual effect. Discuss some of the ways in which light was calculated to act on and within the Pyramids. Discuss one theory of light and shadow in Stonehenge.

The Mandala. The sun, the flowers, the tunnel of continually dissolving centered shapes, the peacock — they all echo the pull to the middle, the magnetic draw of the mandala.

What is a mandala? What is the effect of centrality on consciousness? Discover and list at least ten manmade mandalas. Create a simple mandala pattern. Complete it in some original way other than crayons or paints, e.g., use cloth, rice, grass, glass, etc.

Dissolves. The transitions in *Radiance* are all dissolves, which heightens the sensation of congruence. In a dissolve, when two images interface, a third image becomes predominant at some point. This intermediate image is usually abstract and evocative.

Using colored cellophane or tissue, cut out a set of shapes. Play with these against a white background, noticing the continually changing image created by the overlay.

Does Art Have Gender? The personalness is heightened by the feminine perspective, female voice, flowing images, receptive tone. Do you think of certain works of art or art forms as masculine or feminine? Discuss.

Some Helpful Readings

Arguelles, Jose and Miriam. *Mandala.* Profusely illustrated overview of the mandala, a symbol of wholeness appearing in every culture. Shambhala Publications, Berkeley, CA, 1972, 140 pp.

Birren, Faber. *Color: A Survey in Words and Pictures from Ancient Mysticism to Modern Science.* University Books, Seacaucus, N.J., 1962.

Hess, T., and John Ashberry (ed.). *Light: From Aten to Laser.* A compilation of illustrated articles on light in art; subjects include the pyramids, Byzantine, Gothic, landscape, dreams, electric art, etc. The MacMillan Company, New York, 1971, 170 pp.

Kandinsky, Wassily. *Concerning the Spiritual in Art.* Wittenborn & Co., New York, 1947, 92 pp.

——. *The art of Spiritual Harmony.* Dover, New York, 1976. Two of the only books specifically on this subject.

Mookerjei, Ajit. *Yoga Art.* Exquisite reproductions of art designed to ignite the inner spirit and invite union with the cosmic. New York Grahpic Society, N.Y., 1976.

Samuels, Mike, M.D., and Nancy. *Seeing With the Mind's Eye.* The history, techniques and uses of visualization. Bookworks, Berkeley, CA, 1975, 331 pp.

Filmmaking

Some questions and projects evolving from *Radiance:*

Mixing Media. *Radiance* combines paintings, people, video synthesized images, nature, laser light, kirlian photography, kinetic mandalas, and long dissolves.

What are the problems and advantages, dangers and opportunities of mixing media so broadly in such a short film?

Effect of Narration. Documentary style films are traditionally narrated by men. Here we have a woman's voice.

How do you feel about a female narrator? What, if any, differences are touched in the viewer's mind, hearing a woman rather than a man?

Do you feel there was too much or not enough explanation?

The narrator is also the writer and director. How would you or do you feel about narrating your own work?

Editing with Varied Rhythm. Visual transitions and musical cross-fades have an inner rhythm. Watch the film, observing the way in which the words, music, and images are continually varied in relation to each other.

How might you have handled any of the transitions or timing differently?

Shooting Slides. Generally, a slide is shot as a still. In looking at this film, notice how much camera movement is actually possible.

Discuss your experiences, concerns and/or the possibilities of shooting slides.

Use of Dissolves. There is one cut in this film. Most of the dissolves are long, and intentionally crafted. A great deal of consciousness goes into that third image created by the transparent overlap of the first two.

As you can see with *Radiance*, a magical intermediate set of images emerges, especially with the mandalas and centered flowers.

Project for studying the dissolve process:

Each person brings in several slides that successfully overlap. Using two slide projectors, superimpose these and study the way in which the new image is created. If possible, use a dissolve unit to observe the progression from one image to another.

Then, arrange the slides randomly, dissolving unrelated images with each other and see what happens!

Music. The musical selections range from Bach to Tibetan Monks to lyric guitar to electronic synthesizer.

Do the juxtapositions from a range of cultures and styles work for you? Discuss your reactions.

Watch the film, listening carefully to the musical selections and noting their effect, and assess the appropriateness of each selection. Offer specific alternatives for those sections in which you feel the scoring could be differently handled.

Cinematic Autobiography. *Radiance* is autobiographical.

What are some of the pitfalls of autobiographical cinema?

What are some opportunities this perspective provides?

Music

In *Radiance*, the music is used to heighten, dramatize, support and express a wide range of moods and cultural experiences. In Appendix A are listed the sections, with the music accompanying each set of visual images.

Listening to the Music. What mood or impression do you get from each piece? How do you feel about each selection in relation to those pictures with which it appeared? If you do not feel the selection maximally served the visual image, recommend what kind of music you would choose, noting any specific titles you might have included. Perhaps bring a cassette recording of your choice to the group. Share your process of selection. Listen also to the cross-fades, as each piece blends into the next. Share your impressions with the group.

Exercise

Combining Music with Images (requiring a slide projector and cassette recorder for playback).

Each person select three different slides, choose three pieces of music — one for each image, record the musical selections onto a cassette tape in the order you will present the pictures.

For the Presentation: without words, project the images, one by one, playing each piece of music.

Group discussion of each person's presentation:

1. Did the music and images fit appropriately?
2. What were the emotions people felt?
3. How did the whole sequence seem? Dramatic? Stilted? Flowing?

Food For Thought: *Radiance* uses 17 very different selections of music in a 22-minute film. Discuss your reactions and impressions of so varied an offering.

Some Helpful Readings

Hall, Manly P. *The Therapeutic Value of Music.* Music therapy as practiced in a range of cultures since ancient times. Philosophical Research Society, Los Angeles, 1955, 45 pp.

Heindel, Max. *Musical Scale and the Scheme of Evolution.* An esoteric treatise by the founder of the Rosicrucian order. Rosicrucian Fellowship, Oceanside, CA, 1949, 96 pp.

Heline, Corrine. *Music. The Keynote of Human Evolution.* Relationship of consciousness and music through history. New Age Press, La Canada, CA, 1965, 144 pp.

Khan, Hazrat Inayat. *The Mysticism of Sound.* Music, as a key to infinity. Health Research, Mokelumne Hill, CA, 1923, 94 pp.

Scott, Cyril. *Music: Its Secret Influences Throughout the Ages.* Investigates the subtle implications of music. Samuel Weiser, Inc., New York, 208 pp.

LEADER'S GUIDE

FOR USE WITH THE 16MM FILM/VIDEOCASSETTE

The Wonder of Dolphins

11 MINUTES ■ COLOR ■ A MICHAEL WIESE FILM PRODUCTION

INTENDED AUDIENCE

This film is designed for use by the widest possible audience. It is useful in elementary science courses; junior and senior high school classes in science, communications and futurism; and is entertaining and enlightening for a general adult audience.

PRIOR TO SHOWING THE FILM:

Preview the film and study the leader's guide.

VOCABULARY/DISCUSSION WORDS FOR ELEMENTARY STUDENTS:

sonar	communicate	behavior	perceive
scuba	sensitive	amplified	pressure wave
	interspecies		expedition

FILM CONTENT:

The introduction to this motion picture enumerates some of the extraordinary attributes of dolphins. They can swim 30 miles an hour; dive 1,000 feet deep; communicate with each other through high frequency sounds; "see" distant objects through a kind of sonar; and they have evolved brains larger than those of human beings.

The second section of the film introduces a baby dolphin and explains how the young are born alive underwater and must surface to breathe. The mother nurses her baby every 15 minutes for a year and a half, and protects it from sharks. Dolphins, and their cousins the killer whales, seem to be interested in humans and friendly towards them.

The third segment of the film documents the expedition of a group of young people who sail into the Bermuda Triangle to try to establish a close personal relationship with dolphins in the open environment of the ocean. The dolphins respond to the sounds of an underwater piano, and for three days, humans and dolphins swim and play together.

The conclusion of the film raises questions about future relationships with these intelligent and apparently friendly creatures.

302

SUPPLEMENTARY INFORMATION:

The term "dolphin" can be confusing because there are two creatures that bear that name — one is a fish, the other is a mammal in the whale family. The dolphins featured in this film are mammals. Sometimes porpoises are referred to as dolphins, but this is inaccurate. The porpoise is a different aquatic mammal in the whale family.

Dolphins are a relatively old life form; they have existed for about 50 million years. Most dolphins are less than ten feet long, have pronounced beaks, and are equipped with large dorsal fins. They feed mostly on fish, and some types of dolphins have as many as 200 sharp teeth. In general, they travel in large schools and are gentle and sociable.

Captive dolphins have been trained to perform tricks to entertain visitors to marine parks, but recent research indicates that these animals are capable of far more profound and subtle intellectual activities. Some noted scientists believe that dolphins may well be more intelligent than human beings.

In recent years the U.S. Navy has trained dolphins to recover objects from the ocean floor; scientists at the Communication Research Institute have taught dolphins to repeat entire sentences and to count aloud in English (although the animals do not understand the meanings of the words they are parroting); dolphins have demonstrated a capability for abstract reasoning; and efforts are currently underway to utilize computers to create a new language of sounds which may allow humans and dolphins to communicate directly.

As scientist John Lilly has expressed it: "The whales and dolphins may have more to teach us than we have to teach them."

GROUP DISCUSSION QUESTIONS AND ACTIVITIES:

Assuming that dolphins are able to communicate abstract ideas among their kind from generation to generation, what kinds of things might we learn from this life form that has existed on earth for 50 million years?

Try to construct the first conversation that might take place between humans and dolphins. What sorts of questions might each party ask the other?

Discuss the kinds of joint projects that humans and dolphins might engage in for the benefit of both.

If humans are eventually able to develop a spoken language with which we can converse with dolphins, what other applications might we find for this type of language development?

303

The sperm whale has a brain six times larger than that of a human being. Is it possible that the intelligence of these mammals is so far superior to ours that they could not communicate with such primitive and dull-witted organisms as humans? How might this affect the ways in which we perceive ourselves and our relationship to other forms of life?

RELATED CENTRON FILMS/VIDEOCASSETTES

One Species Among Many
Animals of a Living Reef
Animals of Africa
Animals of Asia
Animals of Australia
Animals of North America
Animals of South America
Animals of the Arctic
Elementary Natural Science — The Gray
    Squirrel's Neighborhood
Elementary Natural Science — Owls
Elementary Natural Science — The Eastern Cottontail
Elementary Natural Science — Hawks
Elementary Natural Science — Songbirds
Elementary Natural Science — Small Predatory Mammals
Grassland Ecology — Habitats and Change
Cave Ecology
Lakes — Aging and Pollution
What Ecologists Do
Populations
Energy and Living Things

RELATED CENTRON SOUND FILMSTRIP PROGRAMS:

Environmental Awareness
Environmental Studies Series
Concepts in Ecology
Poetry of the Seasons

CENTRON FILMS
1621 w. 9th • box 687 • lawrence, kansas 66044 USA • 913/843-0400

DOLPHIN

Objectives

To observe and appreciate the intelligence, playfulness and life of the dolphin.

To consider the benefits from communication with another creature of equal or greater intelligence than human.

To explore the historical perspective of human/dolphin relationships.

Synopsis

For centuries we have believed we were the only ones on earth with a mind and soul . . . perhaps there are other such creatures.

Dolphins, like humans, are warm blooded, air-breathing and give birth to live young. They live in all the oceans of the world. Aristotle was the first to study the behavior and biology of the dolphin and recognize their intelligence. He noted they "careth for man and enjoyeth his music."

Dolphins were once land animals, and some 50 million years ago returned to the seas where they evolved streamlined aquatic bodies and highly developed brains. When, in recent years, the bottle-nosed dolphin was found to have a brain 30% larger than the human brain and every bit as complex, the U.S. Navy began experiments with dolphins. They found dolphins willing to assist in deep-sea experiments and that—with their highly developed sonar—they could locate objects in dark and murky waters. Some whales were trained to retrieve missiles from the ocean floor.

Buckminster Fuller, philosopher and global thinker, theorizes that since dolphins have been on earth for 50 million years they may, in their large brain, store information critical for human survival.

Most people first see dolphins in marine parks where they are trained to perform tricks. Rarely, however do these antics really demonstrate how intelligent these creatures may really be.

Unfortunately not all dolphins are held in high respect by humans. American tuna fisherman in their drive to net as many tuna as possible, "inadvertently" kill tens of thousands of dolphins each year. The dolphins are caught in the nets and drown. In Iki Japan, fishermen blame dolphins for a decrease in their fish catch and on several occasions have mercilessly slaughtered them.

The tragedy of some dolphins and the potential for greater understanding with others inspire filmmakers Michael Wiese and Hardy Jones to explore existing relationships between humans and dolphins. They visit Flipper Sea School in Florida where humans and dolphins are developing a language and where the dolphins have demonstrated their ability to reason abstractly. It is certain that the future of such learning experiments will hold benefits for both humans and dolphins.

But research has always taken place with captive dolphins. What about wild dolphins who live in the open seas? Even Jacques Cousteau had been unsuccessful in trying to film wild dolphins—they would swim away as soon as *Calypso* divers got into the water.

Wiese and Jones meet a treasure diver who tells them of a spot he knows where dolphins might be found. Since dolphins receive much of their information through sound—music may be a way of attracting dolphins to the divers.

An underwater piano is designed by Steve Gagne for this purpose. After many days of sailing in the Bahamas, the location is reached—but there are no dolphins in sight. Steve enters the water and begins playing chords and melodies on his piano. Suddenly, some 50-60 dolphins come swooping in to explore the piano and join their human friends in a spectacular underwater ballet. For three days the human swimmers find ways of relating to the dolphins—through movement and by playing flutes and clarinets to the dolphins through underwater speakers. This is the first time wild dolphins in play with humans have been documented on film.

The dolphins are indeed playful, graceful and fun and welcome the humans into their home. We have yet to discover what we may learn from these intelligent creatures who have been on earth so long, but there is every indication that they are willing to meet us half-way.

Applications

Communication What is the value of learning to communicate with a creature so different from ourselves? Could relating to dolphins somehow prepare us for communication with beings from outer space? How real do you think that possibility is? Discuss ways in which communication between humans and dolphins might take place. What constitutes communication? What might dolphins be able to tell us that would be of practical value to humans? Imagine the first conversation between humans and dolphins. Write it out. Do you think their language will be anything at all like human language? Carl Jung has said that "man is an enigma to himself. He lacks the means of comparison necessary for self-knowledge. The possibility of comparison and hence of self-knowledge would arise only if he could establish relations with quasi-human mammals inhabiting other stars" (or perhaps the seas?). What are similarities between humans and dolphins? What are the differences? Are there overlaps? How might the dolphin's perception of reality differ from human perception of reality?

Magazine and Newspaper Articles

Both *HARDWARE WARS* and *DOLPHIN* received a great deal of press coverage. Once articles of the film appeared in the major newspapers and magazines, the smaller ones picked up on it, felt they discovered it, and wrote articles of their own. Therefore, it's better to contact the larger publications first.

It's interesting how many different perspectives various writers may have on your work. I found that, after spending a year or two on a film, I had developed one point of view about it. But once the film was released and articles started appearing there were almost as many points of views as there were articles. Every reviewer or feature writer found something different to write about. Sometimes I'd be impressed by a writer's angle. Other times, I couldn't believe the stupidity of a writer's concern.

RollingStone

"ALL THE NEWS THAT FITS"

June 15th, 1978 · No. 267

'Hardware Wars' spoofs the Force

'Romance, rebellion and household appliances'

SAN FRANCISCO

HERE'S ONE *STAR Wars* spinoff George Lucas wasn't counting on: *Hardware Wars*, a thirteen-minute parody that is becoming the hottest short subject to hit the screen since Steve Martin's *The Absent-Minded Waiter*.

The film, made last fall on an $8000 budget by San Francisco writer/animator/actor Ernie Fosselius, was little more than a local laugh until Pyramid Films of Los Angeles picked up distribution rights and made 200 prints. Now, through a deal with United Artists Theatres, it will be shown in a dozen theaters in California.

Hardware Wars, which is coproduced by Michael Wiese and Laurel Polanick, takes the form of a "Coming Attractions" trailer for a "spectacular space saga of romance, rebellion and household appliances." The first scenes are of a toaster, a steam iron and an egg-beater doing intergalactic battle. The stars are Artie Deco, who resembles a vacuum cleaner; 4-Q-2, a British-accented Tin Man; Princess Anne-Droid, who wears fresh cinnamon rolls in her hair; Darph Nader, a heavy breather no one can understand; Augie "Ben" Doggie, "venerable member of the Red-Eye Knights," who fights with a luminous sword powered by flashlight batteries; Fluke Star-bucker, spacey boy wonder, and Ham Salad, a mercenary pilot who is found in a weird "fern bar" populated by a species known as "singles." Salad is the "intergalactic wise-ass," and in the heat of one battle, when the Princess scolds him, "You'll get us all killed!" he sneers: "Ex-CUUSE ME!" As the announcer promises, "You'll laugh! You'll cry! You'll kiss three bucks goodbye!"

The Wookie Monster, Fluke, Augie and Ham on their way to save Princess Anne-Droid

And what does George Lucas think of this? "He has a copy," said Fosselius, who in fact arranged for Lucas to have one. "I think he went over it frame by frame with his attorneys." Lucas, however, has no plans to sue. A spokesman for the director said Lucas thought the parody "was a cute film."

Fosselius, who is thirty-two and whose credits include animation work for *Sesame Street*, now plans to cash in on *Hardware Wars* merchandise. Aside from the usual T-shirts, toys and disco versions of the main theme, there's a watch "that tells the time, date and the amount the film's grossing."

—BEN FONG-TORRES

It's also disorienting if you believe everything you read. One day you may be touted as a cinematic genius. The next day you may read that your film is a waste of time and money and that the world would be better off if you quit making movies. You have to treat this great inflow of opinions like a game. And it is a game. A publicity game. Sure it's great if someone writes something nice about your film. But important thing is that they write something at all. (Sometimes a bad review can create more interest in a film than a good one.)

Set aside a specific amount of time to promote your film. (Include this in your budget as part of your job so you can get paid for it.) It could be a month or two. And then speak to anyone who can help publicize it: newspapers, magazines, TV and radio talk shows.

It's fun. When good interviewers ask good questions you will discover things about your film that you never knew. But after a while, you catch yourself saying the same things over and over. And then you may say things that you've heard others say. After a while you won't be able to find anything new to say. Soon after that, if you feel you've talked to the most influential media, it may be time to stop. Then, by the time you burn out, you can feel that you did as much as possible. Sometimes you can do interviews with syndicated columnists whose articles appear in dozens or even hundreds of other newspapers. This way you cover Maine to Oregon with one stop. Time the release of interviews and reviews so they will do the most good, like before your theatrical release or television broadcast. Otherwise you may waste your only shot. (They'll only write once about your film.)

(I've included a few of the articles about *DOLPHIN*. I thought they might be of interest to those readers who've spent the last hundred pages reading about *DOLPHIN* but have not seen it and have no idea what I've been talking about. At last count there were about 150 articles published on the film.)

New Film: DOLPHIN

By Win Murphy

ARISTOTLE SAID IT centuries ago: "Dolphins careth for man and enjoyeth his music." Filmmakers Michael Wiese and Hardy Jones have proven Aristotle correct.

In their new film, *DOLPHIN: A Human-Dolphin Celebration in the Open Sea,"* Wiese and Jones set out on an odyssey to photograph dolphins, not in typical amusement park tanks, but in their natural environment—the open sea. Remembering the words of Artistotle about dolphins enjoying man's music, they decided to try something no one else had—to find out if it was true that wild dolphins would respond to music.

Their expedition comprises the main body of their film, *DOLPHIN*. Joining the two filmmakers were Ric O'Feldman, trainer of the famed dolphin, Flipper; Steve Gagne, sound engineer who designed a special underwater piano for this unique experiment; Jack McKenney, underwater cinematographer for the film *The*

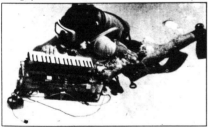

Deep as well as the TV special *The Wreck of the Andrea Doria;* underwater photographer James Hudnall, who photographed humpback whales for "National Geographic" and cameraman John Knoop.

The film begins with information on this sea mammal from ancient times in lore and legend to modern-day facts. We learn about the size of the dolphin brain (far bigger than a human's), the dolphin's memory and intelligence capabilities, facts about their sonar ability and dolphins' perception of eighty percent of tion's first try at communicating with dolphins through music is both disappointing and unsuccessful. But after search and research and contacting many dolphin experts,

their world through sound. We see dolphins in captivity; able and willing to communicate with man and to decifer abstract problems in what might well be called a new kind of dolphin math.

The main body of the film *DOLPHIN* is the exciting experiment with underwater musical sounds. Would they respond , as Artistotle indicated they do? The film takes us to Hawaii, where the expedi-

including John Lilly, they find a special sea spot off the Bahamas where dolphins romp freely and man rarely invades due to difficult navigational terrain. From their big, two-masted sailing ship, divers and cameramen submerge into the blue-blue Bahama waters and take us beneath the sea to the ocean floor, where curious but friendly dolphins sized up the intruders with their dolphin sonar ability, and decided it was okay to stay. Steve Gagne had difficulty at first with his specially designed, waterproof mini-piano, but modified it for ease of handling and then took it into the sea. Playing like a modern-day Lorilei, he attracted a few dolphins, then more and even more.

The high point of the film is the ballet-like swimming of the dolphins as they appear to dance and play to the music in graceful underwater choreography that Agnes DeMille would envy. They glide in twos, fours, and sixes, swooping and diving in rhythm and pattern in response to the new phenomena of underwater music. This particular area of ocean floor was fascinating; it looked like a vast, white-shag carpet, with clean white sand and no glimpse of seawead, shells or undersea life in sight. Contrasted to the brilliant

blues of the water, the dolphin ballet has the perfect setting for an underwater sequence of breathtaking beauty.

There are also some disturbing sequences; we see footage of many dolphins destroyed by tuna fishermen as well as the recent mass slaughter of dolphins at the hands of Japanese fishermen, leaving blood-soaked beaches as an aftermath of their massacre. The producers hope the film will serve to influence legislation leading to the protection of dolphins and whales at the next meeting of the International Whaling Commission in London.

Theme music for the film is a lyrical ballad called *Dolphin Song,* written and sung by expedition member, Morgan Smith, and Mary Earle. Earle also experimented with music by playing a flute on the boat and, with an underwater microphone, attracted and entertained the dolphins in the waters below. Shots from beneath the water looking up provide a dolphin's-eye view of the water surface and boats going by above.

DOLPHIN opens up in the mind of the movie-goer a dolphin consciousness and sense of respect and affection for this friendly sea creature with the perpetual smile on its face and untapped intelligence.

ISSUE NUMBER 18 — AUGUST 1979

Stephen Gagne plays the underwater piano he constructed in order to attract the elusive dolphin for the documentary film, "Dolphin."

'Dolphin' a film of intelligence, love

"Dolphin," directed by Hardy Jones and Michael Wiese. Produced by Wiese and written by Jones. Music composed and conducted by Basil Poledouris. Underwater piano built and played by Stephen Gagne. Showing through Thursday at the J Street Cinema.

Movie Review

By RICHARD SIMON
Staff Writer

The intrepid men and women aboard the William H. Albury have achieved what no other adventurers—not even Jacques Cousteau—have been able to do.

In a stretch of the Atlantic Ocean near Bermuda — a stretch made inhospitable by wind and tide constantly blowing and surging—they have danced with dolphins.

UNTIL that moment, the dolphin has remained for all of its millions of years aloof from mingling with man in the dolphin's natural habitat.

The achievement of the crew aboard the Albury is the high point of the film, "Dolphin," but is not its only distinction.

"Dolphin" stands both as a labor of love and as a film of intelligence.

MICHAEL Wise and Hardy Jones, two Bay Area filmmaker, started with more than a romantic urge to cavort with dolphins when they undertook the project.

They envisaged—like Jane Goodall with the chimpanzees of the African veldt—mingling with the dolphin in his natural environment.

They had a plan. Based on their knowledge that the dolphin perceives approximately 80 percent of his world through his hearing, they hoped to lure him with music.

FOR THAT purpose, they secured the help of Stephen Gagne, creater and performer of an underwater piano.

The experiment worked, and the interaction between the dolphins and the underwater pianist provides one of the many lighhearted moments in the film.

BUT THERE is more to the film than idyllic moments. The film begins with the tracing of the evolution from his pre-historic past to the present. For millions of years, a narrator says with gratitude, the dolphin had no natural enemies. It is only in the past 30 years that man has made himself the enemy of the mammal,

THERE ARE painful—but fortunately, brief—scenes Japanese fishermen entrapping masses of dolphins and then clubbing them to death—much in the manner of those Canadian fishermen who "harvest" harp seals annually. This is even more painful because the Japanese fishermen are not slaughtering the dolphin for monetary gain but to exterminate what they consider a threat.

EQUALLY disturbing are the scenes that reveal the dolphins caught by fishermen intent on the tuna. A cruel anomaly of nature is that tuna swim beneath the dolphins, and fishermen catch an inordinate number of dolphins while "harvesting" tuna.

There has been some progress in separating the catches, but not enough to end the willy-nilly destruction of the dolphin.

MORE THAN sentiment is at issue. As Buckminster Fuller argues, the dolphin may be as intelligent as man. He may help man to find new and better ways to live upon the planet. The Navy, in fact, is undertaking some projects based on its awareness of the extraordinary powers of the dolphins.

LATER THIS summer, the film will be shown at a meeting in London of the International Whaling Commission in the hope that it might influence legislation to protect both the dolphin and his cousin, the whale.

If the commission can be moved by a film, this one should move it.

309

A PBS-TV Special Probes Man's Best Underwater Friend

Dolphin. If the universe were made up of opposites surely the opposite of shark would be dolphin. As if to fool us, the dolphin wears a dorsal fin on its back, which knifes through the water in the same way as does its menacing cousin's. But as if to give us a clue to their opposing natures, the shark wears its tail vertically and the dolphin wears its horizontally, as do all sea mammals. And, as if to make us laugh at the difference, the dolphin wears a perpetual smile.

Although the folk lore of man and dolphin's proximity on the high seas in times of emergency abound, in point of fact there is very little on film to document this strange rapport. Where the shark likes to come in for a nudge or even an attack, and can be baited more easily than perhaps any other creature, the dolphin is among the shyest and most skittish of beings, and the only thing which ever seems to work in baiting them is to hit them where they live: sensitivity and playfulness.

Nothing seems to delight a dolphin more than playing in a bow wake, or leaping at a highspeed run right out of the water as if for sheer sport. Dolphins are long since famous for their cooperation and trainability in captivity. But efforts to get close to dolphins in their own environment have proven illusive and frustrating, perhaps because those who have attempted contact have forgotten this playful, intuitive approach.

That is until, "Dolphin," a stunning and sensitive film by Hardy Jones and Michael Wiese, with underwater footage by Jim Hudnall and Jack McKenny. (See McKenny's story "Corrected Underwater Optics" in this section) shown as a one-hour PBS special sponsored by Atlantic Richfield in August, 1980. "For centuries we have be-

lieved we were the only ones on earth with a mind and soul . . . perhaps there are other such creatures," read their flyer. And their film is what could be considered preliminary proof that indeed, they are right.

There is something else which has always appealed to animals, at least as far as legend is concerned, and that is "music hath charms to soothe the savage breast." Perhaps on the premise that music is in fact the universal language, Wiese and Jones set out to determine whether the music of humans could tempt a response out of this whimsical sea creature.

Steve Gagne , a former rock and roll engineer, designed and built the first underwater piano, and plunged into the depths, swimming as he played. The result was as fanciful as it sounds — the dolphins came. They loved it. They even seemed to dance to it. They almost seemed to reach out for this acoustical message.

Hardy Jones is a journalist, who has spent considerable time researching dolphins, and the precarious situation certain groups of the species are in — notably those near the island of Iki in Japan. Since his collaborative effort with Wiese, he has gone on to do "Island At The Edge," a film documenting his experiences while living with the Japanese fishermen who brutally beat the dolphins, who, they claim, are cutting seriously into their own food supply. "They don't come off culprits," explained Jones of the Fishermen. "They have no understanding that the dolphins are special. They feel, 'They have big brains? So what?' "

And he has another film in the works, to be called "A Year With The Dolphins," for which he says "Dolphin" serves as an introduction. While "Dolphin" broke new

310

ground, he would now like to add two new elements to the open-ocean dolphin work. One, a scientific component, a means of testing and proving some of the success recorded in the first film. And two, he would like to do a film with a much faster pace, and sell it to a network. And indeed the leisurely pace of "Dolphin" is perhaps one of the elements that made it suitable for PBS.

Michael Wiese is a San Francisco filmmaker, who is best known for his extremely popular short, "Hardware Wars." He has travelled the world extensively, and who in the early 70s optioned Japanese novelist Kobo Abe's book "Inter Ice Age 4," an extraordinary aquatic science fiction tale involving dolphins. "Actually the beginning of my interest in dolphins was even before that," he explained. "In 1969, I was living on the beach in San Francisco and saw a very sick dolphin up on the beach. I don't know what came over me, but I empathized, and I knelt down beside the dolphin and started stroking its head and saying inwardly 'I really hope you make it out there, and here's some strength.' The dolphin started making some sounds, almost as if it were saying 'thank you' — it kind of shocked me and frightened me at the same time. We pushed the dolphin back into the water and he made it back out to sea. The thing was — did it really communicate to me? Did I make it up, or what's going on with dolphins anyway? From there I went to all the marine worlds and read all (Dr. John) Lilly's books.

"Hardy was the catalyst for me," Wiese continued. "I don't think I would have done a dolphin film on my own. He brought to it the intellect, the understanding, the contacts, and was a real go-getter as far as lining things up. My job — I raised most of the money for it, brought in most of the investors, and really saw to the completing of the film, the picture and the music. He's come to this from journalism, from investigative reporting. And I come to it from filmmaking." Obviously, the combination of skills was a highly successful one.

Since the object of the film was to make contact with the dolphins in the wild, a voyage to appropriate waters was crucial to the project. The story of the voyage is the story of the film, as told by Wiese, and by Morgan Smith, another expedition member, whose major contribution — a firm conviction in the power of intuition — proved to be another crucial element in the making of "Dolphin."

On Location — How did the project begin?

Michael — We started by looking at dolphin films. We thought for a while that we could compile other people's material. But we learned that there really wasn't much of anything — Cousteau hadn't done it at that time — even Hudnall's stuff of dolphins was something like 50 feet away.

On Location — Why did you feel the need to study the dolphins in open water?

Michael — Once you explore dolphins in marine parks, you say well this is sort of a false situation. What are dolphins like in the wild? Would they relate to us? They seem to be real curious about us, and want to interact with us, when we're feeding them fish, and when they're dependent upon us for survival but what about on their own turf?

On Location — Do you think it made a difference to the trip that women came along?

Michael — At first there was a female energy missing from the trip. There were 11 men, and only one woman who had planned to go. Then Morgan came along, and came right out and said, "I think this is a very chauvinistic trip, do you have any women going?" And I said well it's going to be rough, and I just work with men . . . Hardy and I were bugged by this thing. We were scrambling to get our money. We were told about this woman who had a dream about dolphins, and I said, Oh well, whatever it takes. She dreams about dolphins? Great. I don't care.

Morgan — They thought I was bogus. They thought I was a 55-year-old fruitcake.

Michael — But, I had heard stories that dolphins responded to women in a different way than they responded to men. It was like — well, she's got a good point there.

On Location — Morgan, what do you think you added to the trip?

Morgan — Hardy was kind of being the hardcore intellectual talking about how this film was going to take place. I remember him talking about the idea of setting up a computer language, and reaching dolphins that way, and a very intellectual approach to dolphins. And I remember this little bulb in my head, going, "That's not how it's going to happen. That may be a by-product of the intuitive communication, but they're here to teach us intuition. We're here to be children in their presence."

311

On Location — To ask some nuts-and-bolts questions — how did you get your film on PBS?

Michael — PBS was an extremely frustrating system to work with, and I had much higher expectations going in. They had run a whale special, which was their second highest rated show ever — it had tremendous public response. I was certain that, since our show was similar in a way, and since we had such marvelous footage and productions qualities as high as that, that we would find that kind of acceptance. Well, I don't think it has much to do with the show — it had to do with the whole system.

On Location — What would have made PBS more interested in really getting behind the project?

Michael — The problem was that PBS had not funded it. It was all privately funded, so they had no investment. If they had had even a little money in it at the *production* level, —

On Location — They would have seen to their investment. So they really didn't help with promotion?

Michael — It's Atlantic Richfield who did a tremendous promotion campaign, doing half-page ads in TV Guide in 13 major cities, which another corporation would probably not do. And this lead to PBS sending elaborate press kits to over 600 newspapers and magazines.

On Location — Aside from the PBS airing, are there other markets for the film?

Michael — There are many. The pattern went like this. First, we showed it to one market — we did a run in San Francisco theaters and at cities mostly throughout the West. It did well in ocean cities, and seemed to drop off inland.

Second. We got non-theatrical distribution with Films Inc. and also arranged distribution in Canada, at English-speaking schools.

Third. We did pay TV. Show Time was interested originally, but when they dropped out we found some smaller pay stations to take it.

Fourth was the PBS test run. Fifth was the PBS national broadcast, which puts us in the position to go nationally in syndication — that would be sixth. Seventh is foreign TV sales, and eighth, further down the line, will be video disk.

You've got to think of it as a pie, and that you're going to get income from each area. A ninth area that is starting to pick up is stock footage, showing excerpts from "Dolphin" on different shows — "Mysteries of the Sea" (see article this section) was one. "Amazing Animals" is interested, as is "American Sportsman."

On Location — Will you make all your money back on "Dolphin"?

Michael — It looks like "Dolphin" will make its money back over a much longer period of time than we imagined. But it's done phenomenally well in foreign markets — we've sold it to BBC, Ireland, Switzerland, Germany, South Africa, Japan, Australia, New Zealand, Hong Kong and it's been sold to the Armed Forces Network. And then I cut a children's version of it called "The Wonder of the Dolphin" with all new footage which is being shown in schools.

On Location — What do you think was the smartest thing you did during the making of "Dolphin"?

Michael — We didn't ask others whether we were right or wrong. Had we asked other people they would have told us our approach was all wrong. Fortunately, we didn't know!

Morgan — There was no mistake in that.

On Location — Did you spend time with dolphin experts?

Michael — Yes, we still felt we'd find somebody who had already done it. In the process of talking to all the experts about it — we spent a long time with Lilly, we talked to Lou Herman, Steve Letterwood, a number of people who are dolphin experts. But we were learning more about experts than we were about dolphins. And I had this great desire to really be with dolphins and see what that was like, and see if we could look into their eyes and see if we could get behind that eye and find out what was going on with them.

On Location — How did you think you'd be able to do this?

Michael — We needed a way to relate to them, and we heard that Paul Winter and Paul Spong had played music to orcas, and we thought well, music is certainly going to be the way. They're acoustical creatures, with sonar with which they can communicate long distances underwater. At that point Steve Gagne. happened into our lives. He said how about an underwater piano? Would you be interested? And we said 'Oh, yea!' So he built this thing, and it went through several evolutions. It was the craziest thing. We tested it out, and it was totally mad!

Morgan — By the time we were in the Bahamas (where the voyage took place) he literally, from the time we boarded that boat, spent every spare minute down below tinkering with it.

Michael — It was at the last minute he actually got it together. It's interesting, I'm thinking now about how humor kept coming into it. It was totally ridiculous. Innocent, childlike. You know, a ship of fools, going out in the Bahamas with an underwater piano, and a mad scientist, and a rock and roll ex-engineer.

Morgan — On the hunch of a treasure diver.

Michael — That was the other thing! We were told by a treasure diver, Bob Marks, who appears briefly in the film, who wrote books such as "Diving For Pleasure And Treasure" — kind of a pirate character — that we would find dolphins if we went out to this area. After we were out there four or five days, and we hand't seen one dolphin yet, I started saying, well let's talk about Bob Marks for a minute. Maybe he just wanted to send us off into this dangerous water.

Morgan — And maybe he's back there laughing.

Michael — And here we are, high rolling a lot of money getting this expedition out here, investors . . .

On Location — But he was right! It sounds like there were two parts to the voyage — first the anxiety! Then the successful contact.

Morgan — During the first part, the closer we got to the actualization, the heavier it got, the more intense the wondering.

Michael — Somehow I guess on the inside, my hopes couldn't have been greater. But on the outside, you know the rational part, I'm saying Michael who are you trying to kid!

Morgan — Well, what's at stake begins to enter your mind.

On Location — But you both trusted your communicating abilities. Michael you just went ahead and talked to the dolphin on the beach. And you, Morgan, you went ahead and tried transmitting mental images to the dolphins at the Flipper Sea School.

Michael — Well nobody said you shouldn't try that. In fact as the film progressed, we were really willing to try anything. And I think innocence had a lot to do with the big pay off.

Morgan — I do too. There is one way to prove it, ultimately, which is, when we went out to meet the dolphins, and to make a film about them, it was an exchange. We weren't just going out there for a vacation. We actually had something we were offering them, and they came.

Michael — We were so on purpose to make this film.

Morgan — We didn't have any other agenda. We didn't have jobs to do, we were totally there for them. Whereas other people have gone out on pleasure cruises, to see the dolphins, or to swim with them, and the dolphins have not come. So I think there is proof, or at least enough to my satisfaction. We had to make a leap of faith.

On Location — What's an example that convinces you that you communicated with the dolphins?

Michael — I saw a shark and the dolphins intervened between me and the shark, which was phenomenal. It was one of my first dives with the dolphins. I swam in the water and I was saying — sort of like my communications with the stranded dolphin on the beach — "we're here to make a film about dolphins, we really need your help, it's going to be your movie . . ." I was going through all this kind of thing, and this shark darts into the picture. I think it's a dolphin at first, but it's kind of darting around, and it scares me to death.

And I could tell at that point that the dolphins really picked up on my emotional state, because a whole wall of them moved in, eight or 10 of them, and kept between me and the shark, I was terrified, trying to get back to the boat — and the dolphins kept the shark away from me. We got some great footage that day! ●

By MARA PURL

On Location®
The Film & Videotape Production Magazine

OCTOBER 1978

New/Age

VOL. 4, NO. 5

Film/Bud Brainard

Radiance: The Experience of Light

"...The message that we are all radiant beings reaches more than the intellect—it rushes directly to the heart..."

When five hundred people buy out a theater to see a 22-minute film, one should take note. That many people packed into the New Varsity Theater in Palo Alto, California, to see the new film, *Radiance: The Experience of Light*. Hundreds more were turned away at the door.

The film is an exploration of light, from the strictly physical radiation of the sun and stars to the spiritual glow of saints and mystics. A beautiful blending of nature, art, gentle music, and soft narration leads the viewer to discover light not only in the environment and in the spiritual world of holy people, but within all living creatures. Therein lies the impact of the film. The message that we are all radiant beings reaches more than the intellect—it rushes directly to the heart.

Radiance has been a long time in the making. Ten years ago Dorothy Fadiman, the writer, director, and narrator of the film, had a striking experience of inner light. In her own words, "An incredible illumination flooded my body. Every cell seemed electrified. I had a pure sense of being connected to the universe. I felt a responsibility to communicate this to people from then on."

True to her word and vision, Fadiman began compiling accounts of other people who had similar illuminations. Over the

years, she gathered a wealth of material on the subject. Then, two years ago, she joined forces with a gifted filmmaker, Michael Wiese, whose previous films had earned her a number of awards and drawn such notable supporters as Salvidor Dali and the American Film Institute. Working together, Fadiman and Weise developed the multimedia production *Do Saints Really Glow?* Shown at a wide variety of conferences and symposia, this production generated a devoted following. Adding the talents and contributions of other photographers, artists, and filmmakers, the original show *Do Saints Really Glow?* evolved into the film version of *Radiance*.

The film itself is a striking visionary experience, but its impact reaches far beyond sights and sounds. The key to the film's success is that audiences *feel* the production as much as they see and hear it. Marilyn Ferguson, editor of *Brain/ Mind Bulletin*, called the film "a peak experience": "I was moved to tears by its beauty and authenticity," she says. "It's an aesthetic and spiritual high if there ever was one."

■

Radiance: The Experience of Light is available from Pyramid Distributors (Box 1048, Santa Monica CA 90406). Rental costs $40.00; a print sells for $350.00.

Bud Brainard is a free-lance writer and medical researcher at George Washington University in Washington, D.C.

LIMITED PARTNERSHIP AGREEMENT

The Limited Partnership Agreement

This is one version of the Limited Partnership Agreement. Some versions run dozens of pages, others are relatively short, like the sample that follows. *This sample is not intended for legal purpose but only as an example of a structure for film financing.* Consult your lawyer to design an agreement for your own purposes.

The Limited Partnership Agreement

This Limited Partnership Agreement is entered into as of January 1, 1984.

By this Agreement the parties form a Limited Partnership and agree to the terms and conditions of this Agreement.

ARTICLE 1

General Partners. The partners are:

Limited Partners. The names and addresses of the Limited Partners are set forth on Exhibit A, attached hereto.

ARTICLE 2

The name of the partnership shall be: *BIG GROSS PRODUCTIONS.*

ARTICLE 3

The purpose of the partnership shall be to produce and distribute the motion picture, *THE BIG GROSS*, and to engage in all activities reasonably incidental thereto.

ARTICLE 4

Each Limited Partner irrevocably constitutes and appoints each General Partner as his or her attorney-in-fact, in his or her name, place, and stead, to make, execute, acknowledge, record, and file any of the following documents:

1. The original and any modification or amendment to the certificate of limited partnership and any other instrument that may be required to be recorded or filed by the partnership; and

2. All documents that may be required to effectuate the dissolution and termination of the partnership; and

3. A fictitious business name statement.

It is expressly understood and agreed by each limited partner that the grant of this power of attorney is coupled with an interest and shall survive the delivery of an assignment of the limited partnership interest.

In the event of any conflict between the provisions of this limited partnership agreement or any amendment to it and any document executed, acknowledged, sworn to, or filed by a general partner under this power of attorney, the limited partnership agreement and its amendments shall govern.

ARTICLE 5

An amendment to the certificate of limited partnership may be signed, personally or by an attorney-in-fact, by:

1. A general partner and the new limited partner if the amendment is caused by the addition of a new limited partner;

2. A general partner, the substituted limited partner, and the assigning limited partner if the amendment is caused by the retirement, death, or insanity of a general partner and the partnership business is continued.

ARTICLE 6

The partnership's principal place of business shall be at *BIG GROSS PRODUCTION CENTER, 1234 Video Lane, San Rafael, CA., or such other place as the general partners determine in the future.*

ARTICLE 7

The partnership shall begin as of the date of this agreement and shall continue until the first of the following events:

1. January 1, 1994;

2. The distribution, sale, or abandonment of all partnership properties and assets;

3. The election pursuant to Article 23 by the limited partners to terminate the partnership;

4. The election by the general partners to terminate the partnership.

5. The resignation, death, bankruptcy, insolvency, or incompetency of the general partners, unless a successor is elected by all the limited partners.

ARTICLE 8

Contribution to capital shall be in units of Five Thousand Dollars ($5000); the minimum permitted contribution shall be one unit.

Each of the limited partners has contributed the amount of cash set forth opposite his/her name in Exhibit B, attached hereto.

ARTICLE 9

Limited partners shall not be required to contribute any additional capital to the partnership.

ARTICLE 10

The general partners shall have the right to admit additional limited partners.

ARTICLE 11

An individual capital account shall be maintained for each partner. Each partner's capital account shall consist of his or her original capital contribution increased by any additional capital contributions and his or her share of partnership profits, and decreased by distributions in reduction of partnership capital and his or her share of partnership losses.

ARTICLE 12

If any limited partner shall, with the general partners' prior consent, make any loan to the partnership or advance money on its behalf, the loan or advance shall not increase the lending partner's capital account, entitle the lending partner to any greater share of partnership distributions, or subject him or her to any greater proportion of partnership losses. The amount of the loan or advance shall be a debt owed by the partnership to the lending partner, repayable on the terms and conditions and bearing interest at the rate agreed on by the lending partner and the general partner.

ARTICLE 13

Subject to Article 16, the partnership's net profits shall be credited 50% to the general partners.

The remaining 50% shall be divided as follows: a) For each $5000 contributed by a limited partner he or she shall receive 5% of the remaining 50% of the net profits (or 2.5% of the total net profits).

b) If the General Partners do not require the total budget of $100,000 to be raised through limited partners' contributions due to additional funds being raised by the general partners from other sources such as grants, advances by distributors, networks, and sponsoring corporations, etc., then limited partners shall receive a bonus equal to one-half (1/2) of the profits earned by the unsold limited partnership shares with the remaining one-half (1/2) retained by the general partners.

The losses of the partnership shall be charged to the limited partners in proportion to each partner's capital account.

ARTICLE 14

The partnership's net profit or net loss shall be determined by the accountant who regularly audits the partnership books, in accordance with generally accepted accounting principles, as soon as practicable after the close of the calendar year.

ARTICLE 15

Distributions of partnership profits shall be limited to those amounts that the general partners shall from time to time determine. Any such distribution shall be in proportion to the partners' shares in the partnership's net profits.

ARTICLE 16

No general partner shall be entitled to any share of partnership profits until each limited partner has received from the partnership distribution in an aggregate amount equal to his or her total partnership contributions.

In the event of dissolution, the partners shall continue to share profits and losses during the period of liquidation in the same proportions as before. Proceeds from the liquidation of the partnership assets shall be applied in the following order:

1. Payment to creditors of the partnership, not including payment to limited partners on account of their contributions or to general partners;

319

2. If the distributions to each limited partner under Article 16 have not in the aggregate equalled the total capital contributions of each limited partner, there shall be distributed to each limited partner an amount equal to the difference between the sum of the distributions under Article 16 and each partner's total capital contributions;

3. Payments to general partners other than for capital and profits;

4. After the payments called for herein have been made, the balance shall be divided equally between the general and limited partners. Each limited partner's share of such distribution shall be in proportion to his or her share of the total contributions to capital made by limited partners.

ARTICLE 17

The liability of each limited partner for partnership losses shall in no event exceed the aggregate amount of that limited partner's capital contributions required by this agreement and any additional contributions actually made.

ARTICLE 18

At all times during the term of the partnership, and beyond that term if the general partners deem it necessary, the general partners shall keep or cause to be kept books of account in which each partnership transaction shall be entered fully and accurately. All partnership books of account, together with executed copies of the certificate of limited partnership, the fictitious business name statement, this limited partnership agreement, and the amendments to any of these documents, shall be kept at the partnership's principal office and shall be available during reasonable business hours for inspection and examination by the partners or their representatives, who shall have the right to make copies of any of those books and documents at their own expense.

ARTICLE 19

At the end of each calendar year the books shall be closed and statements reflecting the financial condition of the partnership and its net profit or net loss shall be prepared by the accountants that the general partners shall, in their sole judgment, employ at the partnership's expense. Copies of the financial statements shall be given to all partners.

ARTICLE 20

The general partners shall deliver to each limited partner, within 45 days after the end of each partnership taxable year, a statement of affairs that shall include:

1. A balance sheet and profit and loss statement of the partnership as of the close of the taxable year.

2. A statement showing the capital account of each partner as of the close of the taxable year and the distribution, if any, made to each partner during the year; and

3. The amount of partnership income reportable by each partner, or the amount of partnership loss deductible by each partner, for federal and California income tax purposes for the taxable year.

At any time during the term of the partnership, limited partners with a majority interest in the partnership capital may, at their discretion, require an audit of the partnership books at the expense of the partnership, by certified public accountants selected by those limited partners; provided, however, that not more than one such audit shall be made during any taxable year of the partnership.

ARTICLE 21

The partnership business shall be managed by the general partners. Limited partners shall have no right to transact any business on its behalf.

ARTICLE 22

The general partners, without prior written consent or ratification of all the partners, shall have no authority to:

1. Do any act in contravention of the certificate of limited partnership.

2. Do any act which would make it impossible to carry on the ordinary business of the partnership;

3. Confess a judgment against the partnership;

4. Possess partnership property or assign a general partner's rights in specific partnership property, for other than a partnership purpose;

5. Admit a person as a general partner.

ARTICLE 23

Any of the following actions shall require approval of all partners possessing an aggregate interest of 70% or more in the capital of the partnership:

1. Removal of a general partner.

2. Termination of the partnership.

3. Amendment of this agreement.

ARTICLE 24

One or more partnership bank accounts shall be established and checks on the accounts shall be signed by any one of the general partners or their designated agent. The general partners are authorized to execute standard bank documentation to establish these accounts on the partnership's behalf.

ARTICLE 25

None of the general partners shall be liable to any limited partner because of any act or failure to act if the act or omission is within the scope of the authority conferred on general partners by this agreement or by law and does not constitute malfeasance or misfeasance. Without limiting the foregoing, the general partners shall not be personally liable for the return of any other contribution to the partnership made by any limited partner.

ARTICLE 26

The general and limited partners, either individually or collectively, may participate in other business ventures of every kind, whether or not those other business ventures compete with the partnership, except the distribution or any other exploitation of the motion picture.

ARTICLE 27

On the death, disablement, resignation, or removal of a general partner, the partnership business shall be continued by the remaining general partner. The executor, guardian, or other successor to the partnership interest of the former general partner shall be a limited partner.

ARTICLE 28

On the death of a limited partner, his or her executor or administrator shall have all the rights of a limited partner for the purpose of settling his or her estate or, if his or her limited partnership interest is held in joint tenancy, the right and liabilities of the deceased joint tenant shall pass to the surviving joint tenant.

ARTICLE 29

The general partners may assign, pledge, encumber or otherwise transfer all or any part of his or her interest as a general partner in the partnership.

ARTICLE 30

A limited partner may not sell, assign, or transfer any part of his or her partnership interest smaller than four units, as defined in Article 8, and only after complying with the following requirements:

A. Transfer of a limited partner's interest shall be by a written instrument in form and substance satisfactory to the general partners; and

B. A counterpart of the instrument of transfer, executed and acknowledged by the limited partner and accepted by his or her assignee shall be filed with the partnership; and

C. By written notice setting forth the purchaser's name and the terms on which the interest is to be sold offers the general partners the opportunity to purchase the interest or portion thereof that is offered for sale on the same terms within seven (7) days.

If neither general partner exercises the right to purchase the interest, that right shall be given to the limited partners for an additional 14-day period, beginning on the day that the general partners' right to purchase expires. Each of the limited partners shall have the right to purchase, on the same terms, a part of the interest of the offering partner in the proportion that his or her capital account bears to the total capital accounts of all the partners who wish to participate in the purchase; provided, however, that the participating partners may not, in the aggregate, purchase less than the entire amount offered for sale by the selling partner.

If neither general partner nor the limited partners exercises their rights to purchase the interest, the offering partner may, after twenty-one (21) days from the date the notice is given and on the terms and conditions stated in the notice, sell or exchange his or her partnership interest to the purchaser named in the notice.

ARTICLE 31

No limited partner has the right to demand or receive property other than cash in return for his contribution.

324

ARTICLE 32

The partnership agreement and any amendment thereto may be executed in several counterparts and all so executed shall constitute one agreement which shall be binding upon the parties hereto, notwithstanding that all of the parties are not signatory to the original or the same counterpart.

ARTICLE 33

Any dispute or controversy arising under this agreement or in connection with the winding up of the partnership business shall be settled by arbitration. In any such dispute, counsel for the parties shall act as arbitrators. In the event counsel cannot reach a resolution of the dispute within twenty-one (21) days of the date the dispute is submitted to them for arbitration, they shall select a third arbitrator. If no agreement on the third arbitrator exists, a third arbitrator shall be selected by the Arbitration Committee of the American Arbitration Association. Arbitration shall be held in San Francisco or any other place agreed upon by all parties to the dispute.

Any dispute over arbitrability may be decided by the arbitrators.

Any partner may enforce the award rendered in any court of competent jurisdiction.

Any submission to arbitration as herein provided shall be accompanied by all records, papers, correspondence, bills of accounts, and all other pertinent or relevant exhibits respecting the presentation of the case.

IN WITNESS WHEREOF, the parties to this limited partnership agreement have executed it effective as of the day and year first above written.

GENERAL PARTNERS

LIMITED PARTNERS

325

EXHIBIT A

General Partners

Limited Partners

EXHIBIT B

CONTRIBUTIONS TO CAPITAL

Name	Amount	No. of Units

FOREIGN TELEVISION "DEAL MEMO"

Foreign Television 'Deal Memo'

Sale No: 667
Salesman: Swifty
Date: October 12, 1983

Market: United Kingdom
Station: BBC
Licensee: British Broadcasting Corporation

Title: 'BIG GROSS', one hour special
B/W or Color: Color, 16mm
Language: English

License Fee: $US 15,000

Payable as follows: Due and payable in full upon signature of agreement.

Term of License commences: January 1, 1984, or on the date of the first telecast of a picture, whichever first occurs, **and terminates:** one year thereafter.

Episode No. or Title: 'THE BIG GROSS'

Original Telecasts: 1
Repeat Telecasts: 0
Total Telecasts: 1

First Playdate: Now scheduled for January 1984

Ship Attn: BBC Television, London Heathrow Airport
Address:

Via: Air Collect **Special Instructions:** None

Promotion Material To:＿＿＿＿＿ **From:**＿＿＿＿＿

327

Remarks: 1) print costs and M&E track included in the license fee, 2) BBC has option of rerun at 50% of original license fee, within license term, 3) BBC will issue its own standard contract and forward it as soon as possible.

Licensor Signed:

Licensee Signed:

STOCK FOOTAGE LICENSE

Stock Footage License

Michael Wiese
Michael Wiese Film Productions
Box 406
Westport, CT, 06881

Re: *'THE BIG GROSS'*
January 1, 1984

Dear Michael:

The following confirms our agreement (the 'Agreement') with respect to certain film material (the 'Footage') which *BEST PRODUCTIONS* may select for use in the motion picture tentatively entitled *'The Making of The Big Gross'* (the 'Picture'):

1. You (hereafter referred to as 'Owner') warrant that the Footage subject to this license agreement, and described in subparagraph (a) below, is owned by you and that you have the absolute and unencumbered right to grant to *BEST PRO-DUCTIONS* all rights granted herein.

(a) Excerpts from *'THE BIG GROSS'*

2. Owner agrees to make available to *BEST PRODUCTIONS* respective positive prints and duplicating material of all Footage designated by *BEST PRODUCTIONS*. *BEST PRODUCTIONS* agrees to pay all laboratory charges and duplicating costs in connection therewith and shall be billed directly by the applicable laboratory.

3. Within 60 days, after *BEST PRODUCTIONS* shall have received an answer print of the Picture, *BEST PRODUCTIONS* shall furnish Owner with a schedule describing the Footage and the number of feet thereof actually incorporated by *BEST*

329

PRODUCTIONS into the Picture. Said schedule (Schedule 'A') shall be attached to our respective copies of this license agreement and shall be a part thereof.

4. With respect to the Footage hereunder actually incorporated by *BEST PRODUCTIONS* into the Picture, Owner grants to *BEST PRODUCTIONS* the non-exclusive right forever and throughout the universe to use and incorporate the same into the Picture with the right perpetually and throughout the universe and in all languages to reproduce by any art or method now known or hereafter devised, including film and tape, and to record, perform, broadcast and project without limitation as to the number of times and by any known or hereafter devised method, the Footage in and in connection with the theatrical or non-theatrical television, radio, publishing and any other form or presentation of the Picture in any media and for any purpose and in connection with the advertising, publicizing and exploitation of the Picture. Without limiting the generality of the foregoing, *BEST PRODUCTIONS* shall have the right to edit, interpolate or use the Footage in any manner whatsoever in connection with the Picture, including, without limitation, the right to synchronize music, voices, sounds, or any other portion of the sound track of the Picture, with the Footage or any portion thereof as *BEST PRODUCTIONS* in its sole and complete discretion shall determine.

5. Owner will indemnify, defend and hold *BEST PRODUCTIONS*, its parent, affiliates, subsidiaries, agents, representative, and associates, and the officers, directors, and employees of each of them harmless from and against all losses, costs, damages, judgements, liabilities and expense (including, without limitation, attorney's fees and costs and any payments that may be due any music publisher, writer, musician, director, actor, union, guild or other party) arising from all claims whatsoever and whenever brought, which may be brought directly or indirectly upon *BEST PRODUCTIONS* use of the Footage.

330

6. Upon condition that Owner shall fully perform all of the services required to be performed by Owner hereunder, Producer shall accord Owner on-screen credit, substantially in the form of *'Additional photography courtesy of The Big Gross, a film by Michael Wiese'*. No casual or inadvertent failure to comply with the provisions of this Paragraph nor any failure by third parties to comply with their agreements with Producer shall constitute a breach of this Agreement. Owner shall be limited to Owner's remedy at law for damages, if any, and shall not have the right to terminate or rescind this Agreement or to in any way enjoin or restrain the production, distribution, advertising or exploitation of the Picture.

7. In full payment for the rights herein granted to *BEST PRODUCTIONS* and for the warranty of the Owner herein contained, *BEST PRODUCTIONS* agrees to pay to Owner and Owner agrees to accept the following: Two Thousand Dollars ($2000.00) for up to eighty (80) 16mm feet of Footage actually incorporated by *BEST PRODUCTIONS* into the final answer print of the Picture.

8. *BEST PRODUCTIONS* agrees to make a minimum payment of $2000 (for specified Footage under 80 feet) on or before January 15, 1984 to Owner. Any footage beyond 80 feet shall be charged to *BEST PRODUCTIONS* at $25 per 16mm foot.

Very truly yours,

AGREED TO AND ACCEPTED:

OWNER:

BEST PRODUCTIONS

331

FILM DISTRIBUTORS

These contact lists are very transitory. They could very well have changed by the time you read this. Companies come and go, move locations and change phone numbers very quickly. Names of executives are not listed as they come and go even more frequently. You might try asking for the "director of acquisitions", "director of programming" or "marketing director". These lists should give you a broad range of contacts from which you can begin your search for distribution. Good luck. Now go get 'em.

ABC CIRCLE FILMS, 2040 Avenue of the Stars, 5th Floor, Los Angeles, CA 90067, (213) 557-6860

ALIVE, 8271 Melrose Avenue, Los Angeles, CA 90046, (213) 852-1100

ATLANTIC ENTERTAINMENT GROUP, 8255 Sunset Boulevard, Los Angeles, CA 90046-2400, (213) 650-2500

BUENA VISTA/TOUCHSTONE, 500 S. Buena Vista Street, Burbank, CA 91521, (818) 840-1000

CANNON GROUP, INC., 640 San Vicente Boulevard, Los Angeles, CA 90048, (213) 658-2100

CINECOM INTERNATIONAL FILMS, 1250 Broadway, 33rd Floor, New York, NY 10019, (212) 239-8360

CINEPLEX ODEON CORPORATION, 1925 Century Park East, Suite 300, Los Angeles, CA 90067, (213) 553-5307

CINETEL FILMS, INC., 9200 Sunset Boulevard, Suite 1215, Los Angeles, CA 90069, (213) 550-1067

333

COLUMBIA PICTURES INC., Columbia Plaza, Burbank, CA 91505, (818) 954-6000

CROWN INTERNATIONAL PICTURES, INC., 8701 Wilshire Boulevard, Beverly Hills, CA 90211, (213) 657-6700

DE LAURENTIIS ENTERTAINMENT GROUP, 8670 Wilshire Boulevard, Beverly Hills, CA 90211, (213) 854-7000. Also: 720 Fifth Avenue, Suite 100, New York, NY 10019, (212) 399-7700

EXPANDED ENTERTAINMENT, 2222 S. Barrington, Los Angeles, CA 90064, (213) 473-6701

FOX INC., 10201 W. Pico Boulevard, Los Angeles, CA 90035, (213) 277-2211. Also: P.O. Box 900, Beverly Hills, CA 90213

HEMDALE FILM CORPORATION, 1118 N. Wetherly Drive, Los Angeles, CA 90069, (213) 550-6894 and 550-6856

HBO PICTURES, 1100 Avenue of the Americas, 10th Floor, New York, NY 10036, (212) 512-1000

INTERNATIONAL FILM MARKETING, 9440 Santa Monica Boulevard, Suite 707, Beverly Hills, CA 90210, (213) 859-3971

ISLAND PICTURES, 9000 Sunset Boulevard, Suite 700, Los Angeles, CA 90069, (213) 276-4500

LORIMAR TELEPICTURES CORPORATION, 10202 W. Washington Boulevard, Culver City, CA 90232-3783, (213) 280-8000

MGM/UA, 10000 W. Washington Boulevard, Culver City, CA 90232, (213) 280-6000

MIRAMAX, 18 E. 48th Street, Suite 1601, New York, NY 10017, (212) 888-2662.

NEW CENTURY/VISTA FILM CO., 1875 Century Park East, Suite 200, Los Angeles, CA 90067, (213) 201-0506

NEW LINE CINEMA, 575 Eighth Avenue, 16th Floor, New York, NY 10018, (212) 239-8880. Also: 1116 N. Robertson Boulevard, Suite 808, Los Angeles, CA 90048, (213) 854-5811

NEW WORLD, 1440 S. Sepulveda Boulevard, Los Angeles, CA 90025, (213) 444-8100

ORION PICTURES INTERNATIONAL, and ORION CLASSICS, 711 Fifth Avenue, New York, NY 10022, (212) 758-5100. Also: 9 W. 57th Street, New York, NY 10019, (212) 980-1117. Also: 1888 Century Park East, Los Angeles, CA 90067, (213) 282-0550

PARAMOUNT PICTURES CORPORATION, 5555 Melrose Avenue, Los Angeles, CA 90038-3197, (213) 468-5000. Also: 1 Gulf & Western Plaza, New York, NY 10023, (212) 333-4600

ROSEBUD RELEASING CORP., 8670 Wilshire Boulevard, Beverly Hills, CA 90211, (213) 652-8459

SAMUEL GOLDWYN COMPANY, 10203 Santa Monica Boulevard, Suite 500, Los Angeles, CA 90067-6403, (213) 552-2255

SKOURAS INTERNATIONAL, 1040 N. Las Palmas, Hollywood, CA 90038, (213) 467-3000

TRANS WORLD ENTERTAINMENT, 6464 Sunset Boulevard, Suite 1100, Hollywood, CA 90028, (213) 461-0467

TMS PICTURES, INC., 11111 Santa Monica Boulevard, Suite 1850, Los Angeles, CA 90025, (213) 478-4230

TRI STAR PICTURES, 1875 Century Park East, 7th Floor, Los Angeles, CA 90067, (213) 201-2300. Also: 711 Fifth Avenue, 12th Floor, New York, NY 10022, (212) 758-3900

UNITED ARTISTS PICTURES, INC., 450 N. Roxbury Drive, Beverly Hills, CA 90210, (213) 281-4000

UNIVERSAL PICTURES, 100 Universal City Plaza, Universal City, CA 91608, (818) 777-1000. Also: 445 Park Avenue, New York, NY 10022, (212) 759-7500

VESTRON INC., 1010 Washington Boulevard, Stamford, CT 06901, (203) 978-5636. Also: 9255 Sunset Boulevard, Suite 420, Los Angeles, CA 90069, (213) 551-1723

WARNER BROS., 4000 Warner Boulevard, Burbank, CA 91522, (818) 954-6000

VIDEO MANUFACTURER/SUPPLIERS

A. I. P. DISTRIBUTION INC, 10726 McCune Avenue, Los Angeles, CA 90034, (213) 559-8835.

ABC VIDEO ENTERPRISES, 2040 Avenue of the Stars, Los Angeles, CA 90067, (213) 557-6600

ACADEMY HOME ENTERTAINMENT, 1 Pine Haven Shore Road, Shelburne, VT 05482 (800) 972-0001.

ADLER VIDEO MARKETING INC., Old Dominion Drive, #360, McLean, VA 22101, (703) 556-8880

AIMS MEDIA, 6901 Woodley Avenue, Van Nuys, CA 91406, (818) 785-4111 or (800) 367-2467

ARTHUR CANTOR FILMS, 2112 Broadway, Suite 400, New York, NY 10023, (212) 496-5710

AMERICAN HOME VIDEO LIBRARY, 1500 Broadway, Suite 1807, New York, NY 10136, (212) 869-2616

AVIATION A. V. LIBRARY, 3100 Airport Avenue, Santa Monica, CA 90405 (213) 399-0616.

BARR FILMS, 12801 Schabarum Avenue/P.O. Box 7878, Irwindale, CA

BEACON FILMS INC., 21601 Devonshire Street, Evanston, IL 60202, (800) 322-330

BENNETT MARINE VIDEO, 730 Washington Street, Marina Del Rey, CA 90292 (213) 821-3329.

BEST FILM AND VIDEO CORP., 98 Cutter Mills Road, Great Neck, NY 11021, (516) 487-4515

BFA EDUCATIONAL MEDIA, 468 Park Avenue South, New York, NY 10016, (212) 684-5910

BLACKHAWK FILMS, 595 Triumph Street, Commerce, CA 90040, (319) 323-8637

BOOK OF THE MONTH CLUB, INC., 485 Lexington Avenue, New York, NY 10017, (212) 867-4300

BOOKSHELF VIDEO, 301-B W. Dyer Road, Santa Ana, CA 92702, (714) 957-0206

BULLDOG FILMS, Oley, PA 19547, (212) 779-8226

BUDGET VIDEO, 1540 N. Highland Avenue, Los Angeles, CA 90028, (213) 466-2431

CABIN FEVER ENTERTAINMENT INC., ;100 West Putnam Avenue, Greenwich, CT 06830 (203) 661-1100.

CANNON VIDEO, 640 San Vincente Blvd., Los Angeles, CA 90048, (213) 658-2148.

CAPITAL CITY/ABC VIDEO ENTERPRISES, 1825 7th Avenue, New York, NY 10019, (212) 887-6655

CBS VIDEO CLUBS/CBS VIDEO LIBRARY, 1400 N. Fruitridge Avenue, Terre Haute, IN 47811. Also: 1211 Avenue of the Americas, New York, NY 100036, (212) 975-4875

CBS/FOX VIDEO, 1211 Sixth Avenue, New York, NY 10036, (212) 819-3200

CELEBRITY HOME ENTERTAINMENT, 6320 Canoga Avenue, Penthouse Suite, Woodland Hills, CA 91367, (818) 715-1980.

CENTERPOINT DISTRIBUTION INC., 434 S. First Street, San Jose, CA 95113, (408) 993-9388.

CHRONICLE VIDEO CASSETTES, 4628 Fawn Hill Way, Antioch, CA 94509, (213) 858-0141

CHURCHILL FILMS, 12210 Nebraska Avenue, Los Angeles, CA 90025, (213) 442-5500

CINEMA GUILD, 1697 Broadway, Suite 802, New York, NY 10019, (212) 246-5522

CINERGY ENTERTAINMENT, 858 12th Street, Suite 8, Santa Monica, CA 90403, (213) 451-2513.

CLASSIC FAMILY ENTERTAINMENT, 9333 Oso Avenue, Chatsworth, CA 91311, (818) 993-3238.

COLISEUM VIDEO, 430 W. 54th Street, New York, NY 10019, (212) 489-8130

CONCORD VIDEO INC., 801 S. Main Street, Burbank, CA 91506-3305, (213) 271-5705.

CORINTH VIDEO, 34 Gansevourt Street, New York, NY 10014, (212) 463-0305

CORONET/MTI, a division of Simon and Schuster, 108 Wilmot Road, Deerfield, IL 60015, (312) 940-1260 or (800) 621-2131

COVENANT VIDEO, 3200 W. Foster Avenue, Chicago, IL 60625, (800) 621-1290

CRITIC'S CHOICE VIDEO INC., 1020 31st Street, Suite 130, Downer's Grove, IL 60515-5503, (312) 969-8895

CROWN VIDEO, 225 Park Street, New York, NY 10003, (212) 254-1600

DIRECT CINEMA LIMITED, Box 69589, Los Angeles, CA 90069, (213) 656-4700

DISCOUNT VIDEO TAPES, 3711 Clark Avenue, Suite B, Burbank, CA 91521 (818) 843-3366

DISNEY HOME VIDEO, 500 S. Buena Vista Street, Burbank, CA 91521, (818) 840-1000

DO-IT-YOURSELF, 712 Euclid Avenue, Charlotte, NC 28203, (704) 342-9608

EASTMAN KODAK CO., 343 State Street, Rochester, NY 14650-0001, (716) 724-3242.

EMBASSY HOME ENTERTAINMENT, 1901 Avenue of the Stars, Los Angeles, CA 90067, (213) 553-3600

FAITH FOR TODAY, 1100 Rancho Conejo Boulevard, Newbury Park, CA 91320, (805) 499-4363

FAMILY HOME ENTERTAINMENT, 21800 Burbank Boulevard, Woodland Hills, CA 91365, (800) 423-7455

FANLIGHT PRODUCTIONS, 47 Halifax Street, Boston, MA 02130, (617) 524-0980

FILMS FOR THE HUMANITIES, INC., P. O. Box 2053, Princeton, NJ 08543, (609) 452-1128

FIRST RUN VIDEO, 3620 Overland Avenue, Los Angeles, CA 90034, (213) 838-2111.

FORUM HOME VIDEO INC., 2400 Broadway Avenue, Suite 100, Santa Monica, CA 90404, (213) 315-7800.

GENESIS HOME VIDEO, 15809 Stagg Street, Van Nuys, CA, 91406, (800) 344-1060.

GREENLEAF VIDEO INC., 3230 Nebraska Avenue, Santa Monica, CA 90404 (213) 829-7675

HANNA-BARBERA HOME VIDEO, 3400 Cahuenga Blvd., West, Hollywood, CA 90068, (213) 969-1246.

HARMONY VISION, 116 N. Robertson Boulevard, Suite 701, Los Angeles, CA 90046, (213) 652-8844

HBO VIDEO INC., 1370 Avenue of the Americas, New York, NY 10019, (212) 977-8990

HEALING ARTS HOME VIDEO, 1229 Third Street, Suite C, Santa Monica, CA 90401, (213) 458-9795.

HI-TOPS, 5730 Buckingham Parkway, Culver City, CA 90230, (213) 216-7900

HOLLYWOOD VIDEO INC., 15951 Arminta Street, Van Nuys, CA 91406, (818) 908-1274.

HOME VISION, A FILMS INC. CO., 5547 N. Ravenswood, Chicago, IL 60640, (312) 878-2600.

HORIZON ENTERTAINMENT GROUP, 801 South Main Street, Burbank, CA 91506, (818) 841-9697.

IMAGE ENTERTAINMENT INC., 6311 Romaine Street, Hollywood, CA 90038-2617, (213) 468-8867.

INCREASE VIDEO, 8265 Sunset Boulevard, Suite 105, Hollywood, CA 90046, (213) 654-8808

INDEPENDENT UNITED DISTRIBUTORS (IUD), 430 W. 54th Street, New York, NY 10019, (800) 223-0313

INDEPENDENT VIDEO SERVICES, 401 East Tenth Avenue, Suite 160, Eugene, OR 97401

INTERNATIONAL FILM EXCHANGE, 201 West 52nd Street, New York, NY 10019, (212) 582-4318

INTERNATIONAL VIDEO ENTERTAINMENT (IVE), 15400 Sherman Way, Suite 500, Van Nuys, CA 91406, (818) 908-0303.

INTERNATIONAL VIDEO NETWORK, 2242 Camino Ramon, San Ramon, CA 94583, (415) 866-1121.

IRS VIDEO, 633 N. La Brea, Los Angeles, CA 90036

J2 COMMUNICATIONS, 10850 Wilshire Boulevard, Suite 1000, Los Angeles, CA 90024, (213) 474-5252 or 10 W. 66th Street, New York, NY 10023, (212) 874-5716.

JOURNAL FILMS INC., 21601 Devonshire Street, Evanston, IL 60202, (800) 323-5448

KVC HOME VIDEO, 7225 Woodland Drive, PO Box 68881, Indianapolis, IN 46278, (317) 297-1888.

KAROL MEDIA, 22 Riverview Drive, Wayne, NJ 07470, (201) 628-9111

KARTES VIDEO, 10 E. 106th Street, Indianapolis, IN 46280, (317) 844-7403

KID TIME VIDEO, 2340 Sawtelle Boulevard, Los Angeles, CA 90064, (213) 452-9006

KULTUR, 121 Highway 36, West Long Beach, NJ 07764, (201) 229-2343.

LASERDISC CORP. OF AMERICA, 2265 E. 220th Street, PO Box 22782, Long Beach, CA 90801-5782, (213) 835-6177.

LAWREN PRODUCTION INC., 21601 Devonshire Street, Evanston, IL 60202, (800) 323-9084

LIBERTY PUBLISHING CO., INC., Suite B-3, 440 South Federal Highway, Deerfield, FL 33441, (305) 360-9000.

MAGNUM ENTERTAINMENT INC., 9301 Wilshire Blvd., #602, Beverly Hills, CA 90212-5413, (213) 278-9981.

MALJACK PRODUCTIONS, 15825 Rob Roy Drive, Oak Forest, IL 60452, (800) 323-0442, (312) 687-7881.

MASTERVISION, 969 Park Avenue, New York, NY 10028-0322, (212) 879-0448.

MCA HOME VIDEO, 100 Universal City Plaza, Universal City, CA 91608, (818) 777-4300.

MEDIA HOME ENTERTAINMENT, 5730 Buckingham Parkway, Culver City, CA 90230, (800) 421-4509, (213) 216-7900.

MEDICAL ELECTRON EDUCATION SERVICE INC., 21601 Devonshire Street, Evanston, IL 60202, (800) 323-9084

MEGEL & ASSOCIATES, 3575 Cahuenga Boulevard West, Suite 249, Los Angeles, CA 90068, (213) 850-3306

MGM/UA HOME VIDEO, 10,000 W. Washington Blvd., Culver City, CA 90232-2728, (213) 280-6000.

MIRAMAR, 1333 N. Northlake Way #H, Seattle, WA 98103, (206) 545-4337.

MONTEREY HOME VIDEO, 7920 Alabama Avenue, Canoga Park, CA 91304, (818) 888-3040

MORRIS VIDEO, 2730 Monterey Street, #105, Monterey Business Park, Torrance, CA 90503, (213) 533-4800.

MTI TELEPROGRAMS, 3710 Commercial Avenue, Northbrook, IL 60062, (800) 323-5343

MYSTIC FIRE VIDEO, PO Box 1202, Montauk, NY, 11954, (516) 668-1111.

NATIONAL AUDIOVISUAL CENTER (GSA), Washington, DC 20409, (301) 763-1881

NATIONAL HEALTH VIDEO INC., 12021 Wilshire Boulevard, Suite 550, Los Angeles, CA 90025, (213) 472-2275

NELSON ENTERTAINMENT, 1901 Avenue of the Stars, Los Angeles, CA 90067, (213) 553-3600

NEW AGE VIDEO INC., P.O. Box 669, Old Chelsea Station, New York, NY 10113, (212) 254-1482

NEW DAY FILMS, 7 Harvard Square, Brookline, MA 02146, (617) 566-5914

NEW STAR VIDEO, 260 S. Beverly Drive, Beverly Hills, CA 90212, (213) 205-0666.

NEW WORLD VIDEO, 1440 S. Sepulveda Blvd., Los Angeles, CA 90025, (213) 444-8100.

NFL FILMS, 330 Fellowship Road, Mt. Laurel, NJ 08054, (609) 778-1600

NIGHTENGALE-CONANT CORP., 7300 N. Lehigh Avenue, Chicago, IL 60648, (800) 572-2770

NORSTAR VIDEO CORP., 1580 Old Bayshore Highway, San Jose, CA 95112, (408) 280-0522

NOSTALGIA MERCHANT, 6255 Sunset Boulevard, Hollywood, CA 90028, (213) 216-7900

ORION HOME VIDEO, 410 Park Avenue, 7th Floor, New York, NY 10022, (212) 888-4518.

PACIFIC ARTS VIDEO, 50 La Cienega Boulevard, Suite 210, Beverly Hills, CA 90211, (213) 657-2233

PARAMOUNT HOME VIDEO, 5555 Melrose Avenue, Hollywood, CA 90038, (213) 468-5000

PBS VIDEO, 1320 Braddock Place, Alexandria VA 22314, (800) 424-7963

PENNSYLVANIA STATE UNIVERSITY, Audio Visual Services, Specialty Services Bldg., University Park, PA 16801, (814) 865-6314

PERENNIAL EDUCATION INC., 21601 Devonshire Street, Evanston, IL 60202, (800) 323-9089

PHOENIX FILMS/BFA EDUCATIONAL MEDIA, 468 Park Avenue South, New York, NY 10016, (212) 648-5910

PIONEER VIDEO, 200 West Grand Avenue, Montvale, NJ 07645, (201) 573-1122

POLARIS, 2 Park Avenue, 24th Floor, New York, NY 10016, (212) 684-3232

PREMIERE HOME VIDEO, 6824 Melrose Avenue, Hollywood, CA 90038, (213) 934-8903.

PRISM, 1875 Century Park East, Suite 100, Los Angeles, CA 90067, (213) 277-3270

PROFESSIONAL RESEARCH INC., 21601 Devonshire Street, Evanston, IL 60202, (800) 421-2363

PYRAMID FILM AND VIDEO, Box 1048, Santa Monica, CA 90406, (213) 828-7577

RANDOM HOUSE VIDEO, 201 E. 50th Street, New York, NY 10022, (212) 872-8030.

RCA/COLUMBIA HOME VIDEO, 3500 W. Olive Ave., Burbank, CA 91505, (818) 953-7900

REPUBLIC PICTURES HOME VIDEO, 12636 Beatrice Street, Los Angeles, CA 90066-7004, (213) 306-4040.

RHINO HOME VIDEO RECORDS, 2225 Colorado Blvd., Santa Monica, CA 90404-3721, (213) 828-1980.

SBI VIDEO, 4901 Forbes Road, Lanham, MD 20706, (301) 459-8000

SIMITAR ENTERTAINMENT INC., 3955 Annapolis Lane, Plymouth, MN 5547, (612) 559-6660.

SONY VIDEO SOFTWARE, 1700 Broadway, New York, NY 10019, (212) 757-4990

SPINNAKER SOFTWARE, One Kendall Square, Cambridge, MA 02139, (617) 494-1200

TEACHING FILMS INC., 21601 Devonshire Street, Evanston, IL 60202, (800) 323-9084

TERRA-NOVA FILMS, 9848 S. Winchester Avenue, Chicago, IL 60643, (312) 881-8491

THE KITCHEN, 512 W. 19th Street, New York, NY 10011, (312) 443-3793

THORN EMI/HBO VIDEO INC., 1370 Avenue of the Americas, New York, NY 10019, (212) 977-8990

TIME-LIFE VIDEO, 1271 Avenue of the Americas, New York, NY 10020, (212) 552-5940

TODAY HOME ENTERTAINMENT INC., 9200 Sunset Boulevard, Los Angeles, CA 90069, (213) 278-6490

TOUCHSTONE HOME VIDEO, 500 S. Buena VIsta, Burbank, CA, 91521, (818) 560-5941.

TRANSWORLD ENTERTAINMENT USA, 3330 Cahuenga Blvd W, Suite 500, Los Angeles, CA 90068, (213) 461-0467.

TRAVELNETWORK, P.O. Box 11345, Chicago, IL 60611, (312) 266-9400

TURNER ENTERTAINMENT COMPANY, 6 East 43rd Street, New York, NY 10017, (212) 558-7404.

TWIN TOWER ENTERPRISES INC., 18720 Oxnard Street, SUite 101, Tarzana, CA 91356, (818) 344-8424.

NATHAN TYLER PRODUCTIONS, 451 D Street, Boston, MA 02210, (617) 439-9797

UMBRELLA FILMS, 60 Blake Road, Brookline, MA 02146, (617) 277-6639

UNIVERSITY OF CALIFORNIA, Extension Media Center, 2176 Shattuck Avenue, Berkeley, CA 94704, (415) 642-0460 and 642-5578

USA HOME VIDEO, 7920 Alabama Avenue, Canoga Park, CA 91304, (818) 888-3040

VESTRON VIDEO, PO Box 10382, 1010 Washington Boulevard, Stamford, CT 06901, (203) 978-5400

VIDAMERICA, 235 E. 55th Street, New York, NY 10022, (212) 355-1600

VIDEO CASSETTE MARKETING, 137 Eucalyptus Drive, El Segundo, CA 90245

VIDEO DATA BANK, 280 South Columbus Avenue, Chicago, IL 60603, (312) 443-3793

VIDEODISC PUBLISHING INC., 381 Park Avenue South, Suite 1601, New York, NY 10016, (212) 685-5522

VIDEO GEMS, 731 N. La Brea Avenue, Los Angeles, CA 90038, (213) 938-2385 or (800) 421-3252

VIDEO MARKETING CONCEPTS, 7410 Santa Monica Blvd., W. Hollywood, CA, 90046-5605, (213) 850-6500.

VIDEO NATURALS, 2590 Glen Green, Suite 6, Los Angeles, CA 90068

VIDEO PIPELINE, 11850 Wilshire Blvd., Suite 200, Los ANgeles, CA 90025, (213) 479-7766.

VIDEO PUBLISHING HOUSE INC., 10011 E. Touhy Avenue, Suite 580, Des Plaines, IL 60018, (312) 827-1191

VIDEO SCHOOLHOUSE, THE, 167 Central Avenue, Pacific Grove, CA 93950, (408) 375-4474

VIDEOTAKES, 220 Shrewsbury Avenue, Red Bank, NJ 07701, (201) 747-2444

VIDEOTAPE CATALOG, SMW Video Inc., 803 Russell Boulevard, #2, Davis, CA 95616, (800) 547-0653

VIDEO TREASURES INC., 1767 Morris Avenue, Union, NJ, 07083, (516) 231-8383.

VIDEO YESTERYEAR, P.O. Box C, Sandy Hook, CT 06482, (203) 426-2574

VIDMARK CORP., 2901 Ocean Park Blvd., Suite 213, Santa Monica, CA, 90405, (213) 399-8877.

VIRGIN VISION, 6100 WIlshire Blvd., 16th Floor, Los Angeles, CA 90048, (213) 857-5200.

WALT DISNEY HOME VIDEO, 500 S. Buena Vista Street, Production Bldg, Rm #12, Burbank, CA, 91521-0001, (818) 560-1859.

WARNER HOME VIDEO, 4000 Warner Boulevard, Burbank, CA 91522, (818) 954-6000

WESTERN PUBLISHING CO., 1220 Mound Avenue, Racine, WI, 53404-3336, (414) 633-2431.

WIZARD VIDEO/FORCE VIDEO, 1551 N. La Brea Avenue, Los Angeles, CA 90028, (213) 850-6563

WOOD KNAPP, 5900 Wilshire Blvd, Los Angeles, CA 90036, (213) 938-2484.

XEROX INFORMATION RESOURCES GROUP/PUBLISHING, One Pickwick Plaza/P.O. Box 6710, Greenwich, CT 06836, (203) 625-5675

VIDEO WHOLESALER/DISTRIBUTORS

Video wholesalers or distributors--as they are called in the video trade--are how video suppliers or manufacturers like CBS/FOX or Paramount or the smaller companies deliver their videos to the retail stores and mass merchants. A supplier may employ 15 to 20 wholesalers throughout the country. The videos are sold to the wholesalers at 35-40% off the retail price. The wholesaler makes the sales to the retailer.

Most wholesalers will not take on single programs as they prefer to represent the entire lines of video manufacturers who can supply a steady stream of product, and merchandising materials like posters and point-of-purchase materials. In recent years the video suppliers have cut down on the number of wholesalers they deal with. Some video suppliers have begun to go "direct" to the large retail accounts, thereby cutting out the wholesaler.

AMERICAN VIDEO NETWORK, 830 S. Myrtle Road, Monrovia, CA 91016, (818) 358-7761 or (800) 523-5193

ARTEC INC., 1 Pine Haven Shore Road, Shelbourne, VT 05482, (802) 985-8401

B.A. PARGH COMP. INC., 1283 Murfreesboro Road, Nashville, TN 37217, (800) 227-1000

BAKER & TAYLOR VIDEO, 8140 N. Lehigh Avenue, Morton Grove, IL 60053, (312) 647-0800

BEST VIDEO, INC., 50 N.W. 44th Street, Oklahoma City, OK 73118, (405) 557-0066

BIG STATE DISTRIBUTING CORP., 4830 Lackawana, #121, Dallas, TX 75247, (214) 631-1100

BLACK SWAN ENTERPRISES, 1100 Centennial Boulevard, Suite 248, Richardson, TX 75081, (214) 644-7926

CAPITAL RECORDS VIDEO DISTRIBUTION, 1750 N. Vine Street, Hollywood, CA 90028, (213) 462-6252

CHANNEL 3 Inc., 2901 White Plains Road, New York, NY 10467, (212) 881-7480

COAST VIDEO DISTRIBUTION INC., 500 N. Ventu Park Road, Newbury Park, CA 91320, (818) 884-3800

COMMERCIAL DISTRIBUTORS, 8 Sommerset Street, Portland, ME 04101, (207) 879-5400

COMMTRON, 2450 Bell Avenue, Des Moines, IA 50321, (515) 224-1784

DISCOUNT VIDEO INTERNATIONAL, 1765 Woodhaven Drive, Bensalem, PA 19006, (800) VIDEO-44

EAST TEXAS DISTRIBUTING, 7171 Grand Boulevard, Houston, TX 77054, (800) 231-6648

FIRST VIDEO EXCHANGE, 17503 S. Figueroa, Gardena, CA 90248, (213) 516-6422 or (800) 247-2351

G.G. COMMUNICATIONS INC., 111 French Avenue, Braintree, MA 02184, (617) 843-4860

GLOBAL VIDEO DISTRIBUTORS INC., 7213 N.W. 79th Terrace, Medley, FL 33166, (305) 887-1986 or (305) 887-2000

HANDLEMAN COMPANY, 500 Kirts Boulevard, Troy, MI 48084, (313) 362-4400

HOME ENTERTAINMENT DISTRIBUTORS (a subsidiary of Ingram), 9549 Penn Avenue South, Minneapolis, MN 55431, (612) 887-9500

INDEPENDENT VIDEO INC., 10364 Rockingham Drive, Sacramento, CA 95827, (916) 361-7181

INGRAM VIDEO, 347 Readwood Drive, Nashville, TN 37217, (615) 361-5000

INTERNATIONAL MOVIE MERCHANTS, 25115 S.W. Parkway Avenue, Suite C, Wilsonville, OR 97070, (503) 682-3545

LIBRARY VIDEO COMPANY, Box 40351, Philadelphia, PA 19106, (215) 627-6667

LIEBERMAN ENTERPRISES, INC. (a subsidiary of IVE), 9549 Penn Avenue South, Minneapolis, MN 55431, (612) 887-5300

LISTENING LIBRARY INC., One Park Avenue, Old Greenwich, CT 06870, (203) 637-3616

M.S. DISTRIBUTING COMPANY, 1050 Arthur Avenue, Elk Grove Village, IL 60007, (312) 364-2888

METRO VIDEO, 92 Railroad Avenue, Hasbrouck Heights, NJ 07604, (201) 288-0400

MOVIE TAPE EXCHANGE INC., 9380 Route 130 North, Pennsauken, NJ 08109, (609) 665-5775

MSV DISTRIBUTORS, 40 S. Caroline Street, Baltimore, MD 21231, (301) 675-1400

PRIVATE EYE VIDEO, P.O. Box 2796, Capistrano Beach, CA 92624-0796, (714) 240-5144

SCHWARTZ BROTHERS, INC., 4901 Forbes Boulevard, Lanham, MD 20706, (301) 459-8000

SIGHT AND SOUND DISTRIBUTORS, 2055 Walton Road, St. Louis, MO 63114, (314) 426-2388

SOUND/VIDEO UNLIMITED, 8140 N. Lehigh Avenue, Morton Grove, IL 60053, (312) 647-0800

SOURCE VIDEO, 1100 Hillsboro Road, Franklin, TN 37064, (615) 790-5300

SOUTHERN ELECTRONICS DISTRIBUTORS INC., 4916 N. Royal Atlanta Drive, Tucker, GA 30054, (404) 491-8962

SPRING ARBOR DISTRIBUTORS, 10885 Textile Road, Belleville, MI 48111, (313) 481-0900

STAR VIDEO ENTERTAINMENT, 550 Grand Street, Jersey City, NJ 07302, (201) 333-4600

THE MOVIE WAREHOUSE CO., 605 Harrison Avenue, Leadville, CO 80461, (303) 486-3883 or (800) 535-3400

VIDCOM, 175 W. 2700 S., Salt Lake City, UT 84115, (801) 487-8888

VIDEO BROKERS INTERNATIONAL, 6902 Grand Ave, Maspeth, NY 11378, (718) 457-1617

VIDEO CLOSEOUTS OF AMERICA INC., 261 Central Avenue, Suite 42, Jersey City, NJ 07307, (201) 333-3802 or (800) 221-4391

VIDEO MARKETING AND DISTRIBUTING, 14001 Ridgedale Drive, Suite 290, Minneapolis, MN 55343, (612) 544-8588 or (800) 328-4815

VIDEO MOVIE BROKERS, 7640 Gloria Avenue, Suite C, Van Nuys, CA 91406, (818) 908-8966 or (800) 235-6644

VIDEO ONE VIDEO, 1600 124th Avenue NE, Bellevue, WA 98005, (206) 454-5992

VIDEO PRODUCTS DISTRIBUTORS, 2428 Glendale Lane, Sacramento, CA 95825, (916) 971-1809

VIDEO SHUTTLE NETWORK, 445 Eighth Avenue NW, St. Paul, MN 55112, (612) 639-0622

VIDEO TREND, 12900 Richfield Court, Livonia, MI 48150, (313) 591-0200

VSI DISTRIBUTORS INC., 3333 Commercial Avenue, Northbrook, IL 60062, (312) 498-4130

VTR INC., 173 Industry Drive, Pittsburgh, PA 15275, (412) 787-8890 or (800) 245-1172

VVI DISTRIBUTORS, 2940 Interstate Street/P.O. Box 667309, Charlotte, NC 28208, (704) 399-4660 or (800) 532-0150 and 438-8273

WAX WORKS VIDEOWORKS, 325 E. Third Street, Owensboro, KY 42301, (502) 926-0008

WIN RECORDS AND VIDEO, 76-05 51st Avenue, Elmhurst, NY 11373, (718) 786-7667

ZBS INDUSTRIES, 701 Beta Drive, Mayfield Village, OH 44143, (216) 461-6275

SELECTED DUPLICATORS

Allied Film and Video, Chicago, IL (312) 348-0373

Allied Film and Video, Detroit, MI (313) 871-2222

All Mobile Video, New York, NY (212) 757-8919

C & C Visual, New York, NY (212) 684-3830

Capitol Video Communications, Washington, DC (202) 965-7800

Century III Teleproduction, Boston, MA (617) 267-6400

Communications Concepts, Cape Canaveral, FL (305) 783-5232

Creative Video Services, Street Cloud, MN (612) 255-0033

Dallas Post-Production Center, Irving, TX (214) 556-1043

Devlin Productions, New York, NY (212) 582-5572

Editel/Chicago, Chicago, IL (312) 440-2360

355

Editel/Los Angeles, Los Angeles, CA (213) 931-1821

Editel/New York, New York, NY (212) 867-4600

First Communications, Atlanta, GA (404) 980-9773

Image Transform, North Hollywood, CA (818) 985-7566

Innovision Teleproduction, Lawrence, KS (913) 843-9148

Interface Video Systems, Washington, DC (202) 861-0500

International Production Center, New York, NY (212) 582-6530

Koplar Communications Center, St. Louis, MO (313) 454-6324

Media Associates, Mt. View, CA (415) 968-2444

Midtown Video, Denver, CO (303) 778-1681

MTI, New York, NY (212) 355-0510

Northwest Teleproductions, Kansas City, MO (816) 531-3838

Northwest Teleproductions, Minneapolis, MN (612) 835-4455

PCA Teleproductions, Matthews, NC (704) 847-8011

Polycom Teleproductions, Chicago, IL (312) 337-6000

Skaggs Telecommunications, Salt Lake City, UT (801) 539-1427

Southwest Teleproductions, Dallas, TX (214) 243-5719

Telemation Productions, Seattle, WA (206) 623-5934

Third Coast Video, Austin, TX (512) 473-2020

VCA/Technicolor, Des Plaines, IL (312) 298-7700

Versatile Video, Sunnyvale, CA (408) 734-5550

FOREIGN TELEVISION BUYERS

Foreign Television Program Buyers

These are only some of the many international television buyers. Many of the smaller countries I have not included. Many of these names and addresses may have changed by the time you are ready to use this list but at least you have a place to start. I have not personally used all of these contacts on this list so you should not consider these names as recommendations. (In fact, I'd be interested in hearing from those of you who have recommendations of foreign buyers so I may update this section in future editions of this book.)

ARGENTINA, Primera Television Argentina, Av, Alem 735, Buenos Aires, Argentina.

Compania Argentina de Television S.A., Castex 3345, Buenos Aires, Argentina.

AMERICAN SAMOA, Television of Samoa, Dept. of Education, Pago Pago, American Samoa, 96799.

AUSTRALIA, Australian Broadcasting Commission, 145 Elizabeth St., PO Box 487, GPO. Sydney, N.S.W., Australia 2001. (Government owned.)

Amalgamated Television Services, Pty, Ltd. Television Station ATN, Channel 7, Television Center, Epping, 2121, Sydney, N.S.W, Australia.

Television Corporation Ltd., Television Station TCN, Channel 9, Artarmon Road, Willoughby, 2068, Sydney, N.S.W., Australia.

Nine TV Network Australia, GPO Box 4088, Sydney 2001, Australia. Mr. Russell Watkins.

United Telecasters Ltd, Channel A-10, Epping and Pittwater Roads, North Ryde 2113, N.S.W., Australia.

Herald-Sun TV, Pty, Ltd, Television Station HSV, Channel 7, Corner of Dorcas and Wells St., South Melbourne, Victoria, Australia.

General Television Corporation, Pty. Ltd, Television Station GTV, Channel 9, 22-46 Bendigo Street, Richmond, Melbourne, Victoria, Australia.

Austrama Television, Channel 0, ATC C/Ansett Transport Industries, Ltd, 489 Swanston Street, Melbourne, Victoria, Australia. Mr. John M. Lachlan.

Brisbane TV Limited, Sir Samuel Griffths Drive, Mt. Cootha, Brisbane, Queensland, Australia.

Television Broadcaster Ltd., Television Station ADS, Channel 7, 125 Strangeways Terrace, North Adelaide, South Australia.

TVW Limited, Television Station TVW, Channel 7, Osborne Park Road, Tuart Hill, Perth, Western Australia.

AUSTRIA, Ossterreichischer Rundfunk, GmbH ORG, Argentinierstrasse 30a, 1041 Vienna Postfach 700, Austria.

BELGIUM, Belgishe Radio en Televisie, 52 Boulevard August Reyer, 1040 Brussels, Belgium, Mr. Prosper Ver Bruggen, Mr. Robert Dethier, Mr. Jacques Boigelot, Mr. George Jetter, Mr. R. Wangermee.

Belgishe Radio en Television (BRT), Reyerslaan 52, 1040 Brussels, Belgium. Mr. Jozef Coolsaet.

BRAZIL, Emissora de Televisao Continental, Rue das Laranjeiras 291, Rio de Janeiro, Brazil.

Radio E Televisao Bande, Rua Radiantes N. 13, Sao Paulo, Brazil. Mr. Jorge Joas Saad.

TV Globo, Rua Lopes Unitas 303, Jardim Botanico, Rio de Janeriro, Brazil. Mr. Luiz Eduardo Borgerth or Mr. Jose Roberto Fillippelli.

CANADA, CBC, Toronto, The Nature of Things, Box 500, Station A, Toronto, Canada, M5W 1E6. Buys short subjects to half an hour.

Greene and Dewar Productions, 150 Simcoe Street, Toronto, Ontario, Canada, M5H 3G4. Produces weekly animal show syndicated internationally.

ENGLAND, Affinity Productions, 114 West 86th Street, 7A, New York, NY, 10024. Agents who represent US films in England.

Anglia Television Ltd., Anglia House, Norwich, NR1 3JG, England. Mr. David Little.

ATV Network Limited, ATV Centre, Bridge Street, Birmingham, West Midlands, B1 2JP, England. Mr. Charles Denton.

BBC Television Center, Wood Lane, London W12 7RJ, England. Mr. Gunnar Rugheimer.

BBC-TV, Room 302 Union House, 65-69 Shepherds Bush Green, London W12 7RJ, England. Mr. Alan Howden.

BBC Bristol, Natural History Unit, Broadcasting House, Whiteladies Road, Bristol, BS8 2LR, England. For wildlife documentaries.

BBC, Kensington House, Richmond Way, London W14 OAX, England. For science programs.

Chatsworth Television Ltd, 97-99 Dean Street, London W1V 5RA, England. Mr. Malcolm Heyworth.

Dubai Radio and Colour TV, 7A Grafton Street, London W1X 4HB, England. Mr. John Billett.

Granada Television Ltd., Manchester M60 9EA, England. Jr. Leslie Halliwell.

HTV Wales and West, TV Centre, PO Box 58, Cardiff CFl 9XL, England. Mr. Christopher Grace.

Thames Television Ltd., Thames House, 306-316 Euston Road, London NW1, England. Mr. Tim Riordan, Mr. Jack Saltzman.

Thames TV International, 149 Tottenham Court Road, London NW1, England. Mr. Don Taffner.

FINLAND, Finnish Broadcasting, Kesakatu, 2 Helsinki, 26, Finland.

FRANCE, Antenne 2 Societe National de TV en couleurs, 5 et 7 rue Montessuy, 75341, Paris, France. Mr. Claude Barma.

FR 3, 116 Ave. du President Kennedy, 75016, Paris, France. Mr. Patrick Brion, or Mlle. Michelle Rebel.

TF l, 17 rue de l'Arrivee, 75015, Paris, France. Mr. Jacques Zbinen.

TF 1, 13/15 rue Cognacq Jay, 75007, Paris, France. M. Antonietti.

Telediffusion de France, 116, Avenue du President Kennedy, F75790, Paris, Cedex 16, France.

GERMANY, Deutsche Rundfunk-und Fernsehanstalten, ARD/ Bayerischer Rundfunk, Rundfunkplaz 1, 8, Munich 2, West Germany. Mrs. Waltraud Pusl.

362

Fernsehen der DDR, Winsstr 42, 1055 Berlin, West Germany. Mr. Roland Paul.

ARD-Filmrdaktion, 8 Bertramstrasse, D6000 Frankfurt am Main, West Germany. Mr. Klaus Lackschewitz.

Nordeutscher Runfunk, (NDR), Studio Hamburg, Tonndorfer, Hauptstrasse, West Germany. Mr. Hans Brecht.

Saarlandischer Rundfunk, 66 Saarbrucken, Funkhaus, Halberg, Postfach, 1050, West Germany.

Sender Freies Berlin, Berlin 19, Masurenallee 8-14, West Germany.

Seuddeutscher Rundfunk, 7000 Suttgart 1, Neckarstrasse, 145, West Germany.

Westdeutscher Rundfunk, (WDR), Appelhofplatz 1, 5 Cologne 1, Postfach 101950, West Germany. Mr. Wilfied Reichardt, Mr. Werner Dutsch, Mr. George Alexander.

Zweites Deutsches Fernsehen (ZDF), Essenheimer Landstrasse, 65 Mainz-Lerchenberg, Postfach 4040, West Germany. Mr. Chistoph Holch, Mr. Rolf Schweitzer, Mr. Heinz Ungureit, Mr. Eckart Stein, Miss Ursula Stein, Mr. Manfred Schutze.

GUAM, Guam Television, Pacific Broadcasting, Box 368, Agana, Guam.

HOLLAND, Nederlandse Omroep Stichting NOS0, PO Box 10, Hilversum, Holland.

HONG KONG, Television Broadcasts, Ltd., 77 Broadcast Drive, Kowloon, Hong Kong. Mrs. Stella Wong.

Rediffusion (Hong Kong Ltd.), 81 Broadcast Drive, Kowloon, Hong Kong. Mr. Jock Sloan.

HK TVB International Ltd., Leighton Center, 77 Leighton Road, Hong Kong. Mr. Paul Shields.

INDIA, All India Television, Television Centre, All India Radio, Akashwani Bhawan, 5th Floor, Parliament Street, New Delhi, 110001, India.

INDONESIA, Jajasan Televisi RI (RRI-TV), Senajan, Jakarta, Indonesia.

IRAN, Television of Iran, PO Box 33-200, Av. Pahlavi, Tehran, Iran.

IRAQ, TV Station of the Republic of Iraq, Ministry of Guidance, Broadcasting House, Sathiya, Baghdad, Iraq.

ITALY, Radio-Televisione Italiana, (RAI), Viale Mazzini 14, 00195, Rome, Italy. Mr. Flora Palanti, Mrs. Bruna Cossaro (RAI/Rete 3).

TV Globo, Via Latino Malabranca ll, Rome, Italy. Mr. Jose Roberto Fillippelli.

JAPAN, Nippon Hoso Kyokai (NHK), 2-2-1 Jinnan, Shibuya-ku, Tokyo 150, Japan. (Educational TV system.) Mr. Masaomi Mitsuboshi.

The Yomiuri Television Broadcasting Corp. (YTV), JCIX-TV, Osaka, Japan.

Ashai Broadcasting Co., Ltd. (ABC), JOBX-TV, Osaka, Japan.

Kansai Television Corp., (KTV), JONR-TV, Osaka, Japan.

Mainichi Broadcasting System, (MBS), JOQR-TV, Osaka, Japan.

Fuji Telecasting Co., 7 Kawada-cho, Ichigaya, Shinjuku, Tokyo, Japan.

Ashai National Broadcasting Co. (TV ASHAHI or ANB) formerly NET (Nippon Educational Television), 6-4-10 Roppongi, Tokyo, Japan.

Nippon Television Network, (NTV), 14 Niban-cho, Chiyoda-ku, Tokyo. Mr. Katsuhiro Kirata.

Tokyo Broadcasting System (TBS), 5-3-6, Akasaka, Minato-ku, Tokyo, Japan.

Interlingual-International Inc, No. 7 Mori Bldg., 2 Nishikubo Tomoe-cho, Shiba, Tokyo 105, Japan. Mr. Frank Taniguchi.

Intervision, Inc., 205, 15-6, 7-Chome, Akasaka, Tokyo 105, Japan.

Japan International Enterprises, 17-20- Shimbashi, 6-Chome, Tokyo, Japan.

New Japan Films Inc., 12 Iagura Katamachi, Azabu, Tokyo, Japan.

Sapporo TV Broadcasting, 8-Chome, Chuo-ku, Sapporo, Japan.

Documentary Japan, Inc., Ryoji Hirose, Kalumakasaka 212, 9-2-9 Akasaka, Minato-ku, Japan.

KOREA, Korea Broadcasting System, 33-3, Namsan-Rong, Chung-ku, Seoul, South Korea.

Korean Broadcasting Systems, 1-799 Yoido-Dong, Youngdeungpo-Ku, 150 Seoul, South Korea.

LATIN AMERICA, Alfred Haver, Inc., 321 Commercial Avenue, Palisades, NJ, 07650. Agent for all of Latin America.

365

MALAYSIA, Television Malaysia, Dept. of Broadcasting, Angkasapuri, 2210 Kuala Lumpur, Malaysia. Mr. Wadud Kamaruddin, Mr. Ali Salleh.

MEXICO, Television De La Frontera, S.A., Vincente Guerror num, 704 Ciudad Juarez, Chih, Mexico.

Television Del Norte, S.A., Aparatado Postal num 1833, Monterrey, N.L., Mexico.

Televisa S.A., Avenida Chapultepec 18, Mexico DF, Mexico. Mr. Fernando Diez Barroso.

Television Canal 13, Periferico SUR 4121, Mexico 20 DF, Mexico. Mr. Raul Ostos-Martinez.

THE NETHERLANDS, Documentary Development, VARA-TV, Heuvellaan 33, PO Box 75 1200 AD, Hilversum, The Netherlands. Mr. Frank Diamond.

NEW ZEALAND, New Zealand Broadcasting Council, PO Box 30, 355, Lower Hutt, New Zealand.

Television New Zealand, Centrepoint, Queen Street, PO Box 3819, Auckland, New Zealand. Mr. Barrie Parkin.

NORWAY, Mediavision Distributors, Ann Haley, PO Box 2407, Solli, Oslo 2, Norway. Scandanavian TV and non-theatrical distributor.

Film Department, NRK, Oslo 3, Norway. Pal Bang-Hansen, Miss Berit Rinnan.

Norsk Rikskringkasting, Oslo 3, Norway. Miss Rigmor Hansson Rodin.

PHILIPPINES, Intercontinental Broadcasting Corporation, P. Guevarra Avenue, San Juan, Rizal, Philippines.

Kanlaon Broadcasting System, Inc., Broadcast Plaza, Bohol Avenue, Quezon City, Philippines.

Republic Broadcasting System, E de Los Santos Avenue, Diliman, Quezon City, Philippines.

SINGAPORE, Singapore Broadcasting Corp, Caldecott Hill Tomason Rod, 1129 Maxwell Road, PO Box 1902, 9038 Singapore, Singapore. Mrs. Sandra Buenaventura.

SOUTH AFRICA, South African Broadcasting, Henley Road, 2001 Johannesburg, Republic of South Africa. Mr. Robin Knox-Grant.

SPAIN, Television Espanola, de Prado de Rey, Madrid, Spain. Mr. Mariano Gonzales Arnao, Mr. Segundo Lopez Soria.

SWEDEN, SR 1, Sveriges Radio, S-105 Stockholm, Sweden. Mr. Bo Johan Hultman, Mr. Hans Elefalk, SR 2; Mr. Nils Peter Sundgren, Miss Anna-Ida Winnicka, Mr. R. Bengteric, Mr. Bo Bjelfvenstam, Mrs. Doreen Denning, Swedish Television; Mr. Frank Hirschfeldt, Birgitta Lingsell.

SWITZERLAND, Swiss Broadcasting Corporation, Giacommettistrasse 3, CH-3000, Berne 15, Switzerland. Mr. Yvan Fontana.

TAIWAN, Taiwan Television Enterprises Ltd., No 10, Pa Te Road, Sec. 3, Taipei, Taiwan.

Chinese Television Service, N. 100, Kuang Fu South Road, Taipei, Taiwan.

THAILAND, Thai Television Co., Ltd., Bankhunprom, Bangkok, Thailand.

Bangkok Entertainment Co., 2259 New Petchburi Road, Bangkok, Thailand. Mr. Pravit Maleenont.

Thai Army Television Station, Pahol Youthin Road, Bangkok, Thailand.

VENEZUELA, Televisora Nacional, Apt. 3979, Caracas, Venezuela.

Venevision TV Channel 4, Apartado 60193, Caracas 1061, Venezula. Mr. Irwin Klein.

YUGOSLAVIA, JRT Beograd, Post Office Box 78, 11000 Beograd, Yugoslavia. Mr. Miroljub Filipovic, Mr. Rale Zelenovic.

TELEVISION SELLERS

These are some of the domestic and international television sellers. They attend N.A.P.T.E. and other television conventions yearly in order to sell their programming to broadcasters. Some carry movies, documentaries and off-air television programs. You might start off calling some of these companies and asking who distributes what kind of product. This will narrow your hit list to a manageable size.

In approaching them, write a one page letter with an accompanying one-sheet on the programs you would like distributed. All syndicators and distributors will take a fee ranging from 25-40% for their services depending on the territories covered.

All American Television, 304 E. 45th Street, 2nd Fl, New York, NY, 10017. (Off-network series, documentaries, features, international.)

ARP Films, 342 Madison Ave, #714, New York, NY, 10173. (Cartoons, educational, series, documentaries.)

Baurch Television Group, 7777 Leesburg Pike, #302N, Falls Church, VA 22043. (Horror, children, specials.)

Bavaria Film GmbH, Bavariafilmplatz 7, D-8022, Geiselgasteig, Munich, West Germany. (Children, features, music.)

BBC/Lionhart Television, 630 Fifth Ave, #2220, New York, NY, 10111. (Drama.)

Blair Entertainment, 1290 Avenue of the Americas, NY, NY, 10104. (Specials, sports, children, movies.)

Blair Television, 1290 Avenue of the Americas, NY, NY, 10104. (First run syndication, kid packages, film packages.)

Buena Vista Television, 500 S. Buena Vista St., Burbank, CA, 91521. (Off-network series, animations, series, features.)

Camelot Entertainment Sales, 1700 Broadway, 35th Floor, New York, NY, 10019. (Games shows, magazine and talk shows, feature packages, animations, specials.)

Capital Cities/ABC Video Enterprises, 825 Seventh Ave, NY, NY, 10019.

CBS Broadcast International, 51 W. 52nd St, New York, NY, 10019.

Central Television Enterprises, 35-38 Portman Square, London W1A 2HZ, England 01-486-6688. (Drama, documentaries.)

Center Independent Television (USA), 610 Fifth Avenue, #401, New York, NY, 10020.

Cine-Groupe J.P. Int'l Dist., 1151 Alexandre-de-Save, Montreal, Quebec, H2L 2T7, Canada.

Columbia Pictures TV, 3300 Riverside Dr., Burbank, CA, 91505. (Features.)

Coral Pictures Crop., 6850 Coral Way, Miami, FL 33155. (Spanish, documentaries, specials, children, animation, features.)

Devillier Donegan Enterprises, 1608 New Hampsire Ave., Washington, D.C. 20009.

Excel Telemedia International, 745 Fifth Ave., #1516, New York, NY, 10151-0077. (Features, series, documentaries.)

Filmworld Television, 685 Fifth Avenue., New York, NY, 10022. (Family and horror feature packages.)

Four Star International, 2813 W. Alameda Ave., Burbank, CA, 91505. (Children, family, sports.)

Fox Lorber Associates, 432 Park Ave South, #705, New York, NY, 10016. (Children, music, documentaries.)

Fremantle International, 660 Madison Ave., New York, NY, 10021. (Specials, series.)

Fries Distribution Col, 6922 Hollywood Blvd., Los Angeles, CA, 90028. (Family, children, features.)

Gaylord Syndication, 66 Music Square West, Nashville, TN 37203. (Music, fishing.)

Genesis Entertainment, 5743 Corsa Ave., #216, Westlake Village, CA, 91362. (Documentaries, specials.)

GGP/GGP Sports, 400 Tamal Plaza, Corte Madera, CA, 94925.

Global Vision Group, 550 Biltmore Way, 9th Floor, Coral Gables, FLA, 33134. (Features, mini-series, series, packages, specials.)

Globo TV Network-Brazil, 909 Third Ave., 21st Floor, New York, NY, 10022.

Granada Television International, 400 Madison Avenue, #1511, New York, NY, 10017.

Group W Productions, One Lakeside Plaza, 3801 Barham Blvd., 2nd Floor, Los Angeles, CA, 90068. (Magazine, talk, reality, entertainment, animated, specials and game shows.)

Group W TV Sales, 90 Park Ave., New York, NY, 10016. (Magazine, talk.)

Groupe Multimedia du Canada, 5225 Berri, #300, Montreal, QC, H2J 2S4, Canada.

GTG Marketing, 150 E. 52nd St., 19th Floor, New York, NY, 10022.

Harmony Gold, 8831 Sunset Blvd., Los Angeles, CA, 90069.

Home Shopping Network, 12000 25th Court North, PO Box 9090, St. Peterburg, FL, 33716.

IDDH, 124 Rue de la Boetie, Paris, France, 75008.

Independent Network/Promark, 11150 W. Olympic Blvd., #1100, Los Angeles, CA, 90064.

Independent Television Network, 747 Third Ave., 31st Floor, New York, NY, 10017.

International TV Enterprises, 420 Lexington Ave., New York, NY, 10017.

ITC Entertainment, 12711 Ventura Blvd., Studio City, CA, 91604.

ITEL, 48 Leicester Square, London, WC2H, 7FB, England. (Drama, documentaries.)

JM Entertainment, 133 E. 58th St., New York, NY, 10022.

King World Productions, 1700 Broadway, 35th Floor, New York, NY, 10019. (Game shows, children, talk shows.)

Koch-Silverberg Communications, 1650 Broadway, #510, New York, NY, 10019. (sports, pageants.)

LBS Communications, 875 Third Avenue, New York, NY, 10022. (features, games shows, specials, documentaries, off-network series.)

London Weekend Television International, S. Bank Television Centre, Upper Ground, London SE 1 9LT, England.

Lorimar Syndication, 10202 W. Washington Blvd., Culver City, CA, 90232. (First run series, off-network series, features, children, international, games shows, packages.)

LWT International, South Bank TV Center, London, SEl 9LT, England.

371

MCA,TV, 445 Park Avenue, New York, NY, 10022. (features, network television, children.)

Medallion TV Enterprises, 8831 Sunset Blvd., #100, West Hollywood, CA, 90069.

Medicast Television Entertainment, 2350 E. Devon, #250, Des Plaines, IL, 60018. (Sports.)

MG/Perin, 124 East 40th St., New York, NY, 10016. (First-run series, feature packages, program inserts, specials, children.)

MGM/UA Television Syndication, 10000 W. Washington Blvd., Culver City, CA, 90232. (Series, specials, mini-series, features, films for tv, international.)

MTM TV Distribution Group, 12001 Ventura Pl., #600, PO Box 7406, Studio City, CA, 91604.

Muller Media, 23 E. 39th St., New York, NY, 10016.

Multimedia Entertainment, 75 Rockefeller Plaza, 22nd Floor, New York, NY, 10019. (Magazine, talk, games shows, specials, packages.)

New World Television, 130 E. 59th St., New York, NY 10022. (Features, animation, old tv series, mini-series, tv movies.)

NTV International Corp., 50 Rockefeller Plaza, New York, NY, 10020. (Specials, documentaries.)

Orion Television Syndication, 1888 Century Park East, 6th Floor, Los Angeles, CA, 90067. (First-run series, off-network series, features, packages, mini-series.)

Jim Owens & Associates, 1525 McGavock St., Nashville, TN, 37203. (Music, specials.)

Palladium Entertainment, 444 Madison Ave., 26th Floor, New York, NY, 10022. (First run game shows, series, features, packages.)

Paragon International, 260 Richmond St. West, #405, Toronto, Ontario, M5R 1K5, Canada.

Paramount Domestic TV, 5555 Melrose Ave., Los Angeles, CA, 90038. (Tal shows, features, mini-series, packages, off-network, specials.)

Petry Television, 3 E. 54th St., New York, NY, 10022. (Magazine, music.)

Primetime Entertainment, 444 Madison Ave., New York, NY, 10022.

The Program Exchange, 375 Hudson St., New York, NY, 10014. (Children, off-network series, sports.)

Program Syndication Services, 375 Hudson St., New York, NY, 10014. (Exercise).

ProServe Television, 10935 Estate Lane, #100, Dallas, TX, 45238.1 (Sports, international.)

Qintex Entertainment, 345 N. Maple Dr., Beverly Hills, CA, 90210.

Reel Movies International, 8235 Douglas Ave., #770, Dallas, TX, 75225.

Republic Pictures Corp., 12636 Beatrice St., Los Angeles, CA, 90066. (Specials, international.)

RTVE/Radio Television of Spain, 501 Madison Ave., #604, New York, NY, 10022.

Samuel Goldwyn Television, 10203 Santa Monica Blvd., Los Angeles, CA 90067. (Exercise, music, family, movies.)

Scott Entertainment, PO Box 554, Westbury, NY, 11590. (Features, packages, program inserts, specials, off-network series.)

Select Media Communications, 885 Third Avenue, #1220, New York, NY 10022. (Sports, pageants, awards, program inserts.)

SFM Entertainment, 1180 Avenue of the Americas, 10th floor, New York, NY 10036. (Childrens, series, documentaries, compilations.)

Silverbach-Lazarus Group, 9911 W. Pico Blvd., PH-M, Los Angeles, CA 90035. (Off-network series, first-run series, mini-series, documentaries, specials, features, packages, international.)

Spectrum, 75 Rockefeller Plaza, 22nd Floor, New York, NY, 10019.

S. P. E. X. Group/Media, 8831 Sunset Blvd., Penthouse West, Los Angeles, CA, 90069. (Home remodeling shows.)

Sportsman's Showcase with Ken Tucker, Highway 313, PO Box 872, Brewton, ALA 36427. (Hunting.)

SPR News Source, 5165 Shady Island Rd., Mound, MN, 55634. (Documentaries.)

Studio Hamburg Alelier BMBH, Jenfelder Allee 80, D-2000, Hamburg 70, West Germany. (Music, children, documentaries.)

Sunbow Productions, 130 Fifth Avenue., New York, NY 10011. (Children.)

Survival Anglia Ltd., 113 Park Lane, Brook House, London, W1YY 4DX, England. (Documentary.)

D. L. Taffner, 31 W. 56th Street, New York, NY, 10019.

Telefilm Canada, 144 S. Beverly Dr., Los Angeles, CA, 90212.

Telemedia, 2025 Royal Lane, Dallas, TX, 75229. (Music, compilations.)

Telemundo Channel 2, GPO Box 6222, San Juan, PR, 00936.

Telepool, Sonnenstrasse 21, 8000 Munchen 2, West Germany.

Telerep, 875 Third Avenue, New York, NY 10022.

Teletrib, 875 Third Avenue, New York, NY 10022. (Series, specials, magazine.)

TeleVentures, 1925 Century Park East, S-2140, Los Angeles, CA, 90067.

Television Program Enterprises, 875 Third Avenue, New York, NY, 10022. (Series, mini-series.)

Television Week, Meed House 21, John St., London, WC1N 2BP.

Thames TV International Ltd., 149 Tottenham Court Rd., London, England, WIP9LL.

Tribune Entertainment Co., 435 N. Michigan Avenue, Chicago, IL, 60611.
(First-run series, magazine, talk, movies, events, specials, sports, variety, music, comedy, mini-series.)

Turner Program Services, One CNN Center, Box 105366, Atlanta, GA, 30348-5366.
(Features, first-run, off-network, children.)

TV Horizons, 875 Third Avenue, New York, NY, 10022. (Game shows, series, animations, music, documentaries.)

TV World, 27 Wilford St., London, England.

TVRC Syndication, 245 Fifth Avenue., New York, NY, 10016. (Sports, movies news.)

Twentieth Century Fox TV, PO Box 900, Beverly Hills, CA, 90213. (Features, documentaries, talk, music, compilations, childrens, family, mini-series, first-run, off-network.)

U.S. Nippon Communications, The Plaza, 2 W. 59th St., New York, NY 10019. (Business, Japanese related.)

Uniworld Entertainment, 1250 Broadway, 36th Floor, New York, NY, 10001.

Vestron Television, 2029 Century Park East, #200, Los Angeles, CA, 90067. (Features, packages, specials, docu-dramas.)

Viacom, 1211 Avenue of the Stars, New York, NY, 10036. (Specials, first-run, animated, features, packages.)

Video Yesteryear, Box C, Sandy Hook, CT, 06470. (Documentaries, films, cartoons, foreign films, silent films.)

Wall Street Journal TV, 200 Liberty St., 14th Floor, New York, NY, 10281.

Weiss Global Enterprises, 2055 Saviers Rd., #12, Oxnard, CA, 93033-3693. (Features, documentaries, first-run series, comedy shorts, cartoons, off-network series.)

WesternWorld TV, 10523-45 Burbank Blvd., N. Hollywood, CA, 91601. (Features, children, music, animation, series.)

World Wrestling Federation, 1055 Summer St., Stamford, CT, 06905.

Worldvision Enterprises, 600 Madison Avenue, New York, NY, 1021. (First-run game show, first-run late night variety, comedy, children, live-action, specials, series, features, international, holiday specials.)

Yorkshire Television, 32 Bedford Row, London, WC1 R4H, England.

BIBLIOGRAPHY

PRODUCTION

Video Editing and Post-Production: A Professional Guide, available from Knowledge Industry Publications, 701 Westchester Avenue, White Plains, NY 10604

Professional Video Production by Ingrid Weigand, available from Knowledge Industry Publications, 701 Westchester Avenue, White Plains, NY 10604 (1985)

Reel Power by Mark Litwak, New American Library, New York, NY (1986)

Television Production by Alan Wurtzel, McGraw-Hill, New York, NY (1983)

Television Production Handbook by Herbert Zettl, Wadsworth Publishing Company, Belmont, CA (1984)

The Independent Producer: Film & Television by Hourcourt, Howlett, Davies, Moskovic, Faber & Faber, London (1986)

The Video Production Guide by Lon McQuillin, Howard Sams Publishing, Indianapolis, IN (1983)

Producers on Producing: The Making of Film & Television by Irv Broughton, MacFarland Publishing (1986)

DISTRIBUTION

The Independent Film and Videomakers Guide by Michael Wiese, Revised and Expanded 1986, available from Michael Wiese, 3960 Laurel Canyon Boulevard, #331, Studio City, CA 91614-3791—$20.95 postpaid

Doing It Yourself: A Handbook on Independent Film Distribution by AIVF, Inc. by Julia Reichert, 99 Prince Street, New York, NY 10012 (1977)

Entertainment Industry Economics by Harold L. Vogel, Cambridge University Press, New York, NY (1986)

Making Films Your Business by Mollie Gregory, available from Schocken Books, New York, NY (1979)—$6.95

The Film Industries: Practical Business and Legal Problems in Production, Distribution and Exhibition by Michael F. Mayer, available from Hastings House, New York, NY (1978)—$11.50

Motion Picture Distribution—Business or Racket? by Walter E. Hurst and Wm. Storm Hale, Seven Arts, Hollywood, CA (1975)

16mm Distribution by Judith Trojan & Nadien Convert, available from Educational Film Library Association, 43 W. 61st Street, New York, NY 10023—$6

Distribution Guide by the Independent Film Journal, 1251 Avenue of the Americas, New York, NY

Producing, Financing and Distributing Film by Farber and Baumgarten, Drama Book Specialists, New York, NY (1973)

The Movie Business: American Film Industry Practice by William Bluem and Jason Squire, Hastings House, New York (1972)

BUDGETS

Film Scheduling Or, How Long Will It Take To Shoot Your Movie? by Ralph S. Singleton, Lone Eagle Publishing, 9903 Santa Monica Blvd., Beverly Hills, CA 90212 (213) 471-8066 (Features)

Film Scheduling/Film Budgeting Workbook and Movie Production by Ralph S. Singleton, Lone Eagle Publishing, 9903 Santa Monica Blvd., Beverly Hills, CA 90212 (213) 471-8066 (Features)

Budget Forms Instantly! by Ralph S. Singleton, Lone Eagle Publishing, 9903 Santa Monica Blvd., Beverly Hills, CA 90212 (213) 471-8066 (Features)

Film and Video Budgets by Michael Wiese, available from Michael Wiese, 3960 Laurel Canyon Boulevard, #331, Studio City, CA 91614-3791 (818 905-6367). (Revised 1988)—$18.95 postpaid. (18 budget formats—features, docs, comedy, original programs, etc.)

The Hollywood Guide to Film Budgeting and Script Breakdown by Danford Chamness, available from Stanley J. Brooks Company, 1416 Westwood Boulevard, Suite 201, Los Angeles, CA 90024 (1977). Telephone: (213) 470-2849—$20 (Features)

1987-1988 Brooks Standard Rate Book, available from Stanley J. Brooks Company, 1416 Westwood Boulevard, Suite 201, Los Angeles, CA 90024. Telephone: (213) 470-2849—$28

Production Boards and Strips: For Features and Television available from Stanley J. Brooks Company, 1416 Westwood Boulevard, Suite 201, Los Angeles, CA 90024. Telephone: (213) 470-2849

1989 Motion Picture Almanac & Television Almanac (2 books), available from Quigley Publishing Company, 159 W. 53rd Street, New York, NY 10019

VIDEO

Home Video: Producing for the Home Market by Michael Wiese, available from Michael Wiese, 3960 Laurel Canyon Boulevard, #331, Studio City, CA 91614-3791—$18.95 postpaid

Guide to the Sponsored Video by Doug Duda, et al, available from Knowledge Industry Publications, 701 Westchester Avenue, White Plains, NY 10604 (1987)

Guide to Videotape Publishing, ed. by Ellen Lazer, available from Knowledge Industry Publications, 701 Westchester Avenue, White Plains, NY 10604 (1986)

Video Product Marketplace by Martin Porter, Martin Porter & Associates Publications, Port Washington, NY (1987)

Home Video Publishing: The Distribution of Videocassettes 1986-90 by Presentation Consultants Inc. White Plains, NY: Knowledge Industry Publications, Inc., 1986.

Variety's Complete Home Video Directory, R.R. Bowker, New York, NY (1988)

The Video Tape & Disc Guide to Home Entertainment, National Video Clearinghouse, Inc., Syosset, NY (annual)

Video Shopper, P.O. Box 309, Fraser, MI 48026, (313) 774-4311

DIRECTORIES

1988 Film Directors, 1988 Film Producers, Studios and Agents Guide, 1988 Cinematographers, Production Designers, Costume Designers & Film Editors Guide by Kate Bales, available from Lone Eagle Publishing, 9903 Santa Monica Blvd., Beverly Hills, CA 90212 (213) 471-8066

Motion Picture, TV and Theater Directory, Motion Picture Enterprises, Tarrytown, NY 10591—$4.25

New York Feature Film and Video Guide, 90 Riverside Drive, New York, NY 10024—$5

The Producer's Master Guide, New York Production Manual Inc., 611 Broadway, Suite 807, New York, NY 10012—$69.95 per year

TRADE PUBLICATIONS

AD AGE, 200 E. 42nd Street, New York, NY 10017

ADVERTISING AGE, Crain Communications, Inc., 740 N. Rush Street, Chicago, Il 60611

ADWEEK, 49 E. 21st Street, New York, NY 10010

AMERICAN CINEMATOGRAPHER, 220 E. 42nd Street, Suite 930, New York, NY 10017—$15.95 per year

AMERICAN FILM, The American Film Institute, Washington DC

BACKSTAGE, 5151 Wilshire Boulevard, Suite 302, Los Angeles, CA 90036—$35 per year

BILLBOARD, 9107 Wilshire Boulevard, #2265, Los Angeles, CA 90036. Also: 1515 Broadway, New York, NY 10036—$148 per year.

380

BROADCASTING, 630 Third Street, 12th Floor, New York, NY 10017. Also: Broadcasting Publications Inc., Washington, DC

CHAIN STORE AGE, Lebhar-Friedman, Inc., New York, NY

CHANNELS, 19 West 44th Street, #812, New York, NY 10036

CHANNELS OF COMMUNICATION, Media Commentary Council, Inc., New York, NY

CHILDREN'S VIDEO, John L. Weber for Children's Video Magazine, Inc., Brooklyn, NY

COMING ATTRACTIONS, Convenience Video Corp., Jersey City, NJ

CONVENIENCE STORE NEWS, BMT Publications, Inc., New York, NY

DAILY VARIETY, 1400 N. Cahuenga Boulevard, Los Angeles, CA 90028

DEALERSCOPE, North American Publishing Co., Philadelphia, PA

DIRECT MARKETING, Hoke Communications, Inc., Garden City, NY

DM [Direct Marketing] NEWS, c/o DMN Corp., 19 W. 21st Street, New York, NY 10010, (212) 741-2095

ELECTRONIC MEDIA, 220 East 42nd Street, #1306, New York, NY 10017

ELECTRONIC RETAILING, Fairchild Publications, New York, NY

FILM COMMENT, 140 W. 65th Street, New York, NY 10023

FILM JOURNAL, 244 W. 49th Street, #305, New York, NY 10019

FOLIO, Folio Magazine Publishing Corp., New Canaan, CT

HOLLYWOOD REPORTER, 1501 Broadway, New York, NY 10036. Also: 6715 Sunset Boulevard, Hollywood, CA 90028—$89 per year.

HOME VIDEO PUBLISHER, Knowledge Industry Publications, 701 Westchester Avenue, White Plains, NY 10604

HOME VIEWER, 11 N. Second Street, Philadelphia, PA 19160, (215) 629-1588

INTV JOURNAL, 80 Fifth Avenue, New York, NY 10011

LIBRARY JOURNAL, R.R. Bowker Co., New York, NY

MART, Morgan-Grampian Publishing Co., New York, NY

MILLIMETER, 826 Broadway, New York, NY 10003—$40 per year

MOVIELINE, 1141 S. Beverly Drive, Los Angeles, CA 90035-1139

MULTI-CHANNEL NEWS, 7 E. 12th Street, New York, NY 10003

NEWS & VIEWS, 1560 Broadway, #714, New York, NY 10036

PAUL KAGAN ASSOCIATES, 126 Clock Tower Place, Carmel, CA 93923

PHOTOMETHODS, Ziff-Davis Publishing Co., New York, NY

PHOTO WEEKLY, Billboard Publications Inc., New York, NY

PREMIERE, 755 Second Avenue, New York, NY 10017

PUBLISHERS WEEKLY, R.R. Bowker Co., New York, NY

ROCKAMERICA MAGAZINE, 27 E. 21st Street, New York, NY 10010—$3.50 per issue

SCREEN INTERNATIONAL, 8500 Wilshire Boulevard, Beverly Hills, CA 90211

SIGHT & SOUND MARKETING, Dorbaugh Publications, New York, NY

SPLICE, 10 Columbus Circle, #1300, New York, NY 10019

TAPE BUSINESS, Knowledge Industry Publications, 701 Westchester Avenue, White Plains, NY 10604

TELEVISION DIGEST, Television Digest Inc., 475 Fifth Avenue, Suite 1021, New York, NY 10017

TOYS, HOBBIES & CRAFTS, Harcourt Brace Jovanovich Inc., New York, NY

TV/RADIO AGE, 1270 Avenue of the Americas, #502, New York, NY 10020

TWICE, 5900 Wilshire Blvd, #700, Los Angeles, CA 90036

V, THE MAIL ORDER MAGAZINE OF VIDEOCASSETTES, Fairfield Publishing Co., Inc., New York, NY

VARIETY (weekly edition, also available as a daily), Variety, Inc., 154 W. 46th Street, New York, NY 10036—$75 per year.

VIDEO BUSINESS WEEKLY, 345 Park South, New York, NY 10010

VIDEO INSIDER, 223 Conestoga Road, Wayne, PA 19087

VIDEO MAGAZINE, 460 W. 34th Street, New York, NY 10001, (212) 947-6500

VIDEO MARKETING NEWSLETTER, 12052 Montecito Road, Los Alamitos, CA 90720

VIDEO MARKETPLACE, World Publishing Corp., Evanston, IL

VIDEO PREVIEW, P.O. Box 561467, Dallas, TX 75356-1476, (214) 438-4111

VIDEO REVIEW, 902 Broadway, New York, NY 10010, (212) 477-2200

VIDEO SOFTWARE DEALER, 5519 Centinela Avenue, Los Angeles, CA 90066

VIDEO STORE, 545 Fifth Avenue, New York, NY 10017. Also: 1700 E. Dyer Road, Santa Ana, CA 92705

VIDEO STORE (and ENTERTAINMENT MERCHANDISING), Magacycle Inc., Irvine, CA

VIDEO WEEK, 475 Fifth Avenue, New York, NY 10017

VIEW MAGAZINE, 80 Fifth Avenue, #501, New York, NY

383

VIEW: THE MAGAZINE OF CABLE TV PROGRAMMING, Subscription Services Department, P.O. Box 5011, FDR Station, New York, NY 10022—$36 per year

MARKETING & ADVERTISING

Adweek's Marketers Guide to Media, c/o A/S/M Communications Inc., 49 East 21st Street, New York, NY 10010

Advertising Manager's Handbook, Dartnell Corporation, Chicago, IL

American Demographics, Dow Jones and Company Inc., Syracuse, NY

Ayer Directory of Publications, Ayer Press, One Bala Avenue, Bala-Cynwyd, PA 19004

Bacon's Publicity Checker: Magazine and Newspapers, Bacon's Publishing Company, Inc., 332 S. Michigan Avenue, Chicago, Il 60604, (312) 922-2400

Business Publications Rates & Data, Standard Rate and Data Service, Inc., 3004 Glenview Road, Wilmette, IL 60091

Direct Mail List Rates and Data, Standard Rate and Data Service, Inc., 3004 Glenview Road, Wilmette, IL 60091

The Direct Marketing Association, Inc., 6 E. 43rd Street, New York, NY 10017, (212) 689-4977

The Direct Marketing Market Place: The Directory of the Direct Marketing Industry, c/o Hilary House Publishers, Inc., 1033 Channel Drive, Hewlett Harbor, NY 11557

How to Make Your Advertising Make Money by John Caples, Prentice-Hall, Englewood Cliffs, NJ (1983)

Inside the Leading Mail Order Companies, c/o NTC Business Books, 4255 West Touhy Avenue, Lincolnwood, IL 60646.

Maximarketing, The New Direction in Promotion, Advertising and Marketing Strategy, McGraw-Hill, New York, NY

384

Marketing & Media Decisions, 342 Madison Avenue, New York, NY 10017

Media: The Second God by Tony Schwartz, Random House, New York, NY (1981)

NATPE International Pocket Station Listing Guide, NATPE International, 342 Madison Avenue, Suite 933, New York, NY 10173

Ogilvy on Advertising by David Ogilvy, Crown Publishers, New York, NY (1983)

Response Television by John Witek, Crain Books, Chicago, IL (1981)

Television and Cable Contacts, Larimi Communications Associates, Ltd., 5 W. 37th Street, New York, NY 10018, (212) 819-9310

385

ALSO AVAILABLE FROM
MICHAEL WIESE PRODUCTIONS

PRODUCER TO PRODUCER
The Best of Michael Wiese from VIDEOGRAPHY Magazine

by Michael Wiese

Edited by Brian McKernan,
Editor, VIDEOGRAPHY

Current information about producing, financing, marketing and creativity is vital to the videomaker. Michael Wiese's "Producer to Producer" column in *VIDEOGRAPHY* magazine has provided independent producers with cutting-edge insights on the business of video: program development, production, financing, marketing and distribution.

In an informal and entertaining style, Mr. Wiese draws on his own experience and that of other successful video producers to demonstrate forward-thinking industry practices.

Includes: "Shaking the Money Tree," "Zen and the Art of the Steadicam, Jr.," "Where Do you Get the Money?," "Infomercials: Where's the Info?," "Self-Distribution," "You Can Make Desktop Video–But Can You Sell It?" and much more.

176 pp., illustrations
$19.95, ISBN: 0-941188-15-9

FILM & VIDEO FINANCING
by Michael Wiese

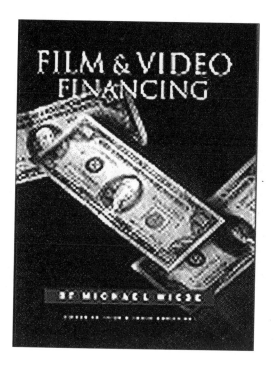

Praised as a book that prepares producers to get the money! A "palette" of creative strategies for producers in financing their feature films and video projects. Interviews with the producers of "sex, lies & videotape," "Trip to Bountiful," and "T2."

$22.95, 300 pp., ISBN 0-941188-11-6

Film Directing
SHOT BY SHOT
by Steven D. Katz

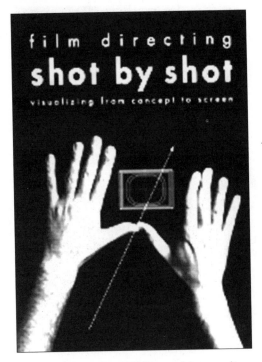

The most sought after book in Hollywood by top directors is filled with visual techniques for filmmakers and screenwriters to expand their stylistic knowledge. Includes storyboards from Spielberg, Welles and Hitchcock.

$24.95, 376 pp., 7 x 10
750 illustrations and photos ISBN 0-941188-10-8

THE WRITER'S JOURNEY
Mythic Structure for Storytellers & Screenwriters

by Christopher Vogler

An insider's look at how master storytellers from Lucas to Spielberg have used mythic structure to create powerful stories which tap into the mythological core which exists in us all.

Writers will discover step-by-step guidelines and learn how to structure plots and create realistic characters. A Hollywood studio head made the rough draft for this book required reading for his entire executive staff.

$22.95, 283 pp.
ISBN 0-941188-13-2